MODERNISM AND THE PROFESSIONAL ARCHITECTURE JOURNAL

The production of this book stems from two of the editors' longstanding research interests: the representation of architecture in print media, and the complex identity of the second phase of modernism in architecture given the role it played in postwar reconstruction in Europe.

While the history of postwar reconstruction has been increasingly well covered for most European countries, research investigating postwar architectural magazines and journals across Europe – their role in the discourse and production of the built environment and particularly their inter-relationship and differing conceptions of postwar architecture – is relatively undeveloped. *Modernism and the Professional Architecture Journal* sounds out this territory in a new collection of essays concerning the second phase of the reception and assimilation of modernism in architecture, as it was represented in professional architecture journals during the period of postwar reconstruction (1945–1968).

Professional architecture journals are often seen as conduits of established facts and knowledge. The role mainstream publications play, however, in establishing 'movements', 'trends' or 'debates' tends to be undervalued. In the context of the complex undertaking of postwar reconstruction, the shortage of resources, political uncertainty and the biographical complexities of individual architects, the chapters on key European architecture journals collected here reveal how modernist architecture, and its discourse, was perceived and disseminated in different European countries.

Torsten Schmiedeknecht teaches design, history and theory at the School of Architecture, University of Liverpool, UK. His research interests include the representation of architecture in print media; rationalism in architecture; and architectural competitions. He is the co-editor of *The Rationalist Reader, Rationalist Traces, An Architect's Guide to Fame* and *Fame and Architecture*. He is currently working on a RIBA-funded project about the representation of (modern) architecture in children's literature.

Andrew Peckham teaches architecture at the University of Westminster, UK. He has co-edited, with Hannah Lewi, a series of annual anthology issues of *The Journal of Architecture* (2016–2018) and is currently editing a book on teaching 'studio': *The Intrinsic and Extrinsic City*. His *Architecture and its Imprint* is due for publication in 2018.

"This is surely the first systematic survey of architectural journals produced across Europe in that vital 20-year period following the war when modernism was in vexed transit from embattled cause to contested orthodoxy. Scholarly country-by-country coverage reveals how the medium of the professional journal functioned as both a mirror and a torch, reflecting while also guiding the inextricable narratives of practice and discourse. Journalism may be but 'the first rough draft of history', yet this fascinating study shows what a rich and compelling draft it can be."

– John Allan, architect and writer

"During the years between 1945 and 1968 professional journals were testing grounds for institutional debates where modernist discourse has been produced and disseminated. Grounded in extensive new research, the essays in this volume by 11 international architectural scholars propose a stimulating interpretation of a medium whose role has been hitherto underestimated. Examining the interferences between journals, design practice and the tasks of reconstruction, the book shows us how professional architectural journals and their owners, editors, contributors and designers shaped architecture culture in the postwar decades."

– Ákos Moravánszky, Professor Emeritus, ETH Zurich, Switzerland

MODERNISM AND THE PROFESSIONAL ARCHITECTURE JOURNAL

Reporting, Editing and Reconstructing in Postwar Europe

Edited by Torsten Schmiedeknecht and Andrew Peckham

Routledge
Taylor & Francis Group

LONDON AND NEW YORK

First published 2019
by Routledge
2 Park Square, Milton Park, Abingdon, Oxon OX14 4RN

and by Routledge
711 Third Avenue, New York, NY 10017

Routledge is an imprint of the Taylor & Francis Group, an informa business

British Library Cataloguing-in-Publication Data
A catalogue record for this book is available from the British Library

Library of Congress Cataloging-in-Publication Data
A catalog record has been requested for this book

ISBN: 978-1-138-94516-6 (hbk)
ISBN: 978-1-138-94522-7 (pbk)
ISBN: 978-1-315-67154-3 (ebk)

Typeset in Bembo
by Out of House Publishing

MIX
Paper from
responsible sources
FSC
www.fsc.org   FSC™ C013985

Printed in the United Kingdom
by Henry Ling Limited

In memory of
Horst Schmiedeknecht
Architect
1937–2015

CONTENTS

CONTRIBUTORS

Christoph Allenspach studied art history at Fribourg/Freiburg and Florence Universities (lic. phil. I). He is a publicist and journalist, and the author of numerous publications on twentieth-century architecture in Switzerland. Editor of *Bauinventar zur Architektur des 20. Jhd.* in the Swiss Canton of Freiburg, he is also a professor of Theory at ZHdK Zürich.

Herman van Bergeijk is an architectural historian who studied in the Netherlands (Groningen) and Italy (Venice). After working abroad and teaching at many universities in the United States, Germany, Italy and the Netherlands, he obtained his PhD in 1995 with a study of the work of the architect and town planner W. M. Dudok. In 1997 he was appointed to the University of Technology in Delft where, in 2004, he became an associate professor in Architectural History. Recent publications include: *Het handschrift van de architect: Schetsen van Nicolaas Lansdorp en tijdgenoten* (together with Michiel Riedijk) (2014); *Aesthetic Economy: Objectivity in Dutch Architecture* (2014); *Jan Duiker, bouwkundig ingenieur (1890–1935);* and *Van warm naar koud* (2016). He is an editor of the cultural journal *Eigenbouwer*, and is currently studying the work of A.J. Kropholler.

Claes Caldenby is professor emeritus in theory and history of architecture at Chalmers Technical University in Göteborg. Since 1977 he has been one of the editors of *Arkitektur, the Swedish Review of Architecture*. He has published a large number of articles and books on twentieth-century architectural history, specialising in Swedish postwar architecture.

Andrew Higgott has taught the history and theory of architecture to undergraduates and postgraduates at the University of East London, the Architectural Association and elsewhere over the past 30 years. Among his recent publications are *Mediating Modernism: Architectural Cultures in Britain* (2007) *Camera Constructs: Photography, Architecture and the Modern City* (co-edited, 2012) and *Key Modern Architects* (2018).

András Ferkai is a professor and architectural historian at the Moholy-Nagy University of Art and Design Budapest (MOME), and member of Docomomo-Hungary. He is an architect, and after ten years of practice he became the editor of the journal *Magyar Építőművészet*. He has been researching and teaching modern Hungarian and Central European architecture since 1990.

Ana Esteban Maluenda is an architect with a PhD in theory and history of architecture, and a professor at the School of Architecture, Universidad Politécnica de Madrid. She has published many articles in the field of twentieth-century architecture and its dissemination, and has attended numerous conferences and lectured at Spanish and foreign universities.

Panayotis Tournikiotis is the professor of architectural theory at the National Technical University of Athens. He has authored books including *Adolf Loos, The Historiography of Modern Architecture* and *The Diagonal of Le Corbusier.* His recent work explores the legacy of Le Corbusier in Greece and the reinvention of the city centre in metropolitan Athens.

Nicholas Bullock teaches at the Architectural Association and the Department of Architecture, Cambridge, where he is also a fellow of King's College. His current research explores the way in which architecture and urbanism reflect the modernisation of France in the 30 years after the Second World War.

Paolo Scrivano holds a PhD from the Politecnico di Torino and teaches at Xi'an Jiaotong-Liverpool University. Among his publications are *Storia di un'idea di architettura moderna: Henry-Russell Hitchcock e l'International Style* (2001), *Olivetti Builds: Modern Architecture in Ivrea* (2001) and *Building Transatlantic Italy: Architectural Dialogues with Postwar America* (2013).

INTRODUCTION

Torsten Schmiedeknecht and Andrew Peckham

> Many of the challenges thrown up by the history of architectural magazines have still to be met – and this at a time when, after two centuries of domination, this type of mechanized publication is being transformed by computerization and rivalled by the new media.
>
> *Jannière and Vanlaethem, 2008, p. 61*

Why, given this context, edit a book on attitudes towards modernism in postwar architecture journals? In the first instance the production of this book stems from two of the editors' longstanding research interests: the representation of architecture in print media, and the complex identity of the second phase of modernism in architecture given the role it played in postwar reconstruction in Europe.

The collection of chapters originated in a proposal to investigate the relationship between modernism and postwar professional architecture journals for the period between 1945 and 1968. Aware of the extent of the material to be researched – PhDs are written on the history of just one journal covering a period of this length – we asked our authors to concentrate on the journal(s) they viewed as the most pertinent or revealing with regard to different national cultures of modernism. Furthermore, we suggested that each contributor might well identify shorter periods within this timeframe, given their approach to the subject.

While the history of postwar reconstruction has been increasingly well covered for most European countries, research investigating postwar architectural magazines and journals across Europe, their role in the discourse and production of the built environment and particularly their inter-relationship and differing conceptions of contemporary architecture postwar, is relatively undeveloped. *Modernism and the Professional Architecture Journal* sounds out this territory in a new collection of chapters concerning the second phase of the reception and assimilation of modernism in architecture, as it was represented in professional architecture journals during the period of postwar reconstruction (1945–1968).

A question of genre

> Periodical: published with a fixed interval between the issues or numbers.
> Magazine: a periodical containing miscellaneous pieces (such as articles, stories, poems) and often illustrated.
> Journal: a periodical dealing especially with matters of current interest.
>
> *Merriam Webster[1]*

While the obvious choice of publication genre is 'professional periodical', and while Sornin et al. (2008) chose to define their focus on architectural 'magazines' in the context of a wider-ranging study (perhaps because architectural publications are 'illustrated' and incorporate a variety of text by different authors), our contention is that 'professional journal' better describes the identity of the majority of the publications selected for study here. Journals tend to have direct connections with 'professional' associations and institutes, or 'represent' the discipline of architecture indirectly in documenting and recording the 'current' nature of practice and building, as news (mediated by editorial policy). It is this, together with their habit of addressing the wider culture of architectural design, sometimes in learned articles, that led us to choose 'journal' rather than 'magazine' to define their identity. As the postwar era developed, an increasingly self-conscious concern with architectural style, fashion and consumerist trends in Western Europe (as opposed to the parallel ideological constraints and practice that eventually prevailed behind the Iron Curtain) moved the character of these publications towards that of the magazine, highly illustrated and more graphically sophisticated. In a general sense, journals evidenced a transition from the priority of 'news' postwar, to an expression of the polarities of 'documentation' and 'debate', and later to a preoccupation with the extremes of polemic and fashion identified with the 1960s.

In 1967 Roland Barthes published his classic study of the fashion industry, *Systeme de la Mode* (*The Fashion System*), in which the concepts of 'written clothing' and the 'endless garment' prefigure the later tendency in architectural theory to typically widen the concept of architecture to encompass its dissemination in the media (Barthes, 1990). This tendency has marked the trajectory of contemporary research interest in architectural publication, so clearly delineated by Sornin and Jannière. Given the crosscurrents within, and acting between, different national cultures and professional affiliations, it would be more accurate to say that within the loose genre of the periodical, publications themselves fluctuated between the characteristics of a 'newspaper', professional or learned journal, cultural or popular magazine. How in this context did the postwar architecture journal balance reporting the imperatives of reconstruction with consideration of inherited attitudes towards interwar modernism, and what evidence is there in the journals of an increasing professionalism, specialisation and sophistication in the manipulation of media (and of photography in particular) during this period?

Collected texts

Professional architecture journals are often seen as conduits of established facts and knowledge (as opposed to the volatility of the avant-garde). The role mainstream publications play, however, in establishing 'movements', 'trends' or 'debates' tends to be undervalued. In the context of the complex undertaking of postwar reconstruction, the shortage of resources, political uncertainty and the biographical complexities of individual architects, the chapters on key European architecture journals collected here reveal how modernist architecture, and its discourse, was perceived and disseminated in different European countries.

The different chapters collected here highlight differences and similarities between journals in order to draw reciprocal conclusions about how the state of a 'contemporary' architecture was perceived at the time. Of particular interest are respective editorial policies, which reflected a shifting relationship between professional pragmatics and cultural diversity, and influenced the more general discourse and the production of the built environment.

How publication format and contents changed over time, and the choice of architectural projects published, has been closely scrutinised and placed in the wider context of the postwar era. Where did the journals position themselves in the ongoing reconstruction debate? How was modernism perceived and in what way was it viewed as an appropriate manner of reconstruction? How was the contemporary architecture of other countries received, and published, as a plausible model?

The texts share some common themes, while identifying distinct differences in the development and role of postwar modernism (and its expression in the journals studied). The variety of responses from the different authors also highlights the limitations of generalising 'the architecture journal'. What becomes clear is that, while commonalities exist, social and political circumstances, as much as geographical differences, determine the nature of discourse and the contribution made of individual journals in the countries concerned. Furthermore, the conditions of publishing, access to resources, financial dependencies, affiliations with professional or political bodies, as much as the personal histories and circumstances of editors, play an important role. Consequently, the threefold relationship between the journal, the profession and postwar reconstruction varies considerably from case to case. In the context of the texts collected in this book, the question of whether a journal is to be seen largely as a conduit of professional architectural practice, or whether it plays an active role in shaping that activity, is met with a variety of interpretations.

Journal complexes

Arguably one can approach the question of the journal as a 'complex' from three different overlapping perspectives.

First, there is the complex external to the journal itself but within which it resides, in the relationship between different journals, their editors, publishers and institutions, in a network of contacts and the juxtaposition of polemic and argument. This is both about commercial acumen, professional probity, cultural dialogue and architectural polemic.

Second, there is the inner structure or relationship between the different parts of the journal, viewed as a complex in the arrangement of textual and illustrative content: covers, editorials, columns; news of, or reportage on, the building industry and professional imperatives; case studies, essays and criticism; construction studies and working drawings or details. All of these tend to follow a particular, or typical, structural logic attached to periodisation, whether that is identified with a requisite editorial stability or (increasingly) a more volatile concern with design fashionability as much as with professional inclinations and the building industry.

Third, there is the question of attribution, representation and identity, which come to bear on the journal. That is to say, with what discourse is it attached or what narrative does it come to, or claim to, represent or project? Is not the journal itself a narrative complex, whether professional, identified with modern architecture or traditional in a conservative sense (the picturesque, the classical-vernacular or the *Heimatschutzarchitektur*)? How are these discourses set in a relative hierarchy to one another, or is there a more explicit ideological axe to grind (whether political in the context of reconstruction, or to do for example with the constitution of craft skills)? This sense of a complex might well be conditioned by an architectural or cultural 'movement', or the national politics in which the journal is embedded.

Jannière and Vanlaethem (2008), in concluding their 'methodological essay', look for new avenues for research on architectural journals: first pointing to an absence of those most representative of political change in the 1960s – a lacuna filled by Colomina's ironically monumental anthology of 'little magazines' *Clip Stamp Fold* (Colomina, 2010) – and second lamenting the tendency to indulge a monographic approach to the most emblematic publications. Pointing to 'international or transnational' journal transactions, they sought an interface between the politically 'representative' and the 'monographic' in arguing that research in this subject area needs to clarify its wider intentions and objectives.

While our collection of texts was influenced by Jannière and Vanlaethem's observations, David Rifkind's monograph on *Quadrante*, the Italian rationalist journal of the 1930s, makes no reference to their book. However, it occupies the interface they identify, in examining *Quadrante*'s ideological context and thematic discourse as both professional and didactic, the subject of its editors but also an artefact conditioned by a wider propagandising role. He notes that the journal, far from iconic, was printed in a compressed form on cheap paper in contrast to the glossy format, sophisticated graphic design and generous spatiality of *domus* and *Casabella* of the same period (Rifkind, 2012, pp. 18–19). Following 'two trajectories' – the chronology of *Quadrante*'s 'political history' associated with its founding editor Pietro Maria Bardi, and in contrast the thematic development of discourses on buildings and projects associated with engineering infrastructure and urban planning – the book serves as an exemplary model.

Editorial influence

The role of editors, as well as their aspirations, their networks and their powers to shape or influence journal narratives, has been extensively discussed in the following papers. The occasional 'conversation' in the form of editorials between Rudolf Pfister of *Baumeister* and Alfons Leitl of *Baukunst und Werkform* in Germany stands out, as the distance between both journals exceeds the rivalry between journals in other countries. Pfister and Leitl also stand for powerful examples of strong-minded and determined editors respectively pursuing their 'missions'. Andrew Higgott illustrates the case of James Richards and his influence – from interwar to postwar years – on editorial policy (and staffing) at *The Architectural Review*, while Nicholas Bullock tells a more personal history of André Bloc and the editorial team at *L'Architecture d'Aujourd'hui*. Examination of their different approaches and opinions, which proved to be both beneficial and at times detrimental to the respective journal's fortunes, is revealing. Panayotis Tournikiotis makes a case for the significant influence on Greek postwar architecture of Constantinos Doxiadis, de facto owner of *Ekistics* – a publication that evolved from in-house bulletin to international journal – and on the other hand the cultured Orestis Doumanis, who was involved with a plethora of journals: *Zygos, Architectoniki, Technika Chronika, Architectonika Themata* and *Themata Chorou + Texnon*. In Spain, as Ana Esteban Maluenda writes, Carlos de Miguel, Juan Miguel Fullaondo and Carlos Flores were the most powerful and influential editorial personalities: the 'balanced' de Miguel, the 'methodical' Flores and the 'vehement' Fullaondo.

A visual medium

Following Andrew Higgott's examination of the visual culture embodied in *The Architectural Review*, one can speculate more widely on how the influence of new codes of photographic publication, or the projection of architecture through photography, manifest themselves in postwar architectural journals. They present a conjunction between photography as a mass medium and the graphic formats adopted by individual publications. While it has been argued that the eclecticism practised by *The Architectural Review*, oscillating between provincial and cosmopolitan identities, influenced the visual culture of the Italian journal *domus*, for example – different professional expectations such as polemical confrontation between journals within particular national architectural traditions, styles or movements, and a more consistent graphic identity or culture of design – all epitomise 'genealogies of the present'. Together they came to represent distinct forms of the realism and an incipient postmodernism that prefaced qualities that emerged in European architecture after 1968. Mario Carpo (1998) coined the phrase 'biblio-space' to characterise the emergence of the printed architectural treatise, and some-such milieu was created in the professional architecture journals of the postwar period.

The differentiation of content remains a central difficulty in reading backdated architectural journals and may be considered in two ways: as a set of general 'thematic' categories (editorial, professional news, projects, buildings, case or technical studies, reviews, criticism, illustrations, building products, advertising, compilations); or as a constituent structure of elements (cover, contents, columns, sections, sub-sections, captions, articles, texts, drawings, photographs, titles, sub-headings, index) which orders the content of each individual issue.[2] Both sets interact to form the overall narrative structure of the journal.

Editorial policy directs this narration and tempers the degree of 'professionalism' involved in the choice of the architecture and buildings to be included (or excluded) in journal coverage. This influence, though, may be less immediately apparent generally, than when a forceful editorial or new graphic format indicates a change in editorship.

One can focus on individual concerns (reconstruction) and isolate areas of interest (a retrospective modernism), but that is necessarily a selective process given the complexity of the journal as an artefact, and it typically involves a relatively narrow focus on pertinent editorial dialogue and the selection of projects and buildings published. It would be wrong to treat the former primarily as a historical issue predicated on professional mores, and the latter as a matter of aesthetic choice. Beyond the intentional parameters of the editors, or the retrospective research interests of the culture critic, sociologist or historian, lies a grey area of orthodoxy. To follow Roland Barthes' conception of the photographic *punctum* (Barthes, 1984), what lies beyond the journal issue's representation of contemporary architecture, in the contingent, the overlooked detail or the journal's ambiguous temporality? How does its institutional constitution affect our view of the rubric of reconstruction and the 'tradition' of modernism represented on its pages? Which prospects presaged what was to come, what archetypes were located in a deeper past, and how revealing is the journal as a totality about the profession and its representation postwar?

Marketing and finance

No two journals are exactly alike, as each owner, publisher and editor seeks to establish a professional marketplace for their product. In addition to the range of content listed above, there are also the specialised concerns of practice administration: competition notices and results; managerial and legal matters; letters from architects and the general public, and new technological developments, which are all part of a content that, in different guises and combinations, forms a professional architecture journal, irrespective of the country of origin. However, the combination varies considerably, not least with regard to their relationship with primary content, that is the editorial position of the journal and nature of the building projects published and discussed (where the stance towards modernism should be most apparent). In addition, a journal's international outlook, whether publishing projects from other countries abroad – at the behest of the editor – or a journal sold in substantial numbers abroad in extending its range of influence, seems, in the latter case at least, to also depend on the country of origin. The UK's *The Architectural Review*, the French *L'Architecture d'Aujourd'Hui* or the Italian *domus* and *Casabella* are cases in point.

While funding and financial viability, and their role in the success and lasting duration – or not – of a journal is discussed as a serious issue in almost all chapters, the picture is not quite as clear-cut when it comes to professional affiliations. The most pronounced dependencies for the journals examined are expressed in the cases of Switzerland, the Netherlands, Hungary, Spain and Greece. While in Greece *Ekisitics* was affiliated with and dependent on Doxiadis, András Ferkai traces the differing fortunes of the Hungarian journals *Tér és Forma* and *Új Építészet*: the former a successful interwar avant-garde journal which faded in the early postwar years, not least due to lack of financial support, while the latter was bankrolled by the communist trade union. In Spain, where the dependencies were particularly pronounced, it took until 1958 for the first journal, *Temas de Arquitectura*, to be published without direct affiliation with any particular professional body or organisation.

Modernism and reconstruction

Although not explicitly formulated as a starting point, the continuity of interwar modernist architecture, was, as could be expected, raised as an issue by all our contributing authors. However, the modernism of the interwar years could hardly be described as one homogeneous movement, and postwar endeavours to reconnect to, or continue within, the modernist canon – identified with modernism's social and political credentials – were distinctly different from country to country. In the UK the shift in editorial policy at *The Architectural Review* from all-out support, in principle, for modernism during the interwar years to a more moderate approach was identified with a 'new humanism' as a 'corrective of prevailing practice'. In Germany, *Baumeister*'s critical approach to the Bauhaus contrasted with *Baukunst und Werkform*'s initial continuity postwar of support for a reconsidered and cautious *Neues Bauen*, and in France *L'Architecture d'Aujourd'hui*'s editor, André Bloc, had a particular fondness for the work of Le Corbusier. These examples are all instructive. In Switzerland, the journal *Das Werk* was, through affiliation with the BSA (Swiss Association of Architects), restricted in its ability to publish modernist projects abroad, having to give precedence in the national context to the work produced by its members, whether or not of a modernist persuasion.

The battle between modernism – progressive or pragmatic – and more conservative regionally oriented voices was evident in most European countries postwar. However, the involvement of journals, as conduits or as active participants, varied. The most extreme positions were to be found in the Netherlands and in Germany (with their strong avant-garde presence during the interwar period).

Professional architecture journals as a particular type of periodical contributed strongly to a perception of modernism as 'a common language' where 'continuity' between pre-war and postwar periods was at a premium, particularly in Italy and Germany. This was complicated by an ideological conflict between a radical modernist legacy and the given identity of traditionalist tendencies, while this divide persisted elsewhere in a less strident form.

Initially, the postwar journals tended to idolise the 'masters' identified with the modern movement of the preceding interwar period: Le Corbusier, Mies van der Rohe, Gropius, August Perret and Aalto all appear in monographic issues or special articles, often introduced with supportive editorials (in one instance of Perret's case, his own). Later they preface, in the critical space given to Colin Rowe in *The Architectural Review* or the discourse of Ernesto Rogers' circle at *Casabella*, new perspectives on interwar modernity, whether within the autonomy of formalist analysis or concerned with the concept of historical 'continuity'. Both register a detachment from diluted versions of the modernist canon acted out in national variants of a social or welfare state architecture.

To what extent does the nature of the journal itself as a modernist construct align with the notion of continuity and with the narrative of its publication? And might that parallel the evolutionary conception of modernism likely to be inherent in the selection of the projects published (and the issues reported)?

In this context, it is revealing to compare modern architecture's involvement in the 'formation' of the fascist state examined in Rifkind's study of *Quadrante*, with its contribution to the postwar European architectural context of 'reconstruction', whether that was in hock to the capitalist imperatives of the Marshall Plan (particularly as experienced in Germany) or in the terms of the evolution of the Labourist British Welfare State. In Germany, architectural culture was immediately distanced from classical monumentality and there remained an antipathy to, and stringent polemic between, exponents of a progressive continuity with the social projects of interwar modernism and those who identified with the conservative values of vernacular tradition. Whereas in Britain, the impact of modernism had been piecemeal before the Second World War and hence the social architecture of the postwar period generally looked to Scandinavian models (with significant exceptions). This acceptable face of a second phase of modernism was habitually blurred, given the editorial predilections of *The Architectural Review* which, in a very different context to the Italian interwar experience, sought legitimacy in a strangely familiar hybridity in which an English provincial conservatism associated with the picturesque could coexist with the formal preoccupations of Colin Rowe and a tempered undidactic variant of the International Style promoted by the likes of Philip Johnson.

This was not only identified with the architecture of the New Empiricism published in the postwar journals, but also with the visuality propagated in the format and the graphic design of *The Architectural Review*, *Casabella* or *domus* in their differing national contexts and cultures of design. The coloured inserts and fold-outs, the framing and typographic nuances, and the preoccupation with furniture, furnishing and industrial design delineated not only a new domesticity but were forerunners of an emergent consumer economy fuelled by style, fashion and an affective taste. The anodyne version of modern architecture that served as its backdrop was displaced by the New Brutalism coined by Reyner Banham in 1966 and associated with the Independent Group and members of Team 10, where the influence of the tactility of *art brut* was manifested in the texture of an architecture, and a graphic style, best characterised in *domus* during the late 1950s.

The accompanying popular culture was deconstructed in a French context by the essays collected in Roland Barthes' *Mythologies* of 1957. Whereas these texts were

attentive to visual detail, photographic representation and the tactility of materials (the seduc-
tion of 'design' and its surfaces in 'The Face of Garbo', 'The New Citroen', 'The Jet-man' or
'Plastic'), their critical agenda was to expose the cultural consequences of an increasingly hege-
monic capitalism that pervaded the 1950s and extended into the pop culture of the 1960s. This
gradually began to be registered in professional architecture journals. They were less attentive
to the events of 1968, however, which tended to be sublimated in subsequent attention to
matters educational (architectural students, education and school building). Curiously, Barthes'
Mythologies was unillustrated (in its English editions). Its visual territory, however, lay in the
growth of popular magazines, traces of which may be found in the architecture journals of the
1950s (not least in their advertisements). In contrast to Barthes' *The Fashion System*, published
incomplete in 1967, structuralism in architecture turned to analysis of form and meaning,
rather than to the metalinguistic implications for architecture of this study of the fashion
industry, its media and publications.

Speaking of 'The Endless Garment', Barthes proposes: 'Imagine (if possible) a woman
dressed in an endless garment, one that is woven of everything the magazine of Fashion says'
(Barthes, 1990). What, we are asking here, does the 'magazine of Architecture' have to say
about its subject? And, does that 'telling' or the wrapping of architecture in the form of the
journal during the postwar period (now a foreign country) preface the endless garment of
an architectural culture that later projects the discipline into a world of publicity, celebrity
and status. This trajectory underpins the republication of journals in books, of which *domus*
is the classic example – primarily because at the time it arguably bridged the divide between
the high, and the popular, culture of design and architecture in postwar Italy (though Paolo
Scrivano takes issue with this perception in Chapter 10). The international reach of a commodity culture, heavily influenced by American mores, was paralleled by a reciprocal inter-
nationalism sought by professional architectural journals like *Casabella*, *The Architectural Review*,
L'Architecture d'aujourd'hui or *Ekistics*, albeit each from their different perspectives.

Outlook

The postwar era brought a host of new journals – notably in Spain, Switzerland, Hungary,
Greece and Germany – competing with established titles. Several of the former picked up
from where they had left off before or after the war, while others, perhaps also in the light of
facing new competition, performed more or less extreme changes of direction. The mid-1960s,
following the demise of CIAM and a questioning of the prevailing pragmatic and commercial
modernism – all but stripped of social idealism – that had emerged in most European countries, also brought with it the emergence of new journals and changes to the more established
titles. In most cases this meant a stronger emphasis on differing forms of urbanism and on
broader cultural issues, but also a questioning of the role of the architect and the profession.

After the events of 1968 everything changed – or was that really the case? The majority of
the chapters that follow argue for a sea change which impacted on the professional architecture
journal in most of Western Europe. Certainly the student revolution affected attitudes towards
urbanism and social architecture; how exactly is unclear, primarily because of the difficulty of
assessing the reciprocal relationship between cause and effect in a retrospective study of journals.

While content, layouts and ideological persuasions changed; some journals continued
in a similar vein, others ceased publication and new journals arrived; the format of the
professional journals seems largely to have remained similar (in principle). Some things did

change. Documentary drawings have today in many cases been all but replaced by glossy photographs, a process that was underway during the 1960s. Competition news and technical drawings – in the form of fold-outs, for instance – are largely due to the omnipotence of the internet, absent today from many contemporary architecture journals. It is hard to imagine a conflict like that of the 'Bauhaus debate', fought out in the pages of the German journal *Baukunst und Werkform* over almost the entire course of 1953, now taking place in any journal. The professional architecture journal (analogue or digital) is evidently declining in subscription numbers, and has lost its comparative value for practitioners. As late as the 1990s, the received view was that architects updated their knowledge of the latest developments if they subscribed to leading national journals – and perhaps an international title or two. The last decades of the twentieth century in Western Europe saw an unprecedented growth in the numbers of registered architects in most countries, and with that an increase in practices and schools of architecture taking out multiple subscriptions. Practices in the UK, for instance, would still employ part-time librarians to organise information sources in the form of data sheets and product advertising accompanying the journals they subscribed to.

While, like its architecture, the all-pervasive digital age was accompanied by an underlying postmodern sense of 'plurality', in fact most of the established titles in the major European economies have survived in one form or another and do contain much what they did 50 years ago – naturally there are exceptions and considerable adaptions to digital culture. Online editions with more up-to-date news sections are published in parallel to print editions; some journals are sent out free and are entirely financed by advertising and professional subscriptions. Is their relevance to the profession diminished? Certainly, editorials are shorter and opinions seem less confrontational (in a culture where 'anything goes'). Although its current role has changed when news is available on the internet long before hard copy has reached an architect's workstation (or hot-desk), the mainstream professional architecture journal, with all that title implies, remains for the time being and in the face of an uncertain future, here to stay. Its retrospective presence remains significant to a historical understanding of the architecture of the postwar era, when the first signs of our current culture were evolving in the formation of journals as much as in the construction of the buildings they chose to publish.

Acknowledgements

Heartfelt thanks from both editors to all the authors for their texts, and their patience with the transnational editing process, given the cultural and linguistic issues involved. We would also like to thank the following for their help and patience during the production process: editorial assistant at Routledge, Kalliope Dalto; copy-editor Gary Smith; and Liz Davey, project manager at Out of House Publishing. Last but not least thanks to Fran Ford at Routledge for commissioning this book.

Notes

1 Periodical; Journal; Magazine (2017). Definitions taken from Merriam-Webster.com. Retrieved September 11, 2017 from www.merriam-webster.com/dictionary.
2 Jannière and Vanlaethem note Jean-Michel Leniaud's comments on 'the peripheries of the discourse' in the sub-section 'Beyond Content: Method' of their essay on *Architectural Periodicals in the 1960s and 1970s*, where 'tables of contents, indexes, regular columns and advertisements are mentioned' (Jannière and Vanlaethem, 2008, p. 44).

References

Barthes, R. (1972). *Mythologies*. St. Albans: Paladin.

—— (1984). *Camera Lucida*. London: Flamingo, pp. 25–26, 43, 94–99.

—— (1990). *The Fashion System*. Berkeley, CA: University of California Press.

Carpo, M. (1998). The Making of the Typographic Architect. In V. Hart and P. Hicks (Eds), *Paper Palaces: The Rise of the Renaissance Architectural Treatise*. New Haven, CT: Yale University Press, pp. 158–170.

Colomina, C. (2010). *Clip/Stamp/Fold: The Radical Architecture of Little Magazines 196x–197x*. Barcelona: ActarBirkhäuser.

Jannière, H. and Vanlaethem, F. (2008). Architectural Magazines as Historical Source or Object? A Methodological Essay. In A. Sornin, H. Jannière, F. Vanlaethem (Eds), *Architectural Periodicals in the 1960s and 1970s*. Quebec: Institut de recherche en histoire de l'architecture, pp. 41–70.

Rifkind, D. (2012). *The Battle for Modernism:* Quadrante *and the Politicization of Architectural Discourse in Fascist Italy*. Venice: Marsilio.

Sornin, A., Jannière, H. and Vanlaethem, F. (Eds) (2008), *Architectural Periodicals in the 1960s and 1970s*. Quebec: Institut de recherche en histoire de l'architecture.

1

SWISS JOURNALS 1940–1965

Mirroring the difficult departure into modernity

Christoph Allenspach

Following the Second World War, Switzerland was in the very fortunate position of having been spared the destruction of a brutal European war. Postwar, the country had no imperative to rebuild bombed cities, but could, after years of scarce resources, commit to economic recovery and the building of new infrastructures. The biggest challenge was the housing shortage in the towns and cities, caused by the influx of people from rural areas.

In the period before the 1960s, the country experienced an unprecedented economic boom and the building sector prospered. However, Swiss architecture found itself in a peculiar situation. During the isolation of the war years a particular Swiss regional style of architecture had emerged, which attracted strong European interest in the postwar years. Simultaneously, young Swiss architects, in order to escape the limitations of the regional style, looked to reconnect with international, especially American, modernism. In the 1950s, these young architects fought for the renewal of a corresponding Swiss modernism. Having achieved their cultural aspirations by returning to the legacy of the Swiss modern masters, they were however, accused of merely being epigones.

The celebrated 'Swiss way' and its limitations

The acceptance of modern architecture, or the *Neues Bauen* in Switzerland, had come late, but lasted longer than in most other European countries. Architects deliberately distanced themselves from the rhetoric of classicist state architectures identified with the dictatorships of neighbouring countries. Modern architecture was seen as resistance to the status quo, and a purely monumental architecture had never been representative of the bourgeois microstate that was nineteenth-century Switzerland. Clients and architects attached importance to sober and pragmatic construction in architecture, and avant-garde experiments remained the exception. In the 1930s, Swiss architects developed a consensus about the concept of a 'moderate modernism', which in 1939 found its culmination in the pavilions built for the federal exhibition in Zurich; affectionately known as 'Landi' (*Landesausstellung*). From then on the *Landi-Stil* was an established term. A traditional style with regional roots, a staid and plain minimalism derived from the simple building types of past master builders was developed in the context of

FIGURE 1.1   Swiss architecture built during the war, *Kantonsspital Zürich*, 1943–1945, *Werk* 11 (1946).
Source: © Amt für Städtebau der Stadt Zürich.

the isolation and defensiveness prevalent during the war years. The building of settlements, the main preoccupation of the building industry, saw the reemergence of the nineteenth-century tenement block; with pitched roofs instead of flat roofs, punch-hole facades instead of horizontal long windows, brick and timber instead of concrete and steel, these simple forms could be built by local brick layers and carpenters in the villages.

After the end of the Second World War, the Swiss government swiftly and somewhat calculatingly responded to the interest in Swiss regionalism that surfaced in Europe. In September 1946, commissioned by the Swiss Federal Council, a number of different institutions presented the *Switzerland – Planning and Building Exhibition* at the RIBA in London.[1] This, as the first major exhibition on Swiss architecture outside Switzerland, incorporated 600 posters and was also successfully shown in Copenhagen, Stockholm, Warsaw, Amsterdam and Cologne. In Switzerland the exhibition was covered extensively in *Schweizerische Bauzeitung* (Furrer, 1946), and briefly in *Werk* (Roth, 1946a). It was not available to a Swiss audience until January 1949, when it was shown in the Kunsthalle Basel.

Hans Hofmann, chief architect of the 1939 'Landi', and professor of architecture at the Eidgenössische Polytechnikum in Zurich (ETH today), in his introduction to the exhibition catalogue, presented the architecture which had emerged in isolation from international tendencies as a logically consistent development of 1930s modernism: 'We gratefully acknowledge that the *Neues Bauen* provided a fruitful basis for the development of a contemporary architecture. The break with tradition forced us to re-evaluate the fundamental problems of building and architecture' (Hofmann, 1946, p. 136). Distancing himself immediately, however, he argued:

> We have kept our distance from *Neues Bauen* and we are able today, with a certain objectivity, to weigh up its advantages and disadvantages. We see the *Neues Bauen* mirroring its time in the then common overestimation of science and technology; a belief in the absolute validity of intellectual thought, and an arrogant, uncritical trust in progress.

For Hofmann, the development during the war was to be seen as a corrective, maturing and complementing the principles of *Neues Bauen*:

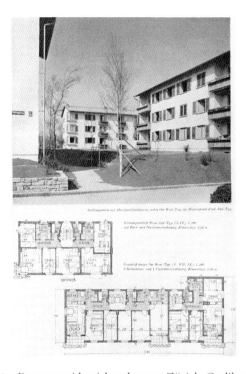

FIGURE 1.2   Postwar residential settlement, Zürich-Oerlikon, by A. &
H. Oeschger 1946, *Werk* 1 (1946).
Source: © Verlag Werk AG, Zürich.

We are searching for a sensible realisation of building tasks, in the context of practical, faultless solutions and artistic design. The search for architectural form is led by construction in accordance to material properties and the aesthetic laws of harmony and proportions.

Hofmann distinguishes between two stylistic categories, one traditional and the other modern:

We distinguish between tasks that come out of a lively tradition, such as the house, the church and so on, and the new tasks which have no tradition, like the factory, the office building, the department store, the train station, the hospital and so on. […]. Generally, brick, tried and tested, and tiled roofs are used for housing… The use of these materials and a modest, self-evident architectural design provide a lively tradition related to the good examples of our farm, and bourgeois town houses, of the past.

Hofmann, 1946, p. 136

Two publications disseminated this regional style in Switzerland and abroad: *Schweizer Architektur: Ein Überblick über das schweizerische Bauschaffen der Gegenwart*, by the architect Hans Volkart, was published in Germany in 1951 (Volkart, 1951); in the same year in Switzerland, *Der Siedlungsbau in der Schweiz*, by the chief architect of Basel, Julius Maurizio, was published (Maurizio, 1951). Both books summed up the dominant organisational types and showed once again the contrast between traditional and modern building types. Urban *Dörfli* (housing estates), many of which emerged after 1940, stood in contrast to utilitarian buildings for industry, administration and infrastructure. Both categories diverged in their respective directions until the mid-1950s.

The folio publication *Moderne Schweizer Architektur 1925–45*, compiled by Max Bill (Bill, 1949), and republished in a second edition in 1949, provided a counterpart presenting exclusively 'modern' buildings, coupled with a plea for architects to dare again to build modern architecture. While the official exhibition represented the built reality of this period, it only reflected a limited picture of architects' current opinions. The younger generation was discontented, as it perceived the architecture of the wartime and the immediately postwar years as traditional and petty bourgeois. In the decade following 1945, this generation began to rediscover, after years of isolation and via the newly available (again) international architecture journals, developments abroad. The architect and aspiring novelist Max Frisch, who had been invited by the Rockefeller Foundation to visit the USA in 1951, wrote, on his return to Switzerland, a sardonic account of Swiss architecture. Having presented this as a lecture to assembled colleagues of the BSA, who had developed the very building types he criticised, he proceeded to publish his attack in their journal *Das Werk*:

> Even the last spout is crafted, and the returning traveler will hardly find a building that doesn't make him think of terms such as: decoration, solid, thorough, cared for, tasteful, safe, clean, […], flawless, respectable, very respectable. Where [else] in the world do people build like this?

This conservative mentality was clearly getting on Frisch's nerves:

> [...] never to want, let alone to do anything radical. […] Taking refuge in detailing – it seems to the returnee – is a character trait of especially our best architecture. Even large projects often seem as if they'd been hand crafted with a coping saw.
>
> *Frisch, 1953*

He had experienced American cities, and the modernism developed during the war by European emigrés like Mies van der Rohe, Gropius, Neutra and Breuer. Mexico City, for example, in his view was an architectonic jungle, but one that contained orchids of modern architecture. In Switzerland, he believed, even an airport terminal would be compartmented to a degree that prevented any suggestion of monumentality. Everything had to be intimate and inconspicuous. Appalled, he insisted: 'I am an urbanite, I am a renter and not a farmer living on his soil.'

Das Werk: mirror of discord post-1945

Das Werk, Schweizer Monatsschrift für Architektur, freie Kunst und angewandte Kunst, founded in 1914 by the *Bund Schweizer Architekten* (BSA) and the Schweizerische Werkbund, was for a significant period the most important publication for architecture and design in Switzerland. Its themed issues were published monthly and it was unusual in that it not only covered architecture, urban planning and garden design, but also interior architecture, art, design, graphic design and fashion. All these disciplines were given generous space, with a focus on developments in Switzerland. The respective editors-in-chief, overseeing the whole spectrum, would heavily shape the contents of the journals. It was only in 1943, with the inauguration of Alfred Roth, that a second editor would supervise the two art publications.[2]

Das Werk was originally founded by young BSA members primarily in order to establish a mouthpiece for their reform-oriented architecture, opposing the neo-Renaissance style of Swiss followers of Gottfried Semper. However, the federation's publication was quickly confronted with the new tendencies of both neo-classicism and modernism. The editors were confronted by the strongly divergent positions of the BSA members, who all insisted on their right to see their work published. Moreover, they sought to influence developments with axiomatic texts. Which kind of architecture was to be the order of the day? Peter Meyer, editor from 1930 to 1942, who shaped the journal's issues with his astute and sometimes polemical commentaries, tried to propagate a third 'Swiss' way, between classicism and modernism, while heavily condemning 1920s classicism, particularly that representative of the German, Italian and Russian states. He was also critical towards the *Neues Bauen*, in which he missed the aspect of monumentality, and the 1930s 'moderate modernism' that was, although acceptable, not the ideal which he tirelessly propagated in his journal. Shortly before his resignation he identified his conception of a modern monumentality in the building for the University of Miséricorde in Fribourg, 'a bold and generous attempt to bring the two most important branches of modernism into a synthesis' (Meyer, 1942).[3] He alluded to the influence of Auguste Perret and Le Corbusier, but his heated plea remained without impact and the Miséricorde building had no tangible influence on the further development of twentieth-century architecture.

His successor, Alfred Roth, who had worked for Le Corbusier and would edit the journal from 1942 to 1959, had a clear editorial direction: besides Le Corbusier, he considered Perret and Frank Lloyd Wright to be 'outstanding artistic personalities' (Roth, 1944, p. 262). Nonetheless, he had little opportunity to promote their modernist inclinations in Switzerland. During and shortly after the war he had, in default of available sources, to rely on speculative sketches and projects of their international projects. Even by 1947 he could only publish a theoretical text by Perret and his house in the Rue Raynouard in Paris; a project for a commercial high-rise in Algiers by Le Corbusier; and a ten-year-old building by Beaudoin and Lods (*Werk*, 2/1947).

In the Swiss context he mainly focused on modern buildings of the pre-war years, and attempted to align himself with the new regionalism. In 1944, and out of frustration, he prompted a discussion on architectural theory to support preparations for postwar years, reconstructing a Europe in ruins, suggesting that 'the attitude towards architecture in smaller European democracies such as Sweden, Finland, Holland and Switzerland, has led to a surprisingly broad development' and that 'the new architecture in each of these countries could, based on particular universal architectural principles, [also] develop specific national characteristics'. With a pragmatic optimism, he added: 'Moreover, we are convinced that our Swiss architecture will therefore find its way out of the current restrictions and a lack of direction, more quickly than one would anticipate' (Roth, 1944, p. 261). In 1946 he published a second edition of his book *Die neue Architektur*, containing 20 international, and Swiss, examples, all from the 1930s (Roth, 1946b).

Alfred Roth fundamentally disagreed with Hans Hofmann (who he would succeed as professor at the ETH in 1958) concerning the degree of recognition Swiss architecture had achieved abroad. In 1947 he argued for 'an overcoming of the material and intellectual constraints caused by the war' (Roth, 1947, p. 182). This reconsideration was 'on the one hand a consequence of slowly normalizing circumstances in Switzerland, and on the other to the

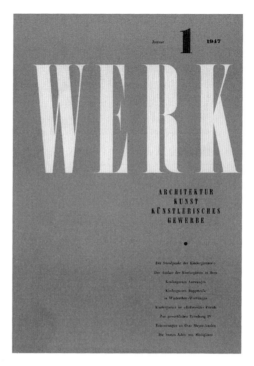

FIGURE 1.3   Journal cover, *Werk* 1 (1947).
Source: © Verlag Werk AG, Zürich.

re-emerging possibilities of comparison with the work in other countries'. This would loosen 'the hardened attitudes and gridlocked opinions that had emerged within the constricted intellectual horizon of the war years'. His favourite concept was *universality*. While it was indeed gratifying that Swiss architecture was being acknowledged positively in other countries, and also was subjected to criticism, he stated: 'The foreign countries, which are burdened with enormous planning and building tasks, expect from a country like ours, which has been spared the horrors of war, more than just the adherence to a relatively high status quo. Being able to work under fortunate conditions, *pioneering model solutions* and *creative achievements* are expected of us' (Roth, 1947, p. 182). The alleged high average quality of Swiss architecture proved on 'closer inspection' to be 'purely material and construction orientated, rather than of a conceptual and architectural character, which isn't exactly anything to be proud of'. He criticised the 'profit orientated business architects, along with the professional bodies', which were, in his view, not concerned with the fundamental questions of contemporary architecture at all. In 1951, writing the last instalment of the column 'Zeitgemäße Architekturbetrachtungen' (Contemporary Views on Architecture), Roth soberly noted: 'Clear visions, sharp and assured judgment, intellectual resilience and breadth, but also outward modesty and inward ambition, are, particularly among the generation of younger architects, the exception' (Roth, 1951, p. 76). He envisaged a future based on 1930s Swiss modernism. In order to demonstrate that it was still possible to gain an overview, his elaborate text attempted to assess new tendencies in other countries. In particular he looked for the influence of Le Corbusier, Gropius, Neutra and Wright, and was also excited by the 'genius' of Alvar Aalto, who made Finland a fortunate exception to the norm elsewhere. In Switzerland itself he could not see any signs of the

FIGURE 1.4   Postwar Modernism, Malagnou-Parc Housing, Geneva, by Marc J. Saugey, 1949–1950, *Werk* 1 (1951).
Source: © Centre d'iconographie de la Bibliothèque de Genève.

longed for renewal of modernism. He was critical of functional, constructive and material complexity, adding: 'Inhibition [in Switzerland] is unfortunately more prevalent than enthusiasm; let alone that we are lacking a natural sense for beauty. Hence it is not surprising that our architecture is seldom buoyant or markedly aesthetic' (Roth, 1951, pp. 75–76).

In order to influence national development, Roth as the *Werk* editor made a genuine effort to publish international modern buildings. But in the national context *Werk* was hand-tied by an obligation to prioritise publication of the works of the BSA members. And despite his critical attitude, Roth was on occasion compelled to praise projects that promised any kind of opening in the debate. He dutifully published staid housing estates, schools and churches designed by his fellow architects, and, at the beginning of 1951, found some recompense in the first modern postwar housing scheme, Marc Saugey's Malagnou-Parc in Geneva, and the first 'high-rise' buildings in Basle and Zurich (*Werk*, 1/1951). In the same issue he dedicated space to a leading article on Mies van der Rohe.

The Schweizerische Werkbund (SWB) had much less trouble publishing modern design and graphic design. In the immediate postwar years the SWB developed dynamic activities and events, associated with numerous designers and graphic designers abroad. In 1949 they promoted the first exhibition *Die gute Form* (Good Form) at the *Mustermesse* Basel (the Swiss Trade Fair), which took place annually until 1967. As early as 1946 a special issue of the journal on the question of form in industrial design was published: an exhibition of Swiss products that had every reason to broker international comparison. In contrast to architecture, there was no need to fight for modern design. Instead, this prompted pedagogical questions concerning how consumers could be 'educated' to appreciate good form. The reflections of the SWB secretary, Egidius Streiff, on 'Formgebung in der Schweizerischen Industrie' (Design in Swiss Industry) (Streiff, 1946), and those by the designer, architect and artist Max Bill on 'Erfahrung bei der Formgestaltung von Industrieprodukten' (Experiences in the Design of Industrially Manufactured Goods) (Bill, 1946), laid the foundations for two decades. Sigfried Giedion contributed 'Stromlinienstil und industrielles Entwerfen in den USA' (Streamlining and industrial design in the USA) (Giedion, 1946).

The exhibition *Die gute Form*, in which the quality of the graphic design stood out, received broad coverage in *Werk*, and there were a series of articles on furniture, housewares, textiles, graphics and exhibition design. The journal contributed significantly to a renewed graphic design culture, which became legendary abroad as 'Swiss Typography'. In 1963 the Werkbund could contently look back at its development over the past 50 years (*Werk*, 10/1963).

Sea change 1955: towards Switzerland's second modernity

The issues of *Werk* from 1955 onwards illustrate the growing influence of Swiss postwar modernism. In previous years Roth had been intermittently able to publish buildings of the older generation of architects – for instance, the distinctive tower of the *Centro Svizzero*, realised by Armin Meili from 1949–1951 in Milan, and certain Swiss factory buildings. However, generally he had to content himself with unbuilt projects by the younger generation of architects (dissatisfied with the status quo) or even with student projects from the design studios of the ETH professors William Dunkel and Hans Hofmann (*Werk*, 1/1953). In 1955 the first apartment buildings (*Werk*, 5/1955)[4] and commercial buildings (*Werk*, 10/1955)[5] designed by the younger generation were published, and in 1956 the pioneering Wasgenring school in Basel by Fritz Haller (1953–1955) (*Werk*, 4/1956), emulating Mies van der Rohe.

Hans Hofmann, adaptable as ever, had several projects published, which revealed the waning of Swiss regionalism (*Werk*, 1/1957).[6] From 1957 regionalism would be irrelevant in *Werk*. The 1958 retrospective held on the occasion of the BSA's fiftieth anniversary showed how much the organisation now identified with modernism. Wartime buildings and those of the immediate postwar period were largely ignored, and the construction of residential

FIGURE 1.5 Second Swiss Modernism, Wasgenring School, Basel, by Bruno and Fritz Haller, 1953–1955, *Werk* 4 (1956).
Source: © Bernhard Moosbrugger/Fotostiftung Schweiz.

settlements, that had played such an important role, was completely excluded (*Werk*, 9/1958). In Issue 11 (1958) the first modern estates appeared, exemplified by the first buildings Atelier 5 built in exposed concrete. The opening issue of 1959 presented sparse, minimalist housing blocks and high-rise buildings with flat roofs, which had over a short period of time replaced normative three- or four-storey pitched roof *Zeilenbau* developments. Because the BSA had changed, given the response to a new generation of architects, *Werk* became the mouthpiece of the new modernism. Strangely, however, buildings designed by engineers were ignored, whether in theoretical debates or the publication of buildings, despite the fact that engineers had accomplished some outstanding achievements in the immediate postwar years. This subject was left to the *Schweizerische Bauzeitung* and the *Bulletin technique de la Suisse Romande*.

Alfred Roth, who in 1958 became Hofmann's successor as professor for design at the ETH, and gradually retreated from his editorial role at *Werk*, was exercising due restraint in his inaugural lecture on the current international developments:

> Where are we, generally speaking, today? In my view we are still at the beginning of a new, possibly very crucial stage of architecture. We can arguably recognise characteristics of a new approach to design, however, it would be too early to detect a broad and solid base of a style of our times.
>
> *Roth, 1958, p. 47*

Le Corbusier's chapel at Ronchamp and his buildings in Chandigarh, and projects by Prouvé, Breuer, Neutra and Saarinen had, in the previous three years, provided an opportunity to hint at the scope of the ongoing international context.

1960: modernist epigones?

'Epigonen. Probleme der Gegenwartsarchitektur' (Epigones. Problems in Contemporary Architecture) was the title of an article in *Werk* Issue 12, 1959, by Benedikt Huber, who had been part of the editorial staff since 1955, and between 1957 and 1961 was editor-in-chief. Huber's axiomatic piece was also aimed at reflecting the current Swiss status quo. His position differed from that of his predecessor:

> Only ten years ago the term 'modern architecture' in principle meant opposition to the normative taste and thinking about architecture […]. Today, the visual appearance of modern architecture determines a large proportion of our environment […]. Modernism today is no longer synonymous with architectural quality in terms of a single concept or form of comprehension. Different perspectives, and distinctions between good and bad architectural quality, now lie within our conception of modern architecture. Consequently the term 'modern' has, in every respect, lost any specific meaning.
>
> *Huber, 1959, p. 419*

The text reads like a swansong to the modern era, which had been characterised by a courageous combative spirit, and by the conviction that the modern was 'new'. He notes that 'disciples' wrongly interpreted 'the great fathers of the *Neues Bauen*':

> We are the younger generation and are fighting with all the attendant difficulties the position brings with it. […]. It is easy to see that the adoption of this heritage is often

only possible in purely formal terms [...]. The little 'Mies van der Rohe' and the little 'Corbusier' are familiar contemporaries.

Huber, 1959, p. 421

There was an evident frustration here, given that the 'moderns' of the second generation had managed to prevail, Huber bemoaning in particular that:

The addiction for the absolute new has become characteristic of our time. [...] In this frenzy for progress other, more fundamental problems are mostly left to one side.

Huber, 1959, p. 422

BSA president Alberto Camenzind went further:

Modern architecture, which had been fought for by a whole generation of architects, has, from one day to the next, vulgarised its forms. A modernism which is no longer substantially motivated has successfully spread everywhere, and the significance of architecture is in danger of being drowned in this excess of 'excitement'.

Camenzind, 1962

These were astonishing words, since *Werk* in the 1960s did publish the buildings of an established and recognised Swiss modernism, and, in particular those of BSA members, all represented in equal measure. In this respect *Werk*, despite any words of warning, maintained satisfaction with what had been achieved and the associated pride of competing internationally on a level playing field. Discussion about the nature of modern architecture had fallen silent. Questions now focused on practical aspects – for example, the large volume of building production or issues concerning general contractors; standardisation; rationalisation and prefabrication; contemporary interpretations of functional types; urban planning and transport; construction research and the education of architects.

From 1962, the new editor, the sociologist Lucius Burckhardt, increased the range of interests and published articles on sociological consideration of human needs in the planning, building and establishment of new settlements and buildings. In hindsight he noted that there was little room for editorial manoeuvre, and that the journal's primary role was to publish buildings designed by BSA members.[7] The majority of themed issues had indeed reflected contemporary building activity in Switzerland and abroad. But Burkhardt and his invited authors often raised critical questions about responsibilities in urban planning and residential occupation. As early as 1961, in an essay called 'Krise der Stadt' (Crisis of the City), he reflected on how, ideally, once city centres had been emptied and taken over by traffic, the modern city might be reclaimed as a viable entity in favour of the 'integration' of the individual (Burckhardt, 1961). At the end of 1962 he critically explored formal questions of the development of industrial and furniture design, maintaining that while he was 'bucking the trend', he did not believe that 'the forms of the industrial world will, as it were, oscillate and asymptomatically maintain a gravitational stasis' (Burckhardt, 1962, p. 420). Individual issues of the journal confronted the task of urban planning and housing (Werk, 11/1962), and utopian urbanism (Friedman, 1963; *Werk*, 7/1963). Over the course of the 1960s, many of these questions would become politicised themes of immediate concern to architects and designers.

Bauen + Wohnen: international rapport, Swiss accent

Bauen + Wohnen, subtitled *Internationale Zeitschrift* and founded in 1947 by the publisher Adolf Pfau, gained a reputation as a journal oriented towards international modernism aiming to position itself as a counterpart to the more mundane *Werk* (Hanak, 2001). However, its development was not linear, and the journal's self-image changed during the initial years of publication. In the first editorial, Alfred Altherr rather ambivalently addressed his fictive readers:

> The main emphasis should be on projects of architects seeking to enhance the development of housing, of the free plan. […] In addition we will give our full attention to the workplace of the housewife: the kitchen and the ancillary rooms with practical equipment. We also want to introduce you to new building materials, products of contemporary industrial production.
>
> *Altherr, 1947*

Bauen + Wohnen accordingly did not see itself as 'a downright specialist journal', but as a 'journal whose task it is to present to the public good buildings and institutions'. The contributing editor Walter Frey concurred:

> Our task should be to demonstrate how furniture and appliances, whose emergent beauty of materials in new forms, conform with the meaning of our lives and yet contain all the advantages of clear functions and practical considerations.
>
> *Frey, 1947*

This was the tenor of the Werkbund's exhibition *Die gute Form*. *Bauen + Wohnen* saw itself as the journal for the cultivated middle class looking to fulfil the dream of a contemporary home. Advertisements for household goods and the generally conventional furniture and interiors featured were clearly directed towards the 'modern' housewife. The competition for the journal was consequently not *Das Werk*, but *Das Ideale Heim*, which had been published with similar aspirations since 1928.

During this period, few open-plan domestic buildings were available to publish, and the editors for the time being tried to fulfil this aspiration by asking eight mainly young architects for proposals producing designs, which resulted, without exception, in schemes traditional in appearance. But it had not been the aim to propagate modern forms like those established by the end of the 1930s. Architect Theo Schmid, writing a column in the journal, evidently had the licence to distance himself from the modern formal idiom in which he would later build. He bemoaned the fact that light, air and sun had become precepts of the 'liberated dwelling', arguing that vain extremists had conceived the house as an abstraction: 'The powerful version of the extraordinary in housing has to be tamed and kept at bay once again' (Schmid, 1947, p. 55).

A new journal's modern self-discovery

Initially *Bauen + Wohnen* called itself *Schweizerische Vierteljahreszeitschrift* (Swiss Quarterly). However, by the end of 1951 only 11 infrequent issues of the journal had been published. The journal's business model, exclusively aimed at the Swiss market, was failing. Although the publisher, thanks to also being involved in the sales of household appliances, managed to market ample advertising space in the journal, subscribers were another question. In contrast to *Werk* and *Schweizerische Bauzeitung*, the new journal lacked the financial backing of a professional body. The publishers exploited the resignation of the editors after only three issues as an opportunity to change course, and the young architect Jacques Schader, who later was to become one of the leading lights of the 'second modernism', edited the fourth issue published at the end of 1948. He remained the sole executive editor until 1955, and was responsible for the journal's international outlook. The cover page now incorporated titles in English and French (*building + home* and *construction + habitation*) and the headings, captions and a summary of the German texts were published in both languages too.

Initially Schader published a range of international modern houses, and – because of the lack of finished buildings – projects by young Swiss architects characterised by flat and mono-pitched roofs. He subsequently opened up the journal to address a broader architectural and urban planning agenda, aimed at a professional audience. Given direct competition from *Das Werk*, *Bauen + Wohnen* now established its own characteristic content and visual appearance. The graphic designer Richard P. Lohse, affiliated with the group *Zürcher Konkrete*, had already acquired responsibility for the graphic concept with the design of the second issue. He developed a radically modern concept employing: three columns; generously sized illustrations; layering photos, plans and text; and coloured overprinting and collages. This significant design format, that immediately announced the journal's modernity on the cover, was part of the tendency later known in other countries as 'Swiss Typography'.[8] Schader

FIGURE 1.6 Journal cover, *Bauen + Wohnen* 1 (1947).
Source: © Verlag Werk AG, Zürich.

responded to the new format with short texts and dry subtitles: brief, situation, solution, plan, construction, cost, etc.

The content and design of the renewed *Bauen + Wohnen* stood in clear contradiction to the international reputation of Swiss architecture. Evidence of a new focus, however, was manifest in 1948 when the official exhibition successfully visited European cities and the travelling exhibition *Siedlungsbau in der Schweiz 1938–1947* toured Switzerland. Instead of continuing to emphasise the 'Swiss' connection, the journal explicitly manifested a desire to build on an international understanding of modernism. The financial disadvantage of not being affiliated with a professional body was now turned to journalistic advantage. While *Das Werk*, besides publishing some modern buildings, was obliged to publish the work of the regional BSA colleagues, *Bauen + Wohnen* could make a more 'radical cut'.

In the fourth issue, an axiomatic essay by Hans Fischli on Swiss housing developments was published, which contradicted a widespread dogma (Fischli, 1948). Fischli had been a first-generation modernist, an adjunct to Hans Hofmann for the 1939 *Landesausstellung*, and the architect of the only genuinely modernist housing scheme in 1940s Switzerland, the *Siedlung Gwad* in Wädenswil. In his text Fischli presented modern settlement and housing types. In their introduction the editors criticised how 'the use and concatenation of approximately the same spatial element, namely the family apartment, causes monotony and uniformity in the overall appearance', noting that Fischli's argument, however, was of a more fundamental nature: 'Out of the circumstances of societal layering and variety, he develops a rich and nuanced building programme, resulting in lively settlement form which corresponds with

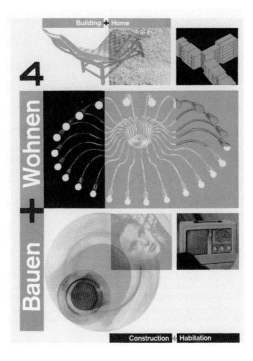

FIGURE 1.7   Journal cover, *Bauen + Wohnen* 4 (1948).
Source: © Richard Paul Lohse Stiftung.

current social, urban planning and architectural demands.' The designs for *Zeilenbau* terraced housing and high-rise blocks with flat roofs must have been provocative at the time. Issue 4 also contained numerous examples of modernist furniture design: by Charlotte Perriand, Charles and Ray Eames, and Eero Saarinen. These designs differed explicitly from the Swiss products, which had been shown in the first Werkbund exhibition *Die gute Form*. By 1950 Fischli was more explicit still in a long (40-page) essay (Fischli, 1950), published in three languages, in which he mapped out a settlement for 25,000 people: the estate of residential buildings, which were interspersed with green spaces, represented, down to the furniture design, a complete vocabulary of international modernist housing types, shops, workshops and kindergarten, bound together by a road network connected to the motorway. This was urban planning according to CIAM principles.

Bauen + Wohnen's content remained restricted to modern villas for several more issues, increasingly publishing American projects. From Issue 8 onwards the whole range of functional types would find their way onto its pages. In Issue 9, Mies van der Rohe received his first critical appreciation in Switzerland, with an overview of his American office buildings and housing schemes; this was followed by an extensive article on steel construction, illustrated with recent Swiss examples. Steel and glass architecture (which had until then found little attention in *Werk*), increasingly became a focus in *Bauen + Wohnen*, while the modern masters and their various 'schools' were also being published: Issue 10, on roof gardens, thoroughly discussed Le Corbusier's design principles and the eleventh issue, on theatres, focused on buildings by Walter Gropius and Frank Lloyd Wright. Readers, who in contrast, sought familiarity with new buildings by Le Corbusier, Richard Neutra and Alvar Aalto, also needed to take out a subscription to *Das Werk*.

International journal in German-speaking countries

With its modern focus, *Bauen + Wohnen* became economically viable, not least due to the general lack of architecture publications and the high demand immediately postwar. From 1952, *Bauen + Wohnen* was published six times a year, which doubled from 1956. The regular publishing schedule correlated with the onset of the journal's distribution in Germany. It was now published in two editions, the Swiss *Internationale Zeitschrift für Bauen + Wohnen*, and the *Deutsche Ausgabe* (German Edition). They shared the main part of the journal with the articles on architecture, which was edited (with a Swiss appendix) in Zurich. The German equivalent was edited in Munich. The publisher, Adolph Pfau, now freed from financial concerns, began to himself contribute to the journal, visiting internationally respected architects and, together with the editors, beginning to establish a network of correspondents and critics. *Bauen + Wohnen* had broken free from the limitations Max Frisch had only recently taken issue with. Issue 6 (1954) began by listing a committee of patrons, among others: Marcel Breuer; Jacob Bakema; Johannes Hendrik van den Broek; Jean Prouvé; Harry Seidler; Jorn Utzon; the Swiss Hans Fischli; and the German Bernhard Pfau; leading modernists of the second generation of the postwar years. The homage and wide-ranging congratulations received by the publisher on his sixtieth birthday in 1968 indicated the international attention now enjoyed by the journal (*Bauen + Wohnen*, 2/1969).[9]

The contents of individual issues became considerably more comprehensive, and shared with most architecture journals issues dedicated to specific functional building types, albeit now broadly supported with representative international precedents. *Bauen + Wohnen* also offered themed issues on pressing concerns, such as prefabrication in Issue 2 (1952). From

1953, detachable construction drawings for one of the published buildings, printed on strong paper, were included. These sheets were intended to encourage architects to familiarise themselves with modern facade technology using prefabricated elements. The journal also published monographic catalogues – for example, on Skidmore Owings & Merrill (*Bauen + Wohnen*, 3/1952),[10] or on Alvar Aalto, who with his brick buildings had become a leading figure among younger Swiss architects. Regularly published architects included Breuer, Seidler, Nervi, Prouvé, Utzon, van den Broek and Bakema, most of whom were members of the committee of patrons. The readers of *Bauen + Wohnen* certainly gained the impression that the world of architecture was now comprehensively 'modern', whereas in *Werk* the contrast between Swiss regional and international, modern architecture would remain in place for some time. However, *Bauen + Wohnen*, by complementing *Das Werk*, began more decisively to influence contemporary Swiss architectural culture. Sometimes both journals would publish the same buildings, but they developed respective preferences: *Das Werk* for the 'school' of Le Corbusier, and *Bauen + Wohnen* for that of Mies. Consequently, building professionals had to read both journals in order to stay well informed on international trends, and the development of new building and construction types.

From 1952 only the addendum to *Bauen + Wohnen* was distinctly 'Swiss'. Since German postwar modernism had not played a role earlier, it now, given the German edition, took increasing precedence. In some issues, Swiss architecture was entirely absent, unless it included modern attributes other than open planning. In the context of work published in *Bauen + Wohnen* it is retrospectively evident when and how the sea change from regional tendencies to a second modernism took place in Switzerland. In the early years, young architects with an inclination towards modernism had the opportunity, despite the lack of a completed oeuvre, to publish innovative designs with some future prospects. The year 1953 saw the first publications of realised buildings designed by the older generation that could stand comparison with international standards – for instance, a factory by Hans Fischli (*Bauen + Wohnen*, 3/1953, pp. 115–119) and an office building by Le Corbusier's pupil Marc Joseph Saugey (*Bauen + Wohnen*, 5/1953, pp. 236–240).[11] From 1954 to 1955, in contrast, it was increasingly the turn of the younger generation to gain commissions and have them published by *Bauen + Wohnen*, thereby gaining an international platform for their design work.[12]

FIGURE 1.8 Freudenberg School, Zurich, by Jacques Schader, 1956–1960,
Bauen + Wohnen, 9 (1960).
Source: © Baudirektion Kanton Zürich.

Theoretical aspirations

In 1955 Ernst Zietzschmann replaced Jacques Schader as editor of *Bauen + Wohnen*. Having already been on the staff for the previous two years, he changed little. The accompanying project descriptions did nonetheless become more elaborate, and there were occasional themed issues typically offering comprehensive discussion of new developments in schools building, industrial architecture or housing. Franz Füeg, the subsequent editor from 1958 to 1961, generated a new emphasis given his theoretical aspirations and deliberately sought out the debate he felt was missing in Switzerland. Shortly before he came on board he attempted to define the term modern in the stand-out essay 'Was ist modern in der Architektur? Strukturanalyse der zeitgenössischen Baukunst' (What is Modern Architecture? A Structural Analysis of Contemporary Architecture) (Füeg, 1958). Just at the point when modern building forms were being reasserted in Switzerland, he was of the opinion that:

> The majority of our architecture which is labeled modern, in truth has nothing to do with modernity. Generally the modern is restricted to new building materials, to the flat roof, or perhaps to contemporary services. The challenge is therefore not only to say what modern architecture is, but rather what an architecture of modernity is.
>
> *Füeg, 1958, p. 31*

Just as the editors of *Werk* would two years later speak of 'epigones', he was not concerned with defending modernism, but attempting to achieve clarification within the contemporary dynamic:

> As modern we denote the architecture of the past sixty years, and the buildings which appear entirely different to that of early epochs. As modernistic we denote architecture which adopts single elements of the modern, but which essentially retains the [syntactic] structural elements of classicism.
>
> *Füeg, 1958, p. 31*

For Füeg the current definition was unsatisfactory because 'In order to distinguish modern and not modern, modern and modernistic; formal and design elements are not sufficient.' Although the development of new architecture could 'not be imagined without concrete, steel and glass, without the flat roof and without the current state of technology', these also typified modernistic architecture. The decisive question, he suggested, was 'how these design elements relate to each other and how this relationship was internally and externally constituted in this structure'. The modern building remained defined in the 'structure' of tectonics, form and space. Füeg identified the concept of open 'free' space as crucial, which had been the *Bauen + Wohnen* credo from its inception. With this definition, Füeg referred explicitly to Sigfried Giedion (Giedion, 1941), and more implicitly to Le Corbusier (Le Corbusier, 1957):

> Space is to be experienced in motion, and not from a fixed location and or a boundary; Windows, facades and whole buildings are not [to be seen] in isolation, but exclusively in relation to other windows, facades and buildings. The crucial [dimension] only happens now in the spatial relationship between the design elements. Space itself is the boundary.
>
> *Füeg, 1958, p. 35*

FIGURE 1.9   St. Pius Church, Meggen, by Franz Füeg, 1964–1966, *Bauen + Wohnen*, 12 (1966).
Source: Photo Roland Schneider © Franz Füeg.

This represented a radically modern notion of space.

With his theory, Füeg demanded that architects question their practice, and as editor pursued this further in axiomatic essays and numerous commentaries in the column 'Am Rande' (In the Margin) (Füeg, 1981).[13] He also managed to acquire texts by internationally well-known architects such as Walter Gropius, Richard Neutra, Luigi Nervi and, astonishingly, Louis Kahn. Füeg decisively shaped the modernist focus of *Bauen + Wohnen* with themed issues on, for example, Konrad Wachsmann, Bakema + van den Broek, prefabrication, industrial buildings and shell structures. His editorial successors, Ernst Zietzschmann with Jürgen Joedicke, continued this perspective, with many substantial texts on functional types, the history of architecture and aspirations for theory. Retrospectively Füeg states that, while the theoretical texts raised much interest in Germany, he could not break the passivity of the Swiss architects.[14]

The SIA journals: encounters with technology[15]

The journals for the building industry most steeped in tradition were those of the *Schweizerischer Ingenieur-und Architektenverband* (SIA; Swiss Association of Engineers and Architects). By far the largest Swiss professional institute for the building industry, the SIA produced three regionally and editorially distinct editions of its 'journal'. In a typically Swiss manner there was one each for German-speaking Switzerland, the Romandy and for Ticino. The French 'edition' had originally been published in 1875 as the *Bulletin de la Société vaudoise des ingénieurs et architectes*, and since 1900 renamed the *Bulletin technique de la Suisse romande*, which became the fortnightly publication of the SIA (and of alumni of the *Ingenieurschule* Lausanne). The weekly German 'edition' the *Schweizerische Bauzeitung*,[16] had been founded in 1883 by the engineer August Waldner, and was published from 1906 by three generations of the Jegher family.[17] The SIA only acquired the *Bauzeitung* in 1966, whereas the Italian *Rivista Tecnica della Svizzera Italiana* had been published monthly since 1910, with some interruptions, representing the SIA's Ticino section.[18] The editorial offices operated independently and rarely reprinted contributions from the other 'editions'.

The SIA journals were a Swiss peculiarity. Despite being addressed to architects and engineers, architecture was, from the outset, always of secondary importance. New buildings were rarely published and were seemingly selected at random. Civil and mechanical engineering were prioritised, given the journals' emergence in the late nineteenth century. The technical schools in Zurich and Lausanne had been opened especially to educate engineers for industry and to undertake the ambitious projects required for the Swiss infrastructure, in particular the railways with their tunnels and bridges, the dams, and the road network. The *Schweizerische Bauzeitung* itself had emerged from the journal *Eisenbahn* (Railway), which had been published from 1874 to 1882. Engineers were in the majority in the SIA, as in the technical schools. Both the *Bauzeitung* and the *Bulletin Technique* were aimed at alumni who also formed the core of the journal's authors. Because the structural engineers were generally well travelled and often spent years on site abroad, the journal was generally up to date on international technical developments and more particularly on developments in the building industry. Even during the war years of the 1940s, when Switzerland was largely isolated, readers could keep themselves informed of civil engineering feats worldwide.

BSA architects and Werkbund designers had founded their own journal, *Werk*, in 1914, in which engineering only played a marginal role. However, it was not the case that architects ignored engineers' concerns. The quality and consciousness towards detail of the Swiss building industry required architects to be well informed on technical and constructional developments in order to be able to handle their projects on site. Within the modernist tradition, incidentally, civil engineered buildings and structures were seen to parallel architecture in their aesthetic virtues.

Over the years *Bauzeitung* and *Bulletin Technique* hardly changed. Their appearance and layout were largely unchanged from the 1940s to the 1960s, and indeed remained much as they had been at the beginning of the twentieth century. The editors ignored modern graphic design; text and advertising remained constrained in two columns, and illustrations, presented in arbitrary formats, were often placed out of context. Factual content was sacrosanct and the texts more elaborate than in architects' journals. Many were scientific papers on questions of concrete or steel construction, the strength and quality of materials or new developments in mechanical or electrical engineering. The papers were supported by mathematical evidence, aimed at an expert audience. The technical installations and the calculations for bridges, tunnels and vaults, were presented in detail. Even the articles on architect-designed buildings were typically structured and illustrated to demonstrate technical issues. Often they contained plans, sections and construction drawings, being well illustrated in terms of site-work and service installations. Architects were more likely to be published if their buildings were of technical interest.

The SIA journals were consequently a rich repository of information on developments in dam, bridge and tunnel building, including details of construction and structure, as much as for more specialist electrical, railway and mechanical engineering, not to mention turbine technology, geological issues, energy and water supply, road construction and lighting and the key issue of prefabrication – but also questions of professional education and legal compliance in the building industry.

Evidently the editors followed a very pragmatic course, publishing state-of-the-art technological achievements. Discussions on steel frame construction had, for example, already appeared in the 1940s and contributions on nuclear installations were published in the early 1950s. Design or societal questions, however, hardly played a role. Colour was seen as no more than a problem of chemistry, buildings were of a neutral 'value' and there was no need to argue about the significance of a regional or modern architecture. Modernity was, as a matter of course, a sign of progress.

From exception to being international establishment

Twenty years after the Second World War ended, Swiss modernism climaxed at the *Landesausstellung* Expo (1964) in Lausanne. To the visitor the exhibitions were likely to have been seen as an optimistic fairground representing Swiss society, economy, education and culture. From an architect's viewpoint, the pavilions represented a pyrotechnic display of Swiss modernism. The Expo architecture, with its ingenious circulation through small-scale and variously shaped volumes, was set to become a myth. The professional journals responded in accordance with their respective editorial positions. *Das Werk* had followed proceedings since the Expo's instigation in 1961 and published the projects for the timber exhibition buildings, making reference to the 1939 'Landi' (*Werk*, 7/1961). Issue 2/1964 offered a comprehensive preview of the pavilions of the individual Expo sections, which were then still being built. Issue 9 was later concerned with the exhibitions and the interiors in themselves. *Schweizerische Bauzeitung* dedicated a large portion of a single issue to the Expo, and was mainly interested in technical aspects, examining construction, transport systems and electricity (*Schweizerische Bauzeitung*, 22/1964). *Bauen + Wohnen* as an international journal with only a limited focus on Swiss architecture ignored the *Landesausstellung*, seen as devoid of significance beyond Switzerland. This attitude was more or less synonymous with the status of Switzerland within the field of international architecture. Alfred Altherr, the first editor of *Bauen + Wohnen*, published the book *Neue Schweizer Architektur* (Altherr, 1965), which, almost 15 years after the plethora of publications on Swiss regionalism, conveyed a very different, contemporary image of Swiss architecture, but the book was largely unnoticed abroad. Swiss architecture was no longer an exception; it had become anchored within international tendencies.

Notes

Translated from German by the editors.

1 The government commissioned the *Schweizerische Kulturstiftung Pro Helvetica*, the *Schweizerische Zentrale für Handelsförderung*, the *Schweizerische Verkehrszentrale*, and the professional bodies BSA, SIA and VLP. The funding was secured by resolution of the Federal Council on 26 April 1946, and loans in 1946 and 1947.
2 Gotthard Jedlicka, professor of art history at Universität Zürich, 1943–1948; Heinz Keller, curator of *Kunstverein Winterthur*, 1949–1968. The art sector is not discussed in this chapter.
3 The building was designed and built from 1938 to 1941 by Denis Honegger and Fernand Dumas.
4 Apartments Riesbacherhof, Zürich, Otto Glaus, 1953–1954.
5 Central-Garage, St. Gallen, Ernst Branschen, 1953–1955.
6 Power Plant Birsfelden, 1953–1954.
7 In conversation with the author.
8 In 1951, 'Swiss Typography' won a gold medal at the ninth Trienniale in Milan.
9 Among others, there were text contributions by Mies van der Rohe, Jacob Bakema, Harry Seidler, Richard Neutra, Heikki and Kaija Siren, Felix Candela and Craig Ellwood.
10 SOM at the time ran the world's largest architecture practice with 322 employees and marked global cities with their steel and glass towers.
11 Hans Fischli, factory in Horgen; Marc Joseph Saugey, office building Mont-Blanc Centre and cinema Le Plaza in Geneva.
12 Among those were housing and school buildings by: Georg Addor; Ernst Gisel; Jacques Schader; Franz Füeg and Fritz Haller.
13 Füeg has published his texts in a collection.

14 Franz Füeg in a note to the author.
15 This essay considers *Schweizerische Bauzeitung* and the *Bulletin Technique*, which were both published frequently, conveying the latest information.
16 Subtitled *Wochenschrift für Architektur/Ingenieurwesen/Maschinentechnik, Organ des SIA, Schweizerischer Ingenieur-und Architekten-Verein und der G.E.P. Gesellschaft ehemal. Studierender der Eidg. Techn. Hochschule*.
17 In the first half of the twentieth century it was edited by August Jegher, Carl Jegher, Werner Jegher (since 1931) and Adolf Ostertag (since 1945).
18 Today the journals are called *Tracés, Tec21* and *Archi*.

References

Allenspach, C. (1999). *Architecture in Switzerland: Building in the 19th and 20th Centuries*. Zürich: Pro Helvetia.
Altherr, A. (1947). Bauen. Bauen + Wohnen, 1 (1), p. 23.
—— (1965), Neue Schweizer Architektur, New Swiss Architecture. Teufen: Verlag Niggli.
Bill, M. (1946). Erfahrung bei der Formgestaltung von Industrieprodukten. *Werk*, 31 (5), pp. 168–170.
—— (Ed.) (1949). *Moderne Schweizer Architektur 1925–45*. Basel: Verlag Karl Werner.
Burckhardt, L. (1961). Die Krise der Stadt. *Werk*, 48 (10), pp. 336–337.
—— (1962). Gestaltung abseits vom Strom. *Werk*, 49 (12), pp. 418–422.
Camenzind, A. (1962). Ein Wechsel in unserer Redaktion. *Werk*, 49 (1), p. 1.
Fischli, H. (1948). Betrachtungen zur heutigen Situation im schweizerischen Wohnungsbau, Swiss Housing Problems. *Bauen + Wohnen*, 2 (4), pp. 2–8.
—— (1950). Wohnungsbau und Siedlungsform, Home Building and Communal Planning. *Bauen + Wohnen*, 4 (7), pp. 2–43.
Frey, W. (1947). Wohnen. *Bauen + Wohnen*, 1, p. 23.
Friedman, Y. (1963). Mobile Architektur. *Werk*, 50 (2), pp. 46–57.
Frisch, M. (1953). Cum grano salis. Eine kleine Glosse zur schweizerischen Architektur. *Werk*, 40 (10), p. 325.
Füeg, F. (1958). Was ist modern in der Architektur? Eine Strukturanalyse der zeitgenössischen Baukunst. *Bauen + Wohnen*, 12 (1), pp. 31–36.
—— (1981). *Wohltaten der Zeit*. Teufen: Verlag Niggli.
Furrer, C. (1946). Die schweizerische Architektur-Ausstellung in London 1946. *Schweizerische Bauzeitung*, 128 (18), pp. 232–234.
Giedion, S. (1941). *Space, Time and Architecture* Cambridge, MA: Harvard University Press.
—— (1946). Stromlinienstil und industrielles Entwerfen in den USA. *Werk*, 31 (5), pp. 155–162.
Hanak, M. (2001). *Funktionalismus im Spiegel der Zeitschrift* Bauen + Wohnen. *Nachkriegsmoderne Schweiz*. Basel: Verlag Birkhäuser.
Hofmann, H. (1946). Gedanken über die Architektur der Gegenwart in der Schweiz. In H. Hofmann, H. Baur, H. Kopp (Eds), Schweizerische Architektur-Ausstellung, Köln. Reprint in C. Luchsinger (Ed.) Hans Hofmann (1897–1957) (pp. 136–137). Zürich: gta Verlag.
Huber, B. (1959). Epigonen. *Werk*, 46 (12), pp. 419–422.
Le Corbusier (1957). Entretien avec les étudiants des écoles d'Architecture. In *LC: La Charte d'Athènes*. Paris: Editions de Minuit.
Maurizio J. (1951). *Der Siedlungsbau in der Schweiz, 1940–1950*. Erlenbach: Verlag für Architektur.
Meyer, P. (1942). Die Neubauten der Universität Fribourg im Rahmen der Architekturentwicklung. *Werk*, 29 (1/2), pp. 33–66.
Roth, A. (1944). Von der Notwendigkeit und vom Nutzen der Architekturtheorie. *Werk*, 31 (9), pp. 261–263.
—— (1946a). Switzerland Planning and Building Exhibition. *Das Werk*, 33 (11), pp. 145–147.
—— (1946b). *Die Neue Architektur, The New Architecture*. Erlenbach: Verlag für Architektur.
—— (1947). Zeitgemässe Architekturbetrachtungen. *Werk*, 34 (6), pp. 182–187.

—— (1951). Zeitgemässe Architekturbetrachtungen: mit besonderer Berücksichtigung der schweizerischen Situation. *Werk*, 38 (3), pp. 65–76.

—— (1958). Inhalt und Form, Anmerkungen zur Situation der Architektur. *Werk*, 45 (2), pp. 46–49.

Schmid, T. (1947). Die Entwicklung des individuellen Wohnraumes. *Bauen + Wohnen*, 1 (1), pp. 55–56.

Streiff, E. (1946). Formgebung in der Schweizerischen Industrie. *Werk*, 31 (5), pp. 138–155.

Volkart, H. (1951). *Schweizer Architektur: Ein Überblick über das schweizerische Bauschaffen der Gegenwart*. Ravensburg: Otto Maier Verlag.

2

POSTWAR EDITORIAL CONVERSATIONS IN GERMANY

Baumeister and *Baukunst und Werkform*

Torsten Schmiedeknecht

Germany has a rich history of architecture journals, dating back to the early nineteenth century.[1] Numerous, mainly independent, journals and magazines came and went, while some journals were, or remain, affiliated with professional bodies or organisations. *Der Architekt* (1952–) is affiliated with the *Bund Deutscher Architekten* (BDA); the journal *Werk und Zeit* (1952–2007) was published by the Deutsche Werkbund.

Amid attempts at political renewal and the search for a new identity on the one hand, and general scarcity of resources on the other, several journals began either publishing again, or were launched in the first decade after the war.[2]

This chapter's primary focus concerns the differences between the journals *Baumeister* (*BM*, founded in 1902, which began publishing again in late spring 1946[3]) and *Baukunst und Werkform* (*BuW*, founded in 1946), examining their respective positions in the context of the German reconstruction debate. While both attempted to contribute positively to the problem of postwar reconstruction, the journals took different positions and identified different means of doing so. It is evident from the published contents that their views differed on how reconstruction should be pursued, particularly in the period between the mid-1940s and the late 1950s. *BM* and *BuW* illustrate different ways journals would position themselves in the debate (through their contents and formats); and the roles they played relative to contemporary conceptions of modernity, modernism and modernisation.[4]

Lipstadt has argued that in nineteenth-century France, architectural 'magazines were not just means of communication, but actually acted as authorities of "distinction" for architects, on the same footing as the profession's established institutions, […] – but less elitist' (Jannière and Vanlaethem, 2008, p. 48). Applied to postwar Germany, I suggest that *BM* and *BuW* were not just merely reflecting consensus views. The positions expressed in and through the journals, particularly towards *Neues Bauen* and *Heimatschutzarchitektur* – despite being part of the general professional (and public) debate on reconstruction – were also resulting from the respective editors' personal histories and agendas.

FIGURE 2.1   Journal cover, *Baumeister* 1 (1946).
Source: Baumeister/Callwey Verlag. Courtesy of Helmuth Baur-Callwey.

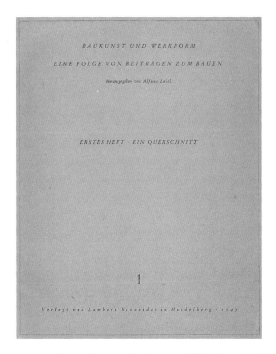

FIGURE 2.2   Journal cover, *Baukunst und Werkform* 1 (1947).
© Verlag Nürnberger Presse.

Postwar context

From the beginning of the twentieth century the 'progressive' *Neues Bauen*, supported by the Werkbund and subsequently the Bauhaus, and *Heimatschutzarchitektur*, which aimed at the development of a traditional and regionally typical architecture, had emerged in parallel and somewhat in opposition to each other. Since the manner of monumental and neoclassical architecture favoured for public buildings during the Nazi period was discredited in the years following the war and therefore did not present an available option for postwar rebuilding, the immediate postwar struggle for influence was to be acted out between traditionalists favouring *Heimatschutzarchitektur*, and modernists propagating the *Neues Bauen*.[5] Von Beyme (1987), Durth (1986) and Frank (1983) have discussed overlaps between the positions taken by traditionalists and modernists in the urban planning debate after 1945. The concept of *Stadtlandschaft* is identified as a lowest common denominator between traditionalist and modernists.[6]

> Some have tried to understand modern architecture as a contrast between two great schools: Garden City movement and Athens Charter or *Neues Bauen*. But have both trends always contradicted each other? [...] traditional architects and town planners preferred the vocabulary of the Garden City movement. [...] supporters of the *Neues Bauen* varied the idea of *Stadtlandschaft*. But even there we find astonishing overlaps. Schwagenscheidt's *Raumstadt* was full of fascistic appeals to the bygone regime. [...] And as much as the terminologies like 'organic' and 'functional' became blurred in the model of the *gegliederte Stadt*, the boundaries between Garden City and *Stadtlandschaft* concepts grew equally hazy in a multitude of ways.
>
> *von Beyme, 1987, pp. 78–79*

The problems arising from the complex biographical connections from the Weimar Republic through the Third Reich to the years of postwar reconstruction, with respect to the hegemony and continuity of one or another 'camp', have been extensively described by Durth:

> The concept of *Stadtlandschaft* [for example] could be applied, by the same architect, on the same drawing board, in the context of reform in the 1920s; as a racist settlement scheme in the conquered East; and as a vision of modest postwar reconstruction.
>
> *Durth, 1992, p. 9[7]*

Similarly, Frank has pointed out that

> Unlike what has been stated by some, German postwar architecture did not continue from where it had left in 1933. From the pre-war era and through the war, postwar building presented an, albeit shaken, but not interrupted continuity of personnel and content. *Neues Bauen* was also represented by architects who had worked in Germany during the Nazi period.
>
> *Frank, 1983, p. 55*

Von Beyme (1987) identified three categories of postwar rebuilding: *rekonstrukiver Wiederaufbau*; *Neubau*; and *traditioneller Anpassungsneubau*. Diefendorf (1993) translated these as: 'reconstruction literally true to the damaged original'; 'completely new building in a modern style'; and 'new building attempting to emulate traditional styles through adaptation to local traditions'. In principle, thus, the question discussed in the architectural press was whether to rebuild (*Wiederaufbau*) or to build (*Aufbau*).

Editors and editors-in-chief

The contemporary impact of the two journals is closely linked to six men. The Munich based *BM*'s editors-in-chief were the architects Dr Rudolf Pfister (1946–1958) and Dr Paulhans Peters (1959–1991). Until 1954 *BuW* was edited by the architect Alfons Leitl, with editors-in-chief Franz Meunier (1947–1952) and Dr Ulrich Conrads (1952–1954). Conrads then took over as editor in May 1954. From 1957 until the last published issue (9/1962), and after which it was 'united' with *Deutsche Bauzeitung* (*db*), Hartmut Rebitzki was the editor-in-chief.[8]

Pfister, who according to Helmuth Baur-Callwey was 'very traditional, always wore a traditional Bavarian jacket and owned a farm near Ruhpolding', had previous editorial experience with the journal *Baukunst*, and, having a background in art history, expressed a keen interest in the history and theory of architecture.[9] He had also previously worked for the Bavarian Office for Historic Preservation and had been a government architect for cultural buildings in Bavaria. Pfister's 1915 doctorate was on residential sixteenth-century dwellings in Würzburg, and he co-authored a book on the prince-bishop residence in Würzburg (Sedlmaier and Pfister, 1923).

Peters, *BM*'s longest serving editor to date, is generally credited with 'turning the journal around', not least through the publication of architecture from other countries. Pfister, however, and despite his commitment to *Heimatschutzarchitektur* and the publication of projects such as the reconstruction of Freudenstadt, had in fact already started this process in the mid-1950s.

Leitl was, in some respect, the antidote to Pfister. His upbringing was 'artistic, cosmopolitan and religious', and his parents were keen to ensure 'an art and humanities based education'. He had originally trained in publishing at *Bauwelt Verlag* and 'from 1933 his articles were published in *Bauwelt* and *Wasmuth*'s *Monatshefte*' (Busmann, 1995, p. 11).

> Through his journalistic activities, he became acquainted with many Berlin architects. In the early 1930s he had particularly close ties with Hans Poelzig's students. He was familiar with, amongst others, Johannes Krahn, Egon Eiermann, Hans Bernhard Reichow, Fritz Jaenecke and Rudolf Schwarz whose work he regularly showed in the *Monatshefte*. These acquaintances […] can be followed through the war and were of importance in the immediate postwar years, some of the friendships lasting until the end of his life.
>
> *Busmann, 1995, p. 11*

From the early 1940s Leitl worked for the architect Herbert Rimpl, whose office according to Busmann 'had a reputation as a hideout [during the war] among the architects committed to the *Neues Bauen*'. As early as 1945 Leitl began, with like-minded architects like Hans Schwippert, to work on the readmission of the Werkbund in the British occupied zone, and in 1947 and 1948 he was the city planner for the town of Rheydt (Busmann, 1995). Leitl subsequently became a successful practising architect while editing *BuW*. From 1946 he was also involved with the *Gesellschaft Oberschwaben* in Aulendorf (Upper Swabia Society), for which he organised, with Hugo Häring, two conferences on the future of architecture and town planning. 'The Upper Swabia Society's aim was to be a meeting point for people and forces committed to new thinking and action' and Leitl 'invited many of the architects of the *Neues Bauen* to the [first] conference in September 1946' (Busmann, 1995, p. 55). His chief concern with *BuW*, in founding the journal with Franz Meunier and the publisher Lambert Schneider, was to project the 'humanitarian content of the modern movement' (Pütz, 2000). Under him, *BuW* became the 'mouthpiece of a carefully considered and tradition conscious modernism' (Durth, 1992, p. 400).

His successor, Ulrich Conrads, moved to *Bauwelt* in the summer of 1957 and would remain its editor-in-chief until 1988, co-founding *Stadtbauwelt*, the quarterly sister publication of *Bauwelt* in 1964.[10] Conrads also initiated and edited the book series *Bauwelt Fundamente*, in which, including his *Programs and Manifestoes on 20th Century Architecture* (1964), he published seminal texts: Le Corbusier's *Towards a New Architecture* (1963), Kevin Lynch's *The Image of the City* (1965), Aldo Rossi's *The Architecture of the City* (1973) and Venturi, Izenour and Scott Brown's *Learning from Las Vegas* (1979), were all translated into German for the first time.

FIGURE 2.3   (a) Rudolf Pfister in *Baumeister* 5 (1951). (b) Alfons Leitl (exact date unknown; photograph presumed to be taken in the late 1940s).
Source: (a) Baumeister/Callwey Verlag. Courtesy of Helmuth Baur-Callwey. (b) Johannes Busmann (1995). *Die revidierte Moderne. Der Architekt Alfons Leitl*. Wuppertal: Müller und Busmann, p. 14. Courtesy of Urban Leitl.

Baumeister and *Baukunst und Werkform*: Pfister, Leitl, *Heimatschutz* and *Neues Bauen*

Up until the late 1950s *BM* is generally seen as the most 'conservative' of the German journals, regularly taking issue with *Neues Bauen* and the Werkbund. *BM*'s first postwar issue was published in May/June 1946, and its *Hauptteil* (core content) consisted of 24 pages, printed on smooth rotogravure paper. It contained six contributions, one being a two-page editorial by Rudolf Pfister in which he set out his interpretation of the current conditions and the task of an architecture journal within the postwar turmoil, issuing a battle cry as to what he feared and desired:

> We awake from a gloomy state of painful waiting, to encounter [our] new personal freedom, and hesitantly we [will need to] learn to use this freedom and realise that it is no longer culpable to be a decent human being. And when we rub our eyes, the first thing we see is: ruins!
>
> Our political state is ruins and helplessness,
> our economic state is ruins and poverty,
> our moral state is ruins and chaos.
> This is the inheritance. [...]
>
> I can see them march, the prophets of a new 'ism' in architecture, amidst literary cries and the motto 'new things want to emerge'. [...]
>
> How can an architecture journal be useful for German architecture? It will not be able to just continue [at the point] where its last issue was defeated by [...] war. Neither will it suffice for it to just report on what is being built – should there even be sufficient to be report on. The journal will have to take a stand and put its cards on the table, it will have to solve educational tasks, and it will [...] fight a passionate battle.
>
> *Pfister, 1946a, pp. 1–2*

The other articles in this first issue included a reprint of a 1935 essay by Karl Scheffler on the profession of the architect; an essay on the housing crisis; another by Pfister on the architect Paul Gedon; an essay on the reacquisition of household goods; and a criticism of the procurement of the memorial at Dachau concentration camp. The double issue also contained four pages of *Tafeln* (plates), printed on heavy cartridge paper, with drawings of the work of Gedon, and a news-like section called *Rundschau* (review) on newsprint. Except for one additional colour plate of a timber-panelled rural interior from 1816, the whole issue was restricted to monochrome, the cover image being a pen and ink drawing of the *Frauenkirche* in Munich by Franz Hart. This structure of core content and review, usually supplemented with 4–8 plates, remained unchanged during the following years. The journal, with a print run of 10,000 copies, was entirely printed in a serif typeface, and the core content and news were both laid out in a two-column format. Considering contemporary circumstances, the issue's illustrations were of (relatively) good quality. According to Hellmuth Baur-Callwey, *BM* did not especially commission photographers, but used photographs supplied by the architects whose projects they published. In contrast, all published drawings were (re)drawn by *BM* staff.[11] From 3/1946, *BM*, at the back of the news section, included one page of advertisements.[12]

BuW, which from the early 1950s would become a monthly journal, was published five times between 1947 and 1949 with a print run of 5,000 copies.[13] Conrads (1994) described the role of *BuW* as the 'voice of those – belonging to the so-called "inner migration" – who tried to continue the modern movement across the 12 years of the "millennial reign" into the future', and Diefendorf (1999) called the journal 'in many ways the standard bearer for modernism'. Regarding the position of the founding editor vis-à-vis modernism, Busmann observed that

> Leitl saw modern architecture's development as irrevocable. Any discussion on building could, for him, only take place in the light of the achievements of the new architecture. In the avant-gardist tendencies of the 1920s Leitl saw a historical necessity which had, in its core, presented architecture in a new context. […] For future building, however, another base, reaching far beyond the roots of modernism, had to be created. The 1920s protagonists had made their contribution. Amongst them, it was only Mies van der Rohe to whom Leitl would refer with respect to design [artistic aspects] in the following years.
>
> *Busmann, 1995, p. 37*

Leitl's first editorial piece – 'Anmerkungen zur Zeit' (Contemporary Comments) – in 1947 was therefore rather cautious regarding the immediate future of the country and the enormity of the task faced by its architects and planners:

> The deep pessimism which has taken hold of us after two years of totally failed reconstruction, makes the worth of every [further] attempt questionable. […] The conditions for making and thinking principle statements regarding planning and reconstruction, for considering work and form or for designing the image of a future order, are obviously very bad.
> The only thing we have plenty of, is time. It seems as if, until we can get [on with] serious building, we have time in abundance. Everything else is lacking: hope, belief, optimism, moral and economic strength, to enable the planned to become real.
>
> *Leitl, 1947, p. 1*

The gloomy response to the daunting task of (re)construction did not prevent the journals from occasionally taking issue with the 'opposition', and there were a few cases during the immediate postwar years when either Pfister or Leitl would write forceful polemics in defence of their own positions, or as a means to take issue with other perspectives. As reconstruction gathered pace, the atmosphere would, on occasion, become combative.

It was not going to be long until Pfister would go into battle and make clear his misgivings on *Neues Bauen*. The Werkbund, and particularly the Weißenhof estate in Stuttgart, was seemingly his *bête noir*, followed closely by the Hansaviertel in Berlin. In contrast, Leitl, and later Conrads, would argue the case for a carefully reconsidered and cautious *Neues Bauen*.

Von Beyme (1987) and Petsch (1979a) have both commented that *BM* had, until 1957, 'the backing' of the BDA. *BuW*, through the composition of its editorial board and the contributing architects and critics,[14] was closely linked to the Werkbund, which, having been forced into line by the Nazis in 1933 and disbanded in 1934, now acquired a new lease of life:

> This journal, which gathers around it the most important exponents of the new Werkbund, will, sustained by their contribution and trust, endeavor to comprehensively capture the Werkbund spirit and to serve it with all our strength.
>
> *Leitl, 1947, p. 6*

In the same issue, the joint declaration 'Ein Aufruf: Grundsätzliche Forderungen' (A Call: Fundamental Demands) was published (*Baukunst und Werkform*, 1947).[15] Five points were co-signed by, among others, the architects Otto Bartning, Richard Döcker, Egon Eiermann, Wilhelm Riphahn, Hans Schmitt, Rudolf Schwarz, Hans Schwippert, Max Taut and Heinrich Tessenow, the publicist Walter Dirks and the chief planner of Frankfurt, Werner Hebebrand. It cautioned 'not to historically reconstruct the destroyed heritage' because 'from new tasks new forms must emerge'. The declaration met with a response from Rudolf Pfister in *BM* 4/1947, in his essay titled 'Um den Deutschen Werkbund' (On the German Werkbund). It is unclear whether the essay was simply in response to the 'Aufruf', or if Pfister, without explicitly mentioning the journal, vented a veiled critique on *BuW* itself. Pfister first took the opportunity to criticise the Werkbund for its 'expansion of aims', particularly into the fields of urban planning and settlements, which he argued had nothing to do with 'the work of creating form' and was 'responsible for the failures of the Weißenhof and Dammerstock'. The *BM* editor-in-chief then took issue with the commanding tone and the use of the term 'must' in the first point of the 'Aufruf', because he felt that

> At a time when even the most experienced experts are still clueless with regards to what future developments will hold […] such expressions of indiscretion reveal a dilettantism one would rather not see at work during the rebuilding of the Werkbund.
>
> *Pfister, 1947, p. 140*[16]

In contrast to the first *BM* issues, *BuW* presented essays and contributions by a host of well-known supporters of *Neues Bauen*, including Schwippert, Bartning, Eiermann and Scharoun. Among the essays, Häring's 'Neues Bauen' claimed an urgency for the movement not merely as a formal imperative but also as an intellectual endeavour underpinning Germany's postwar reconstruction.

BuW, set in a sans serif font – except cover, contents page and image captions – was laid out in a two-column format. The overall impression was that of a scholarly or academic journal, rather than of a professional or trade journal. As was the case with *BM*, and in contrast to many professional journals today, most text contributions were of a considerable length, and some, like Häring's seven-page essay of more than 5,500 words, a text without any illustrations. The journal's first two issues contained no advertising, but by 1949 there were up to six pages incorporated in each issue, mainly containing small ads for building products but also for books. Several were by editorial board members, like Walter Schwagenscheidt's *Die Raumstadt* and Rudolf Schwarz's *Vom Bau der Kirche*, published, as was *BuW*, by Lambert Schneider in Heidelberg.

BuW's second issue, published in 1948, was subtitled on the cover 'Tradition und Wiederaufbau' (Tradition and Reconstruction) and was structured into two parts. Part one was titled 'Rückgriff oder Neubau' (Regression or New Build) and contained a discussion on the nature of the reconstruction of the *Goethehaus* in Frankfurt am Main, which had been destroyed by Allied bombing in March 1944. The official plan of 'reconstruction liter-ally true to the damaged original', completed in 1952, was met with 'words of admonition and warning' by, among others, Walter Dirks and Otto Bartning. In the same issue, Franz Meunier contributed a short text on the recently deceased Paul Clemen, founder of the *Verein Denkmalpflege und Heimatschutz* (Association for Historic Preservation and *Heimatschutz*). Not unlike Pfister in his 'subtle' criticisms of the Werkbund, Meunier, after praising the life and achievements of the conservationist Clemen, ended his text by attributing to him a 'typ-ical German cultural awareness, ultimately lacking intellectual unity, clarity and implicitness' (Meunier, 1948).

Leitl's part of the comments section contained an article titled 'Der Fall Schmitthenner' (The Schmitthenner Case). Having acknowledged Schmitthenner's talents, he criticised his anticipated re-appointment as a professor at the Technical University in Stuttgart, from which Schmittehnner had been removed in December 1945. Leitl concluded with a none too subtle comparison with Mies van der Rohe's moral credentials, noting: 'If we are questioning the kind and quality of the [university] teachers we need today, there cannot be any doubt as to the answer' (Leitl, 1948). In contrast, Pfister's text in *BM* 4/1948, which was also titled 'Der Fall Schmitthenner', began with the question 'What is a "Nazi architect"?', and defended Schmitthenner (a declared enemy of *Neues Bauen*). The Schmitthenner case is symptomatic of the conflict between traditionalist and modernist architects in the first decade after the war. As Frank put it, Schmitthenner had 'undeniably been a Nazi', but the debate surrounding his re-appointment – which in the end never materialised – was first and foremost a fight between modernists and traditionalists. Schmitthenner had officially been cleared regarding his Nazi activities; legally there would have been no issue re-appointing him, and in 1953 he was given full emeritus status by the Technical University in Stuttgart (Voigt and Frank, 2003). Identifying Schmitthenner as a 'Nazi-Architekt' in an article in the *Neue Zeitung* on 25 March 1948 was perhaps not so much about making a case against Schmitthenner personally, but in opposition to the 'extraordinary popularity of the traditional architecture he represented in a particularly qualified way. This architecture was able to express the modesty required for reconstruction in an outstanding manner' (Frank, 1983). In short, there was concern on behalf of the modernist protagonists that the traditionalist architecture propagated by Schmitthenner, which had somewhat got a headstart after the war, would stand in the way of the future and development of *Neues Bauen*.

Although allegiances and loyalties were relatively clear-cut for both journals, there were exceptions, overlaps and perhaps contradictions. Years later, the *BuW* editor-in-chief, Hartmut Rebitzki, would write a conciliatory text on the occasion of Schmitthenner's seventy-fifth birthday (Rebitzki, 1959). Occasionally the past was forgiven!

The second part of the 1948 *BuW* issue was dedicated to the work of Rudolf Schwarz. This was followed by retrospectives on 'modern' architects: Sep Ruf (1/1949), Walter Riphahn (2/1949) and Mies van der Rohe (3/1949). The issue on Mies' work also included an exten-sive report on projects in the modernist idiom in postwar Frankfurt.

BM, in contrast, during this period published essays on, and work by, architects like the controversial Paul Bonatz (another declared enemy of *Neues Bauen*) and Paul Schmitthenner, but also by Hans Döllgast (architect for the reconstruction of the *Alte Pinakothek* in Munich). Interestingly, however, work by Richard Neutra and Emil Steffan (who in the past had worked with Rudolf Schwarz!) was also published.

The 1950s I: Freudenstadt and Hansaviertel.

> The political evaluation of the competing architecture schools employed the simplest clichés, so that nothing stood in the way of its general dissemination. At least from 1950 the conviction that a flat roof meant progress and internationality, whereas a pitched roof was a sure sign of a backward or even chauvinist conviction, was widely spread among the public in the Federal Republic.
>
> *Frank, 1988, p. 26*

Two projects from the 1950s illustrate the differences between the two journals: the Berlin Hansaviertel (*Neubau* – 'completely new building in a modern style') of 1957, and the rebuilding of the small town of Freudenstadt in the Black Forest (*Traditioneller Anpassungsneubau* – 'new building emulating traditional style'). The former, built on the principles of the Athens Charter as part of the *Interbau* exhibition, paralleled the Weißenhof estate 30 years earlier in a latter-day development of the *Neues Bauen*. The original Hansaviertel, a typical example of a nineteenth-century *Gründerzeit* quarter, had been destroyed by Allied phosphor bombs in November 1943 and the area was subject to an urban design competition in 1953. The Hansaviertel was as much a political as it was an urban planning issue.

> The reconstruction of the Hansaviertel was, already before it was linked with the project for an international building exhibition, conceived as a western counter-maneuver to the Stalinallee.
>
> *Dolff-Bonekämper and Schmidt, 1999, p. 15*

In contrast, Freudenstadt (destroyed in April 1945 by French bombs and artillery troops), which Frank (1988) has called the 'last monument of an important historic architectural tendency', stood for the opposite approach to rebuilding.

BuW, and its editor Conrads, completely ignored Freudenstadt's completion in 1955. Only two German journals from the West reported, and both did so positively, on Freudenstadt.[17] *Die Bauzeitung*[18] (2/1955) and *BM*, which dedicated a whole issue to Freudenstadt (2/1955), in which the architect Ludwig Schweizer's efforts were analysed and applauded by Pfister:

> Here, in the small town of Freudenstadt the famous 'opportunity', of which it is often said that regrettably it was not taken up by German towns, here it has been taken indeed. And what has emerged is a uniform town shape which has been planned to the last detail and which […] carries its justification within itself […]. In almost no other German town the war destruction has been turned into a blessing like it did for the small [health resort] town Freudenstadt.
>
> *Pfister, 1955, p. 73*

In issue 5/1954, Pfister had written an editorial titled 'Heimatschutz recht verstanden' (*Heimatschutz* Correctly Understood), in which he tried to explain his view of the term, and his misgivings that 'one only has to say the word to be branded as an arch-reactionary and backward looking sentimentalist'. For Pfister it was in fact the representatives of *Heimatschutz* who were fighting against the 'farmhouse romanticism' of the 'so called farmers', the 'stage

FIGURE 2.4   (a) Journal cover, *Baumeister* 2 (1955). (b) Freudenstadt in *Baumeister* 2 (1955). *Source*: Baumeister/Callwey Verlag. Courtesy of Helmuth Baur-Callwey.

coach romanticism and the carved heart on the window shutter', and who tried to reestablish a meaningful and down-to-earth connection between landscape and built environment (Pfister, 1954). The editorial was followed by *Heimatschutz* projects such as proposals for the renewal of the small town of Schongau or the design for a new savings bank in Ebersberg. However,

> The *Heimatschutz* architecture of the *Stuttgart School*, which dominated all phases of the reconstruction of Freudenstadt, subsequently became irrelevant for town planning in the Federal Republic. It was a double victim of recent German history. Firstly of 'denazification' and secondly of the 'cold war'.
>
> *Frank, 1988*

BM's 'acknowledgement' of the Hansaviertel was expressed in several contributions, published over the course of 1956 and 1957. In the title of an article in issue 3/1956, Pfister rhetorically asked: 'Was geht im Berliner Hansaviertel vor sich' (What is Happening in the Berlin Hansaviertel), only to answer 'not much' in the opening sentence. 'But, at the beginning there was the propaganda!', he wrote, pointing out the contradiction, in his view, between inviting 'world famous' architects to design the Hansaviertel and the desire of Berlin's senator for building, Schwedler, to build economically. For Pfister, citing correspondence between Le Corbusier and Schwedler, in which the architect had expressed his disappointment over the alleged fee of 0.5 per cent of the building contract, the former seriously constrained the latter. Le Corbusier had apparently responded to Schwedler by declaiming that the fee proposal was the 'most extraordinary reading matter I have experienced in my entire life. […]. You asked me to lend my name [to your exhibition] and to share with your city my 40 years of experience in housing'. Pfister, referring to Le Corbusier's Unité project in Marseille, sarcastically remarked that 'as far as we know, Marseille would not be willing to ever pay […] so much again for such a wealth of experience' (Pfister, 1956a).

In the first of five *Interbau* reports (*Berichte*) published in *BM* 6/1956, Pfister opened the article citing Berlin's former chief city planner Martin Wagner's damning critique of the *Interbau* (Pfister, 1956b). Wagner is quoted as having called, among other things, the planned flats 'apartments for filmstars', talking of a 'world record for the increase of building costs', 'the building lunacy in the Hansaviertel' and 'the Hansaviertel's physical and political quagmire'.[19] Reiterating Wagner's arguments throughout much of his article, Pfister fiercely criticised Le Corbusier's proposed 'Typ Berlin', assessing the scheme against CIAM's housing criteria. Asking what 'qualification does Le Corbusier have for housing', he criticised Le Corbusier's contribution to the 1927 Weißenhof as a 'snobbish joke', pointedly noting that in the Swiss journal *Werk*'s view, the building was a 'pleasure which, however, was obtained at the cost of its impracticality'.

Pfister's initial dislike of the Weißenhof and his first critical assessment of the estate dated from February 1928 when he not only criticised the architecture of the estate, but also accused its organisers of deliberately manipulating public opinion. Furthermore, just as in his criticism of the Hansaviertel almost 30 years later, he questioned whether houses built for 'normal' inhabitation were suitable as exhibition objects (Pfister, 1928), incidentally a view shared by Leitl. In his editorial of the January 1950 issue, Pfister reiterated his attack on *Neues Bauen*, referring to the Weißenhof:

> Recognising genuine achievement is not easy, particularly if one does not want to fall back on such convenient criteria as 'modern' or 'backward'. It requires knowledge of the subject matter and experience. But if a well-known publicist still praises, as has happened recently, the Weißenhof today as the highpoint of achievements for the Werkbund, when [in my opinion] it should rather not be mentioned at all, one falls into despair. Such blind ignorance of the truth is, however much the product of idealism, inexcusable.
>
> *Pfister, 1950, p. 41*

The final instalment of Pfister's *Interbau* reports covered, with a short preface, various completed buildings presented in monochrome photographs and line drawings together with a mainly descriptive text. Just as in 1956, he set his sights on the *Interbau*'s press information service and their magazine *Interbau*, accusing it of uncritical propaganda and of fostering a 'personality cult'. He commented that this publicity 'has expanded its field of interest, such that from now on everything in Berlin – a grand ambition – seems to belong to the *Interbau*, whether it is the Charlottenburg Palace or a traffic accident'. Targeting the *Interbau* buildings by Le Corbusier and Niemeyer, he concluded by asking again if it was right that a 'whole city district, into which many millions of taxes were poured, should be allowed to be an exhibition' and noted that it would remain to be seen 'to what degree the garden [landscape] architects can succeed in covering the chaos of the Hansaviertel with a gardener's benevolence' (Pfister, 1957).

Peters contributed two articles on the *Interbau* in 1957. The first one was a short criticism of the accompanying special exhibition 'Die Stadt von morgen' (The City of Tomorrow), wondering why [in contradiction of the principles of the Athens Charter], the topic of work and employment had not been considered: 'Not only leisure and family time are important; firstly […] the workplace and the industrial area[s] and housing must be put in the correct relation to

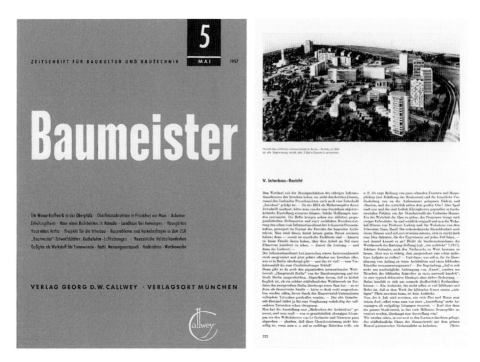

FIGURE 2.5 (a) Journal cover, *Baumeister* 5 (1957). (b) 'V. Interbau Bericht' in *Baumeister* 5 (1957). *Source:* Baumeister/Callwey Verlag. Courtesy of Helmuth Baur-Callwey.

one another' (Peters, 1957a). The second article provided a more expansive exploration of the *Interbau* and its potential problems, to 'show what has been achieved so far and to examine the suggestions and impact this large show is causing'. Peters was, for example, critical of the figure ground plan of the Hansaviertel and he was unhappy with the location of the two new churches as they, in his view, had no meaningful relationship with the rest of the site and the buildings. While praising Aalto's block for its flexibility and believing it would become a future model solution, he nonetheless criticised the apartment layouts in Gropius' building as 'not providing anything new' and noted that 'Gropius demonstrates how one can create a back-yard atmosphere [even] with free standing buildings'. Asking 'what has been achieved', Peters argued that, while the Hansaviertel would in his view eventually achieve a similar status to the 1927 Weißenhof, '1957 is not 1927, and *Neues Bauen* has become a matter of course all over the world'. The *Interbau*, accordingly, should have gone beyond 'the house, [correct] orientation and the planning of the apartment', and have expanded its focus to include the theme of the 'neighborhood'. In his view the Hansaviertel failed to provide a model locale: 'neither in the site plan nor in three-dimensional reality'. What was lacking, he argued, was 'the outstanding thinker, the creative urban designer who could have [...] shown his colleagues the connections out of which a holistic concept could have emerged'. However, despite all his misgivings, Peters emphatically recommended a journey to Berlin, since he believed that the Hansaviertel was of didactic consequence (Peters, 1957b).

While Pfister had been thoroughly dismissive of the ideas behind the Hansaviertel and their execution, Peters obviously sought to engage in a critical debate about 'the city of tomorrow'. His contributions and detailed interest in the completed buildings already pointed to the different tone *BM* would employ when he eventually became chief editor in 1959, albeit by that time *Neues Bauen* and the seminal ideas of the modern movement, or *Heimatschutz*, would no longer be the real issue.

BuW generally displayed a more positive attitude to the Hansaviertel than *BM*, although in a double issue for January/February 1954 it only briefly published the results of the original competition as a matter of fact. In issue 3/1956 Hans Koellmann's sympathetic essay asked the reader to be understanding about the postponement of the *Interbau*'s official opening from 1956 to 1957:

> [...] surely the courage and responsibility to postpone, to be able to show more mature works, deserves recognition over and above the endorsement of inconsiderate temporary solutions. Maybe it is not wrong to show what, at least, has been achieved in the meantime.
>
> *Koellmann, 1956, p. 151*

Opposed to Pfister's view of the *Interbau* as a playground for the avant-garde, Koellmann expressed his misgivings about the negative reception of Le Corbusier's 'Typ Berlin'. He was outraged that the selected international architects should be treated 'in the same way as any run-of-the-mill architect', suggesting that the client should stop haggling over fees with architects of international repute. He closed with the remark that 'It would generally be timely to give up, when looking at the *Interbau* projects, the search for artificial little sensations' (Koellmann, 1956). The general tone of Koellmann's observations was continued, although not without caveats, by Leitl in issues 11/1957 and 12/1957, when the efforts and achievements involved in realising the *Interbau* were analysed: 'The Hansaviertel is definitely not the city of tomorrow, but it is a fantastic achievement as the city of today' (Leitl, 1957a, p. 622). In issue 12/1957 Leitl concluded his generally more measured view of the Hansaviertel with a review of the buildings of Aalto, Vago, Le Corbusier's 'Typ Berlin' and the two new churches by Lemmer and Kreuer (who had won the initial urban design competition for the Hansaviertel), respectively. Leitl was critical but positive, pointing out, for example and as a precursor to any criticism, that neither Lemmer nor Kreuer had had any previous experience with church building. The section on the 'Typ Berlin' called the building the result of the 'mating between Prussian technical organizational skills and thoroughness of the authorities, and a Corbusian esprit' (Leitl, 1957b, p. 716). While Leitl's general observations on the Hansaviertel were not all positive, they differed, however, considerably from Pfister's condemnations. Leitl's review revealed a general curiosity about the project and the hope that the Hansaviertel would become a success.

The 1950s II: the 'Bauhaus debate'

In 1952 Leitl, who by that time had built a significant number of postwar projects, invited Rudolf Schwarz to write a critical commentary on his own (Leitl's) work, to which he proposed to dedicate the final issue of *BuW* that year. The putative essay was titled 'Vom Bauen und Schreiben' (On Building and Writing). Conrads had warned Leitl against publishing his own buildings in the journal, as he thought that this might discredit Leitl's position as editor and as a renowned and respected critic. However, Leitl seemingly felt constrained to simply commenting and writing on other architects' work, while never seeing his own work constructively discussed by critics he respected (Conrads, 1994). Schwarz duly delivered his piece, now titled 'Bilde Künstler, rede nicht' early in December 1952. The title was an appropriation of Goethe's 'Bilde Künstler! Rede nicht! Nur ein Hauch sei Dein Gedicht!' (Create Artist! Don't Talk! Your Poem Shall Be But a Hint!). It was principally a demand that the artist communicate their material with an economy of means and artistic ease, rather than with over-exuberance and 'waffling'.

Leitl, who had promised Schwarz to print the essay without any editorial interference, now decided not to publish it in the issue containing his own work, holding it back instead until the first issue of 1953. Schwarz's essay, although concerned as he had been briefed with 'building and writing', appeared as an all-out polemic against the Bauhaus, functionalism in general and particularly Walter Gropius, whom Schwarz accused of 'not being able to think', in the sense of 'what thinking means in the occidental realm' because 'he never learned [how to think]'. Gropius would, he claimed, never be more than a 'tentative artist' – rather than a 'great master' (Schwarz, 1953). The predominant role played by function at the Bauhaus (in his view at the expense of historical understanding) was one thing; the Bauhaus' (perceived) political orientation another:

> Is it really so hard to discover the gothic being alive in Bartning's Sternkirche, or antiquity in the great work of Mies? What matters to us is that the tradition of our art is alive today, and that it is sustained by the great masters who were, rather than just building a few houses, always more interested in giving mankind its great space, and that they all communicate with each other across all periods and work together on the teaching of the great spirit of humanism.
>
> *Schwarz, 1953, p. 14*

> The worst thing about the Bauhaus was not its failure in technology, but its unbearable phraseology. Very early on they took the theory of function the wrong way, and then they solemnly committed [...] to historical materialism. An artist can do almost anything without ruining his art, he can be a binge or a habitual drinker, he can have six wives simultaneously, [...], and remain an artist. But if he converts to materialism he swallows a poison that will, with absolute inevitability, lead to death.
>
> *Schwarz, 1953, p. 15*

The editor, unsurprisingly, in a foreword distanced himself from several of Schwarz's positions, also publishing an extract from a letter Schwarz had written in response to the reservations *BuW* staff had voiced when they first received the essay. What followed was a heated exchange, known as the 'Bauhaus debate' which was published in *BuW* as a series of articles and letters over the course of 1953.[20] This illustrated *BuW*'s by now more cautious position vis-à-vis the *Neues Bauen*, and the journal's support for a modernism carefully built on traditions. Warning, for example, against the (over-)use of grids in both modern architecture and town planning, Leitl, in issue 1/1953, remarked: 'A terrible notion, which has plagued us for a while, has now become certainty: MODERN ARCHITECTURE HAS OBVIOUSLY PREVAILED. It is high time to think about how we are going to deal with this gratifying fact' (Leitl, 1953).

One contribution to the Schwarz controversy, although not published in *BuW*, came from *BM*'s Rudolf Pfister. His intriguing piece, published in the final *BM* issue of 1953, was titled

'Verwirrung auf der ganzen Linie! Ein Vorschlag zur Güte von Rudolf Pfister' (Confusion Across the Board! A Compromise Proposed by Rudolf Pfister), in which he listed in some detail – and tongue in cheek – a series of issues that *BM* might, retrospectively, have liked to reflect on. Pfister now rather felt obliged, instead, to report on the 'Controversy Schwarz – Bauhaus', at the expense of other, more positive news. According to Pfister, Schwarz (whose work was either ignored or scorned by *BM*) had mercilessly revealed the shortcomings of the Bauhaus and of 'contemporary' modern architecture. Pfister cleverly recounted the sequence of events, quoting from Schwarz's original essay and the various responses to it, to support his own misgivings about modernism and the 'avant-garde'. Having made his point, however, he ended his essay with a direct appeal, in his 'conciliatory proposal' to Alfons Leitl, asking:

> How about if we all – at least for a while – kept our beaks shut and worked silently, without clamour, without propaganda, most [importantly] without 'conversations', without personal attacks, without spitefulness.
>
> *Pfister, 1953*

Having complimented Leitl on the 'exemplary typography of your beautiful journal', he closed the essay wishing him 'a happy new year, [hopefully] in the absence of [any] clever art-claptrap'.

1960s: demise of *Baukunst und Werkform* and emergence of *Stadtbauwelt*

Until Rebitzki became editor-in-chief at *BuW*, the journal retained its scholarly layout, including the sub A4 format, changing to oversized A4 in 1959. From around 1954, how-ever, there was a shift in the importance of the visual formatting, partly due to the need to document the increase in the number of buildings now available for publication. By 1954 the comments section had become shorter, often only running over three pages, in contrast to 14 pages in the first 1947 issue. The substance of the journal during the 1950s (around 60 pages thick), was structured by an initial editorial followed by about two-thirds of each issue dedicated to a single theme, before it concluded with the regular letters, literature reviews, news and various miscellania on the final 15–20 pages.

From the early 1950s until 1957 the journal had been laid out mainly over two columns, employing a traditional typeface, before changing to sans serif typefaces in 1958. At the same time a tripartite layout for the main part, with four narrow columns for the back sections, was introduced together with an irregularly appearing section called *Werkform*, usually consisting of articles on industrial design or other (non-architectural) design matters. This was complemented with the similarly infrequent inclusion of a section on urban planning and design. From 1958 the journal also included technical supplements, consisting of detailed drawings from selected projects printed on cartridge paper. There was also a regular column by Wilhelm Schaupp on the construction challenges of the *Neues Bauen*, registering over a number of years the change of materials and detailing applied in modern architecture.

BuW's visual appearance now seemed more commercial and resembled less the scholarly format of its early years. Contributions were now often shorter, and the issues contained more illustrations and more advertising. Still predominantly in monochrome, full-page and on occasion colour adverts (generally confined to the later sections of each issue) reduced the primary architectural content since the total pagination remained around 60 pages.

From the mid-1950s to the end of the 1960s the erosion of the ideals of *Neues Bauen* and the demise of *Heimatschutzarchitektur* had started to pose new questions. This was reflected, for example, in the journal's critique of functionalism and the search for remedies for the unsympathetic character of the rebuilt city centres.

In 1962, Lewis Mumford's 'The Case Against "Modern Architecture"' (Mumford, 1962a–c) was published in German (*BuW* issues 7 and 8), followed by editorial and subscribers' responses in the next two issues. Mumford's essay was a criticism of modern architecture in general, particularly of the perceived consequences of the machine aesthetic. Rebitzki, by way of responding to Mumford's essay, presented the role of the journal as that of enabling a 'conversation', seeking to encourage debate and inviting readers to participate. Summarising Mumford's main points – a humanist agenda questioning purely technological progress and moderating a no longer new *Neues Bauen* – he concluded that, to enable and foster change, architectural criticism had to become more diligent, knowledgeable and less biased towards 'big names'. There needed in his view to be a new literature available to architects, one specifically engaging biology, sociology, psychology and physiology. This was in line with the general tendencies that would later inform the new journals *Stadtbauwelt* and *ARCH+*, first published in 1964 and 1968 respectively.

Issue 9/1962 was the last *BuW* published, and from 10/1962 the journal was 'united' with *db* (none of *BuW*'s regular writers, however, except Udo Kultermann, contributed to the subsequent *db* issues).[21] *db*, which in its various guises is the longest running German architecture journal, had, when it changed its format and layout in January 1960, declared its ambitions:

> To follow the multiple architectural directions of our time, to publish, to discuss and to disseminate them, is a meaningful task and duty. Thus the journal is going to dedicate itself to the documentation of architectural works, the discussion of […] modern architecture, the passing on of experiences, the representation of contemporary design, form and construction problems, and also to the limitless number of building's technical requirements.
>
> *Schwab, 1960*

After Ulrich Conrads had moved to *Bauwelt* in 1957, he changed the journal's direction. While still providing technical columns and practical information for architects, *Bauwelt* had become more international, and there now was a shift of focus towards fields such as sociology, and coverage of urban design and town planning had increased. In the early 1960s, 'There were increasing signs of the need for reorientation, after the broad consensus of the 1950s on the general principle of the *gegliederte und aufgelockerte Stadt* had lost its power' (Albers, 1988).[22] Consequently, *Stadtbauwelt*, subtitled 'Beiträge zur Neuordnung von Stadt und Land' (Contributions to a Reordering of City and Countryside), was launched in January 1964 and published as a double issue once every three months. While it was possible to purchase individual copies, the issues were also part of the subscription to *Bauwelt*, making *Stadtbauwelt* commercially viable on the one hand, but also increasing the readership with a somewhat 'captive audience'. The second issue of *Stadtbauwelt* reflected the spirit of the time, containing the now seminal text 'Die Unwirtlichkeit unserer Städte' (The Inhospitality of Our Cities) by the psychoanalyst Alexander Mitscherlich, which according to Bartetzko (2008) 'belongs to German urban planning like house-to-house fighting belongs to the student revolt'. While Mitscherlich argued against the functional city and the 'nonsense of segregation [of functions]', he nonetheless did not fall back on the pattern of the traditional city, bemoaning instead 'the inhospitality of our horizontally – instead of bravely vertically – growing cities, which are monotonous rather than melodically composed'. Mitscherlich's general argument, now somewhat commonplace, was that after the destruction of the war had come the 'destruction of reconstruction', not least because, in his view, without a redistribution of landownership, 'new' planning was not going to be possible: 'After the war, we missed the chance to build intellectually better conceived cities. [...] If cities are a self-expression of collectives, then what we are currently witnessing as self-expression is alarming' (Mitscherlich, 1964). Mitscherlich's text, appropriately accompanied by rather gloomy black-and-white photographs of the suburban periphery of Mannheim, set the tone for what was to come.

Towards the end of an era

In the meantime, *BM*, after the change from Pfister to Peters in 1959, had gradually become less 'conservative' and, particularly towards the end of the 1960s, more open to general societal and architectural developments. By 1953 the journal had achieved a print run of 25,000 and was regularly around 80 pages thick, including eight pages of plates showing construction drawings introduced in 1946, and eight sheets laid out and containing information similar in kind to Neufert's *Architect's Data*. The main part of each issue still featured essays and project criticisms, whereas the back of the journal, like the review section, featured shorter essays on technical information, building economy, building laws and regulations. The layout was formatted in two columns throughout, except pages entirely consisting of small adverts, which were arranged over three columns towards the concluding third of each issue. A serif typeface was used throughout, except for the cover title. By 1959 the size of the issues had increased, now generally 65 pages plus 16 construction plates and eight design sheets, all on smooth white paper except for the *Tafeln*, which were printed on cartridge paper. The front section, followed by the *Tafeln* (now in the centre of each issue) was now laid out in a one-column format. The text was still in a serif typeface, with the captions set in sans serif. The concluding sections now regularly started with a column called 'Zeitfragen des Bauens' (Contemporary Building Concerns). Advertisements were still located here, many being full-page and some in colour. Helmuth Baur-Callwey tells of an advertisement with a sparsely clad girl sitting on a pile of roof tiles, causing the local Bishop's building office to cancel its subscription. The issues were generally illustrated with high-quality monochrome photographs and drawings (occasionally in colour).

While there was change, this was gradual. Peters' argument in 'Die perfekte Langeweile' (Perfect Boredom) in the December issue of 1959, for instance, was essentially similar to Pfister's assessment of German architecture in the early 1950s, criticising the 'overpowering mixture of perfection and mediocrity', 'petty bourgeois pseudo-modernisms' and 'fake pomp where real representativeness would have been necessary' (Peters, 1959). By 1964, *BM*'s outlook had become more international and the individual issues had a stronger focus on selected topics. The journal had become considerably thicker, usually around 100 pages per issue, and with additional space dedicated to project reviews, notably including a page of summaries in English.

Peters had continued Pfister's 'tradition' of occasionally provocative editorials, while placing architectural issues in a wider context. Like his predecessor, the new editor-in-chief certainly knew his own mind, voicing his views primarily in his column 'Kritische Anmerkungen von Paulhans Peters' (Critical Comments by Paulhans Peters), within the short news section at the beginning of each issue.

Towards the end of 1964, and resulting from the outcome of a readership survey, Peters published his view of the direction the journal was going to take in 1965 (Peters, 1964). Responding to the evidence that only 13 per cent of readers wished to concern themselves with sociological or urban design questions, and demands that *BM* should publish fewer international projects, he argued for the necessity to publish international projects and for the importance of addressing 'utopian' projects by groups such as the Metabolists or advocates of the Dutch linear city, while continuing to report on the 'contemporary daily problems' of German architects. Peters' article, to a degree, also illustrated the difference between the immediate postwar years, during which there was less variation both in the architecture built and in the ideas published, and the emerging architectural and societal plurality of the late 1960s. By 1968 the journal had fully taken note of the ongoing social, political and cultural changes. Peters also continued to identify with Pfister's general misgivings about some of the ideas of the *Neues Bauen*. In issue 2/1968 he asked: 'Is it not wrong to continue thinking in the hygienic categories of the 1920s, [and] is it not totally absurd to plan variants of *Zeilenbau*, causing not only spatial chaos, but also chaotic inhabitation?' (Peters, 1968c).

The 1968 contents list also included a section on 'sociology, sociography, psychology and futurology'. Peters' editorial 'Wende im Bauen' (A Change of Direction in Building) prefaced issue 6/1968, which had a strong emphasis on participation in architecture, and he announced it as presenting 'analysis and prosecution' at the same time. Analysis because 'the issue tries to highlight the symptoms of change and to test the value of signs pointing in new directions', and 'prosecution' confronting various 'problems', such as 'teaching systems that encourage an artistic hybridity in students, suggesting that architects could provide a better life for later generations through better architecture' (Peters, 1968a). Peters voiced his misgivings about the 'totally wrong education of architects' which turned them into socially marginal figures and that 'in the future even less architecture will be made by architects' (Peters, 1968a).

In the final *BM* issue of 1968, Peters' editorial 'Konfrontation mit der Wirklichkeit' (Confrontation With Reality) assessed the impact of photography on the dissemination of buildings, and architecture being perceived through the media rather than experienced in its physical reality (Peters, 1968b). The issue also contained positive reviews of Stirling and Gowan's Leicester and Cambridge faculty buildings and an illustrated German translation of Christopher Alexander's 'Systems building systems'. Responding to the cultural shifts of the period, the journal incorporated 'Zeitschrift für Architektur / Planung / Umwelt' (Journal for Architecture/Planning/Environment) as its subtitle.

Journals and the status quo: imperative or reflection?

Lipstadt's assumptions concerning the quasi-authority, and thus autonomy, of the architecture journal is not entirely applicable to the German experience of the history and development of *BM* and *BuW*. However, what can be ascertained is that both journals in the first 15 years after the war had established very distinct positions. *BM* voiced support for *Heimatschutzarchitektur*, in the face of accusations of promoting backward thinking. In contrast *BuW*, as a protagonist in support of an ongoing but reconsidered and cautious *Neues Bauen*, presented a format that was more akin to an academic journal than one aimed solely at the

FIGURE 2.6 Journal cover, *Baumeister* 12 (1968).
Source: Baumeister/Callwey Verlag. Courtesy of Helmuth Baur-Callwey.

profession of architecture. Neither position, ultimately, would succeed in dominating the profession, as the first two postwar decades concluded with the incipient commercial modernism of a generally stable economy, something still evident today in many German town centres. The years from 1946 to 1959 were consequently ones in which those responsible for the German journal landscape perhaps offered more extreme positions than would follow in the decade to 1968, despite the emergence of journals such as *Stadtbauwelt* and *ARCH+*.

From the early 1960s *BM* became less 'conservative' and more 'international' under Peters, gaining a critical reputation and thus maintaining a degree of autonomy in the journal market. *BuW*'s early credentials all but disappeared after the journal was 'united' with *db*, which although long running (or perhaps precisely because of it), had less to offer by way of challenging the mainstream in the emergent 1960s. Student revolt, the practice of participation, an environmental consciousness and the merging of the discipline of architecture with social sciences, would follow from the late 1960s onwards, introducing new developments in the history of the professional architecture journal. But that is a different chapter in a story which retains an uncanny prescience for our uncertain future in the age of digital media.

Directly after the end of the war there were fewer journals on the market competing for a finite number of subscribers. News took longer to be processed and influence was much slower to register, on the evidence of, for example, the long drawn-out Bauhaus controversy in *BuW*. Articles and essays were generally longer, and the balance between image and text was, at least until the mid-1950s, more even and occasionally in favour of 'critical' text over image. Perhaps there were fewer distractions for practising architects as the relatively slow speed of the processing of information also affected the building process, and the time architects had to react to changes. If the journals were a reliable guide, architects had more time to read. In both the cases of *BM* and *BuW*, editorials were longer and expressed very strong opinions on key contemporary issues, something less evident in today's cultural plurality.

Professional architecture journals by their nature are required to provide multifarious contents: project features, critique, architectural history, the application of technology, legal practices, knowledge of the economy, product features, letters, competitions, and so on, while needing to have distinguishing features that set them apart from their competitors. The struggle to find an acceptable range of content for readers while still maintaining a position in the market is as difficult today as it was in 1955, with the added complication that today's news becomes yesterday's before it is in print. This could support an argument for the return of a stronger analytical position in the mould of Pfister, Peters, Leitl and Conrads.

Acknowledgements

I would like to thank Helmuth Baur-Callwey and Simon Pepper for their kind help, support and advice on this chapter.

Notes

All translations from German, except where stated otherwise, by the author.

1   See Fuhlrott (1975), who has conducted an excellent study of the architecture journals published in Germany between 1789 and 1918.
2   *Architektur und Wohnform* (1946–1971), *Architektur-Wettbewerbe* (1939–1979), *Bauhelfer* (1946–1950), *Bauen und Wohnen* (1946–1981), *Baurundschau* (1910–1973), *Deutsche Bauzeitschrift* (1953–), *Die Bauzeitung/Deutsche Bauzeitung* (1921–1944; 1948–1959/1960–), *Die Neue Stadt* (1947–1953), *Neue Bauwelt* (1946–1952)/*Bauwelt* (1910–1944, 1952–).
3   *Baumeister* had published through the war until issue 7/8 in 1944.
4   Petsch (1979a) has discussed the problem of national-socialist continuity after the war using *Baumeister* as an example, and (1979b) the reception of the Bauhaus in postwar Germany. Hackelsberger (1985) has commented briefly on *Baumeister*'s 1950s position relative to other journals. Von Beyme (1987) remarked that *Baumeister* had (under Pfister) not covered the Bauhaus on its pages. This is correct except for Pfister's contribution to the 'Bauhaus debate'.
5   Interesting in this context are the recollections of the architect Rudolf Wolters from a 1951 'conciliatory' meeting in Hanover between architects who had been working successfully during the Third Reich, and some of the protagonists of the *Neues Bauen* who had not been able to work, or had had very limited opportunities, between 1933 and 1945: 'Hillebrecht came to talk about contemporary building. It should only be possible to build modern […] in a way appropriate to our times. During the Nazi regime, Hitler had forced his will onto building, like any political power had done before him. But today it would not be possible to build in the same way as during the Third Reich […]: capitals, cornices and bases had to go. This attitude had to be commonly shared and there could be no compromise' (Durth, 1992, p. 394). Wolters had held several leading roles during the Nazi regime, most notably he was heading the *Arbeitsstab für den Wiederaufbau bombenzerstörter Städte* (Task force for the reconstruction of cities destroyed by bombs).
6   There are numerous publications on the architectural developments in Germany from the early twentieth century through to the 1950s and 1960s, including the complex role *Heimatschutzarchitektur* played between 1933 and 1945. See references for the following authors: von Beyme, Busmann, Diefendorf, Durth, Frank, Petsch.
7   This quote does not appear in the first edition published by Vieweg (also see references).

8 *BuW* was, from 10/1962 united with *db,* which mentioned *BuW* on its cover until the end of 1969. *Die neue Stadt* (1947–1953) had been united with *BuW* in 1954, and was mentioned on *BuW*'s cover until that became part of *db.*

9 Helmuth Baur-Callwey in conversation with the author, Munich, 15 September 2016.

10 With Gerd Albers, Kurt Eggeling, Klaus-Jakob Thiele and Klaus Winter.

11 Helmuth Baur-Callwey in conversation with the author, Munich, 15 September 2016.

12 Among job vacancies, there was also a request for old architecture journals 'from home and abroad' from 1920 onwards for a research project!

13 Once in 1947 and 1948 respectively, and three times in 1949. In 1947 and 1948 the covers incorporated the subtitle 'Eine Folge Von Beiträgen Zum Bauen' (A Series of Contributions on Building), whereas for the three 1949 issues the journal was called 'A Quarterly'. The 1947 issue was titled 'Ein Querschnitt' (A Section), and that of 1948 'Tradition und Wiederaufbau' (Tradition and Reconstruction).

14 The first issue in 1947 was published with the support of: Otto Bartning, Egon Eiermann, Werner Hebebrand, Hugo Häring, Georg Leowald, Rudolph Lodders, Rudolf Schwarz, Otto E. Schweizer and Hanz Schwippert. Contributors to the issue were: Schwippert, Bartning, Ludwig Neundörfer, Hans Scharoun, Eugen Blanck, Robert Vorhoelzer, Hugo Häring, Rudolf Lodders, Egon Eiermann, Fritz Schumacher, Georg Leowald, Schwarz, Hermann Mäckler, Johann Hafers and Alfons Leitl.

15 According to Busmann, the 'Aufruf' was written by Leitl (Busmann, 1995, p. 14).

16 The first point of the 'Aufruf' was: 'The large cities must become organised as an association of viable, comprehensible quarters; the old city centre must gain new life as the cultural and political heart'.

17 Hopp (1955), however, also reported positively on Freudenstadt in the East German journal *Deutsche Architektur.*

18 *Die Bauzeitung* was to become *Deutsche Bauzeitung* (*db*) in 1960, and in 1962 amalgamated with *BuW.* Freudenstadt was covered on 15 pages.

19 Pfister quotes from two letters sent by Wagner to four Berlin politicians. The letters were, according to Pfister, published in *Die Baukritik,* a supplement to *Nachrichtendienst für das Bauwesen,* on 3 and 10 February, and 21 April 1956.

20 Involved were, among others: Leitl, Schwarz, Franz Meunier, Hermann Mäckler, Hubert Hoffmann, Paul Klopfer, Louis Schoberth. Also see Conrads (1994).

21 *db*'s history is, since the first publication of *Wochenblatt des Architekten-Vereins zu Berlin* in 1867, relatively more complex than that of any other German journal. The *Deutsche Bauzeitung* eventually subsumed *Die Bauzeitung,* *Der Deutsche Baumeister* and *Baukunst und Werkform. Die Bauzeitung* itself was first published, infrequently, from 1921 to 1942, before its republication in 1948. While in the 1950s it was published as *Die Bauzeitung/Deutsche Bauzeitung,* in 1959 it was subsumed into *Deutsche Bauzeitung.* In the 1930s *Die Bauzeitung* incorporated the subtitle 'vereinigt mit *Süddeutsche Bauzeitung München, Süddeutsche Baugewerks-Zeitung, Deutscher Bauten-Nachweis Stuttgart*'.

22 There is no proper English translation for *Die gegliederte und aufgelockerte Stadt.* Diefendorf (1999) explains: 'This approach received its clearest expression in *Die gegliederte und aufgelockerte Stadt,* published by Johannes Göderitz, Roland Rainer and Hubert Hoffmann in 1957. The date is deceptive […] since the book was drafted during the last years of the war and printed in a small edition which was destroyed at the war's end. […] In their book, we again find model cities that are functionally articulated but organically tied to the natural landscape of hills and waterways.'

References

Albers, G. (1988). Planungsklima. In *Für Ulrich Conrads* (pp. 7–11). Wiesbaden: Vieweg/Teubner.

Bartetzko, D. (2008). Die Stadt, der Prägestock unseres Lebens. *Frankfurter Allgemeine Zeitung.* Retrieved 17 September 2008 from: www.faz.net/aktuell/feuilleton/buecher/rezensionen/sachbuch/die-stadt-der-praegestock-unseres-lebens-1700712.html von Beyme, K. (1987). *Der Wiederaufbau. Architektur und Städtebaupolitik in beiden deutschen Staaten*. München: Piper.

Baukunst und Werkform (1947). *Ein Aufruf: Grundsätzliche Forderungen*, I, p. 29.

Busmann, J. (1995). *Die revidierte Moderne. Der Architekt Alfons Leitl 1909–1975*. Wuppertal: Müller + Busmann.

Conrads, U. (Ed.) (1994). *Die Bauhaus Debatte 1953: Dokumente einer verdrängten Kontroverse*. Braunschweig/Wiesbaden: Vieweg + Teubner.

Diefendorf, J. M. (1993). *In the Wake of War*. Oxford: Oxford University Press.

—— (1999). The West German Debate on Urban Planning. Conference paper given at the German Historical Institute Washington, DC, 25–27 March 1999. Retrieved from: http://webdoc.sub.gwdg.de/ebook/p/2005/ghi_12/www.ghi-dc.org/conpotweb/westernpapers/diefendorf.pdf.

Dolff-Bonekämper, G. and Schmidt, F. (1999). *Das Hansaviertel. Internationale Nachkriegsmoderne in Berlin*. Berlin: Verlag Bauwesen.

Durth, W. (1986 [1992]). *Deutsche Architekten: Biographische Verpflechtungen*. 2nd, revised edition. Munich: DTV.

Frank, H. (1983). Trümmer. Traditionelle und Moderne Architekturen im Nachkriegsdeutschland. In B. Schulz (Ed.), *Grauzonen/Farbwelten*. Berlin: Medusa, pp. 43–83.

—— (1988). Auf der Suche nach der alten Stadt. Zur Diskussion um Heimatschutz und Stadtbaukunst beim Wiederaufbau von Freudenstadt. In H.-G. Burkhardt, H. Frank, U. Höhns, K. Stieghorst (Eds), *Stadtgestalt und Heimatgefühl – Der Wiederaufbau von Freudenstadt 1945–54*. Hamburg: Christians Verlag, pp. 1–31.

Fuhlrott, R. (1975). *Deutschsprachige Architekturzeitschriften*. München: Verlag Dokumentation.

Göderitz, J., Rainer, R. and Hoffman, H. (1957). *Die gegliederte und aufgelockerte Stadt*. Tübingen: Wasmuth.

Hackelsberger, C. (1985). *Die aufgeschobene Moderne: ein Versuch zur Einordnung der Architektur der fünfziger Jahre*. München: Deutscher Kunstverlag.

Hopp, H (1955). Vorbildlicher Wiederaufbau einer Stadt in Süddeutschland. *Deutsche Architektur*, 4 (5), pp. 230–233.

Jannière, H. and Vanlaethem, F. (2008), Architectural Magazines as Historical Source or Object? A Methodological Essay. In A. Sornin, H. Jannière, F. Vanlaethem (Eds), *Architectural Periodicals in the 1960s and 1970s* (pp. 41–70). Quebec: Institut de recherche en histoire de l'architecture.

Koellmann, H.-P. (1956). Internationale Bauausstellung Berlin: Stand der Planung des Hansaviertels. *Baukunst und Werkform*, 9 (3), pp. 151–154.

Leitl, A. (1947). Anmerkungen zur Zeit. *Baukunst und Werkform*, 1, pp. 3–14.

—— (1948). Der Fall Schmitthenner. *Baukunst und Werkform*, 2, pp. 13–14.

—— (1953). Anmerkungen. *Baukunst und Werkform*, 6 (1), p. 5.

—— (1957a). Anmerkungen zum Hansaviertel. *Baukunst und Werkform*, 10 (11), pp. 621–630.

—— (1957b). Nach Schluß der Interbau Berlin. *Baukunst und Werkform*, 10 (12), pp. 714–720.

Meunier, F. (1948). Ein deutsches Gelehrtenleben. *Baukunst und Werkform*, 2, pp. 14–15.

Mitscherlich, A. (1964). Die Unwirtlichkeit unserer Städte. *Stadtbauwelt*, 1 (2), pp. 94–97.

Mumford, L. (1962a). The Case Against Modern Architecture. *Architectural Record*, 131 (4), pp. 155–162.

—— (1962b). Eine Abrechnung mit der modernen Architektur. *Baukunst und Werkform*, 15 (7), pp. 371–373.

—— (1962c). Eine Abrechnung mit der modernen Architektur. *Baukunst und Werkform*, 15 (8), pp. 427–429.

Peters, P. (1957a). Die Stadt von morgen. *Baumeister*, 54 (4), p. 256.

—— (1957b). Über die Interbau Berlin 1957. *Baumeister*, 54 (8), p. 529.

—— (1959). Die Perfekte Langeweile. *Baumeister*, 56 (12), p. 817.

—— (1964). Anstelle eines Jahresabschlußberichtes. *Baumeister*, 61 (12), p. 1379.

—— (1968a). Wende im Bauen. *Baumeister*, 65 (6), p. 613.

—— (1968b). Konfrontation mit der Wirklichkeit. *Baumeister*, 65 (12), p. 1427.

—— (1968c). Vorbilder und Modellfälle oder das Normale und das Absurde. *Baumeister*, 65 (2), p. 103.

Petsch, J. (1979a). Zum Problem der Kontinuität nationalsozialistischer Architektur in den Fünfziger Jahren am Beispiel der Zeitschrift Baumeister. In J. Petsch and W. Petsch (Eds), *Bundesrepublik – Eine Neue Heimat. Städtebau und Architektur nach '45*. Berlin (West): VAS Verlag für Ausbildung und Studium, pp. 41–62.

—— (1979b). Die Bauhausrezeption in der Bundesrepublik Deutschland in den fünfziger Jahren. In J. Petsch and W. Petsch (Eds), *Bundesrepublik – Eine Neue Heimat. Städtebau und Architektur nach '45*. Berlin (West): VAS Verlag für Ausbildung und Studium, pp. 67–83.

Pfister, R. (1928). Stuttgarter Werkbundausstellung 'Die Wohnung'. *Baumeister*, 26 (2), pp. 33–72.

—— (1946a). Unsere Aufgabe. *Baumeister*, 43 (1), pp. 1–3.

—— (1946b). Vorbemerkung der Schriftleitung. *Baumeister*, 43 (4), p. 107.

—— (1947). Um Den Deutschen Werkbund. *Baumeister*, 44 (4), pp. 139–140.

—— (1948). Der Fall Schmitthenner. *Baumeister*, 45 (4), pp. 166–167.

—— (1950). Ein Brief an den Architekturberichterstatter einer großen deutschen Tageszeitung. *Baumeister*, 47 (1), pp. 1, 41–42.

—— (1953). Verwirrung auf der ganzen Linie! Ein Vorschlag zur Güte von Rudolf Pfister. *Baumeister*, 50 (12), p. 821.

—— (1954). Heimatschutz recht verstanden. *Baumeister*, 51 (5), p. 269.

—— (1955). Der Wiederaufbau von Freudenstadt im Schwarzwald. *Baumeister*, 52 (2), p. 73.

—— (1956a). Was geht im Berliner Hansaviertel vor sich? *Baumeister*, 53 (3), p. 173.

—— (1956b). 'Ceterum Censeo'. Notwendige Betrachtungen zur 'Interbau' 1957 in Berlin. *Baumeister*, 53 (6), pp. 407–409.

—— (1957). V. Interbau Bericht. *Baumeister*, 54 (5), p. 332.

Pütz, U. (2000). Der Publizist und Architekt Alfons Leitl ist vor 25 Jahren gestorben. *Deutsche Bauzeitschrift*, 48 (4), p. 12.

Rebitzki, H (1959). Paul Schmitthenner 75-jährig. *Baukunst und Werkform*, 12 (12), p. 720.

Schwab, G. (1960). Vorwort. *Deutsche Bauzeitung*, 65 (1), p. 3.

Schwarz, R. (1953). Bilde Künstler, rede nicht. *Baukunst und Werkform*, 6 (1), pp. 9–17.

Sedlmaier, R. and Pfister, R. (1923). *Die fürstbischöfliche Residenz in Würzburg*. München: G. Müller.

Voigt, W. and Frank, H. (2003). *Paul Schmitthenner 1884–1972*. Tübingen: Ernst Wasmuth Verlag.

Von der Schriftleitung (1955). Freudenstadt, ein Wiederaufbau aus einem Guß. *Die Bauzeitung/Deutsche Bauzeitung*, 60 (2), pp. 37–52.

3

THE FREE BIRD AND ITS CAGES

Dutch architectural journals in the first decade after the Second World War

Herman van Bergeijk

Think, build, write. All of these are just constructions.

The Dutch are known for their frugality. They cut to the chase without bells and whistles, and the same mentality applies to the character of architecture journals in the Netherlands. Before the Second World War, the range of these publications was well defined, each faction having their own professional body and their own views about the design of their own publications. This discussion will not focus on a specific publication. Rather, the attempt is to create a general impression of the situation of journals in the Netherlands, and to illustrate the considered manner in which individual networks were created by people with the same social, societal, political or artistic interests and focus.[1] On the one hand, there were publications such as *de Stijl, de 8 en Opbouw* – 'the only explicitly modernist architectural journal' – and on the other, the more religiously oriented and conservative journals such as *Rooms-Katholiek Bouwblad* (Roman Catholic Building Journal). *Bouwkundig Weekblad* (*BW*; Architectural Weekly) firmly occupied the middle ground as the official journal of the *Bond van Nederlandse Architecten* (BNA; Union of Dutch Architects), the professional association that protected the interests of architecture and the rights of architects. In 1955 the journal *De Bouwwereld* (Building World) came to represent the relatively small *Nederlands Architectengenootschap* (Dutch Architects Association), but remained a minor publication.

Many other journals also found their niche. These were either associated with a certain industry or with the specific vision of an architect and were often short-lived. Several journals that appeared in 1923, for example, did not survive past the first issue. The journal *Bouwbedrijf en openbare werken* (Building Industry and Public Works), well edited by the TU Delft professor J. G. Wattjes, was an exception to this trend, but what transpired after the war?

During the German occupation of the Netherlands, there was a general halt to construction activity. Trade unions came under German control, including professional journals; many swiftly ceased publication. The BNA was renamed the 'Architectural Guild' in 1942 and was placed under the supervision of the *Kultuurkamer* (Chamber of Culture) formed by the occupying Germans. It ceased most of its activities, and publication of its journal was wound up shortly after. However, this did not mean that architects isolated themselves: on the contrary, they met in clandestine or illegal circumstances, exchanging ideas and putative plans. After the war everything would improve: they would come together and not retrench behind their own dogmatic positions. This good-mannered agreement infused the meetings in the city of Doorn's *Maarten-Maartenshuis*, which instituted the so-called Doorn 'courses' founded by the association of Amsterdam architects *Architectura et Amicitia* (A. et A.). The first course, dedicated to the subject of 'the characteristics of Dutch architecture', attracted acute interest and promoted the preservation of a unified Dutch identity. Numerous pre-war factions advocated fraternal dialogue,[2] but this apparent end to discord could not be further from the truth.

During the war, graphic designer Hans Neuburg-Coray wrote in the Swiss journal *Werk*, edited by Alfred Roth and Gotthard Jedlocka, that the 'French, English, German, Turkish, Dutch and Slavic journals were almost always boring and uninteresting' (Neuburg-Coray, 1943). A commonplace view, this did not initially provoke much dispute. It is unclear what lay behind the harsh criticism, for in general, this was not the case. *Wendingen*, the journal of A. et A., had been a very special publication in several respects for many years,[3] and Paul Schuitema's layout of *De 8 en Opbouw* was equally innovative in an increasingly conservative Europe. During the war, however, little opportunity arose to demonstrate graphic skills, which did not change in its immediate aftermath; paper was still rationed and only available in small batches.

In April 1945, the young architect Auke Komter (1904–1982), who had also played a role in the Doorn meetings, was elected as chairman of A. et A. In his opening speech he argued the case that the new A. et A. should continue the association's policy from prior to 1930, when there had been attempts to bring the different architectural movements into contact with each

FIGURE 3.1 Journal cover, *De 8 en Opbouw* 7 (March 1935).

FIGURE 3.2   Journal cover, *Bouwkundig Weekblad Architectura* 1 (December 1945).
Source: © BNA Netherlands.

other (although these were unsuccessful). Opinions were divided following the financial crash of 1929 and found their expression in different journals. Together with J.F. Berghoef, G.H. Holt and A. Staal, Komter conceived a new journal, initiating negotiations with the military authorities and applying for a publishing licence in June 1945.[4] Collectively, they aspired to a journal that could 'withstand the test of criticism' in an international context, and sought collaboration rather than dispute. In December 1945, the first edition of the 63rd volume of the *Bouwkundig Weekblad Architectura* (*BWA*; Architectural Building Weekly) was published as a joint venture with *Maatschappij ter Bevordering van de Bouwkunst* (BvB; Society for the Promotion of Architecture) of the Royal Institute of Dutch Architects and A. et A.

Although by 1919 BvB had already merged with the Royal Institute of Dutch Architects, the publication of the first issue curiously still listed their name. The cover included a photograph of Rhenen, a city reconstructed following an urban plan by the architect C. Pouderoyen, which was featured in the issue. No modernist, he was to become an urban planner influenced by the Delft professor M. J. Granpré Molière. The first page of the sober journal was a tribute to those who had perished during the war, and in particular the architects who had died since 15 June 1941. A statement from the editorial board, chaired by the largely unknown architect-engineer H. G. J. Schelling (1888–1978), followed. His editorial secretary, the architect-writer J. P. Mieras (1888–1956), was clearly the most important figure responsible for the journal.

Compared to the likes of Ernesto Rogers, who put the Italian journal *Casabella* on the international map, Mieras was a middle-of-the-road man with no specific agenda. He had nonetheless been director of the BNA before the war, and was a well-known publicist and

FIGURE 3.3   Portrait of J.P. Mieras, 1948.
Source: *Liber Amicorum J.P. Mieras*, 1958.

critic. Schelling, in contrast, had made a name for himself as architect for the Dutch railways.
Their first editorial emphasised that

> A heavy responsibility rests on our shoulders. In many places, so much has been destroyed
> and severely damaged that a new shape will have to be given to large urban areas. This
> requires much highly responsible work. A great deal of cooperation will be required, a
> great deal of understanding of the opinions of others and especially hard work will be
> needed.

Despite good intentions, cooperation proved difficult and inevitable conflicts arose from too
many divergent visions. The first issue, published in 1946, presented a unified voice for both
the BvB and the BNA, but in the meantime A. et A. had started its own periodical with the
declaration:

> They should realise that the departure of A. et A. from our 'combination' occurred
> without a hint of mutual displeasure. On the contrary, the years of occupation only
> strengthened the bond between the B.N.A. and the association A. et A. Our separate pub-
> lication of periodicals is only motivated by the desire to have architectural publications
> that meet the set objective as effectively as possible and at the highest possible level.

The editors stressed that only 26 issues would appear per year due to the change in paper allocation in 1946. Another followed:

In contrast to the various periodicals that have appeared at this time, in which everything is so attractively restless in the midst of turbulence: the serious word, the principled statement, their lofty promises and their incantation that everything will happen for the good of our subject people; we shall have to be humble and stop using difficult words and creating illusions which we know are to be illusionary. We therefore report, having no intention of coming up with newly current articles, that we are ready to cope with the reconstruction of our periodical and will decidedly not include any special articles on what America has to tell us, or Russia, or Persia, or the Congo. We shall leave the cute [articles] that start with an opening like: 'You should know that [...]', to the enthusiasts. That is all you need to know.

Editorial Board, 1946a

Without alluding to their competitors or even mentioning them directly, the editors of *BWA* made fun of the fanfare with which certain journals publicised themselves. There was no call here for a propagandist purism. *BW*, in contrast, published news from the branches; statements directed at regional governments and the municipalities; wishing to be open to all trends and specifically to reporting on what was being built. But the choices made by *BW* meant that more radical architects were rarely given the opportunity to be heard, and the work of moderate architects predominated. There was also a focus on what was happening in England, in the Scandinavian countries and in the United States. Mieras argued in his article on the Pentagon that the building was the result of a subtle relationship between the American way of life and the challenges and skills of architects – though he did not disguise his criticism of the grand scale with which some architects were preoccupied:

If we keep this relationship in mind, American architects do not 'perform' much more for American society than Dutch architects do for Dutch society. We would feel strange and inadequate in America in the face of challenges such as those of the Pentagon building, but American architects would probably be running around desperately if they had to design something in our entangled ant-like society, which is in our nature and that we must satisfy. There is a macro-cosmos and a micro-cosmos, each with their own internal relationships that, however, do not essentially differ much from each other.

Mieras, 1946b

After the war, the United States was *the* example for many Dutch people. Study groups were sent to the US and impressions of the country, in which sheer size played a dominant role, appeared everywhere. From the manner in which the schematic plan of the Pentagon was published, it was clear that the building was as big as the sum of the Palace of Justice in Brussels, the Paris Opera House, the Houses of Parliament in London, the Town Hall in Stockholm and St. Peter's Basilica in Rome. Such a building, it was claimed, could only be comprehended by contemplating differences in society and the empirical problems that had to be solved: 'It might be good to remember this so as to avoid the Pentagon building – which "gives a real view of the future" – throwing us off balance during our own reconstruction.'

It was only after the journal had featured a range of very diverse contemporary buildings that Mieras felt obliged to write a postscript to an article on the national aviation laboratory by the architects W. van Tijen and H. A. Maaskant, which viewed them as representatives of 'modern building'. Indeed, he says 'the outward appearance of the buildings in this series creates the impression that they were developed from an arbitrary choice, a choice as arbitrary as rummaging in a bag of marbles'. But, Mieras continues, 'the matter is quite different if one realises and feels that outward appearance cannot be any gauge of value in appreciating the essential impact of architecture on the human psychological make-up'. Accordingly, 'good form' had to be sought and 'the greatest enemy of those who search is the philistine; his best friend is the fellow discoverer. And architects are discoverers and should be most aware of this if they think they have found it [this form]' (Mieras, 1946a). Mieras generally chose architects identified with 'middle-of-the-road' architecture and took great care not to occupy too radical a position. He had no particular preference and scarcely paved the way for the representatives of the younger generation, who were anxious to move on.

Clearly, Mieras would have found little support among those architects who declined a conventional perspective, but who were forthright that their approach was correct. These architects believed that the editorial board would not readily accept their viewpoint. Thus they continued their search, but rather than searching for a different architecture, they strove to find different ways of expressing their insights. They found this conviction, on the one hand, in the *Katholiek Bouwblad* (*KB*), and on the other, in the journal *Forum*, founded by A. et A. in 1946.

In a long speech at a meeting of the central administration of A. et A., and before regional delegates, an academic from Delft, Professor H. T. Zwiers looked to maintain unity in pointing out that building was a cultural activity: the architect had a duty to express what society and the community deemed valuable. However, for the architects contributing to the *KB*, this was a religious act. While the more 'avant-garde' architects who found a mouthpiece in *Forum* saw design

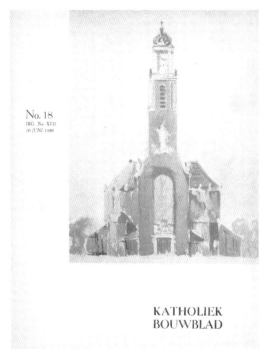

FIGURE 3.4   Journal cover, *Katholiek Bouwblad* 18 (June 1950).
Source: Courtesy Archis.

FIGURE 3.5 Journal cover, *Forum* 1 (1951).
Source: © Forum/A et A.

above all else as a social act, Zwiers offered them no more than a few platitudes, expressing neither enthusiasm nor commitment. *BW* generally avoided controversial or polemic work and barely noted the importance of the other arts. When they were acknowledged, this tended to relate to contemporary developments. Only occasional contributions aroused, instigated and nurtured, rather than suppressed, fundamental debate – though lacking the verve of lively discussions concerning the Bauhaus in the German *Baukunst und Werkform*. *BW* consequently became increasingly dull, over-emphasising minutes of BNA meetings and generally noncommittal in making collegiate judgements.

When the avant-garde pamphlet for visual design *Open Oog* (Open Eye) appeared in the winter of 1947, Mieras notably welcomed it with a bitter comment:

> With *Open Oog* there finally appeared a journal that had been needed for decades, namely a journal that only provides pure and flawless drivel. *Open Oog* did succeed in presenting this purity and flawlessness as having the quality of pure alcohol, which could hardly be more spiritual. *Open Oog* is an avant-garde pamphlet, of which the so-called International editorial board, just like the avant-garde cavaliers of the past, fearlessly entered into battle to overcome the reactionary.
>
> *Mieras, 1947a*

It is surprising that someone usually as mild-mannered as Mieras took aim at this journal, which hardly posed any real threat to the status quo. *Open Oog*, just as the journal *i10* prior to the war, barely mustered a readership and consequently proved innocuous. But Mieras lacked

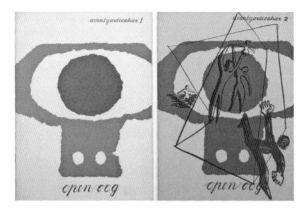

FIGURE 3.6   Journal covers, *Open Oog* 1 and 2 (1946).

any appreciation for this thin periodical that, among other individuals, counted on support from the left-wing Mart Stam and Willem Sandberg. The latter, who created the striking initial design, was a friend of the young architect A.E. van Eyck (1918–1999). A second issue, published with a similarly dynamic cover, severely criticised the dogmas of the so-called Delft School, in the form of a manifesto. Mieras once again could not resist aiming a barb at the journal, but without directly naming it. His ironic article 'Progressief' ridiculed what 'progressive' really meant (Mieras, 1947b), and shortly after the avant-garde periodical died a silent death.

The short life of *Open Oog* in no way meant that the more radical architects were silenced. On the contrary, in 1947 the journal *Forum* published the views of an unknown group of young architects who aimed to 'break through the reactionary sphere, which they observed in the national architecture'. They contended that architecture should not only meet conventional needs, but also itself generate new responsibilities related to social justice, freedom and cooperation (*Forum*, 1947).

Although *Forum*'s initial editorial board was hardly more progressive than that of *BW*, they devoted more space to young architects and to discussion of architectural awards. Following K.L. Sijmons' criticism of the reconstruction plan of Middelburg, a dispute about design principles with his co-editor Berghoef ensued. The upshot was that Berghoef later retired from the editorial board, to be replaced by A. Boeken, who took a less conservative position. Subsequently the direction of the journal barely changed, mainly because Mieras also joined the editorial board, as a representative of the Institute of Dutch Architects. Nonetheless, Van Embden did recognise the significance of the new city plan for Rotterdam in a 'controversial article', which presented an example of how a city should be constructed in a modern manner (Van Embden, 1946a). Mieras once again took the well-tried middle ground and, in doing so, could count on appreciation from various camps, evidenced in the *Liber Amicorum* issue, which appeared two years after his death. W.M. Dudok, S. van Ravesteyn, M.J. Granpré Molière and J. H. van den Broek (1898–1978) each contributed on the question of 'The artistic and social position of the architect' (Van den Broek, 1958).

However, Mieras' influence within *Forum* was limited, since he was not the editorial secretary – a position held by the art historian and curator of the Rijksmuseum, Th.H. Lunsingh Scheurleer. The provisional board of A. et A. wrote in the introduction to the first issue: '*Forum* should find other ways to serve the same objective that brought together the participants in the Doornsche meetings of *Architectura et Amicitia*: deepening architectural insight and jointly studying the best views and expressions.' In order to do this, the periodical sought to include related 'arts', enhancing its content and potentially opening up new perspectives; perhaps the liberal arts could liberate architecture from the intolerable yoke of tradition.

Within the provisional board, J. Bakema acted as a representative of the younger generation. Generally the editorial board of *Forum* endorsed the view of the provisional board, and indeed the introduction to the first issue re-stated its constitution: to 'allow all currents in architecture to freely express themselves without bias'. The situation prior to the war, in which every movement worked in isolation, was to be avoided. The editorial board noted that with the arrival of the new monthly journal 'the sequence of architectural periodicals' was concluded 'in an organic manner': the periodical *Bouw* (Building) mainly focused on technical and socio-economic concerns, while *BW* was a trade journal. Emphasis was placed on the 'cultural aspect of construction' and the board soon added a direct social imperative; building for the development of society was clearly a key issue.

It was striking that within A. et A.'s own provisional editorial board only W. de Bruyn came from a Catholic background, and Catholics were absent from the editorial board of *Forum*. The presumed unity between the different factions was evidently already lacking. This was heightened by the appearance of the first postwar issue of the *KB* in October 1946, which summarised the history of the periodical:

> Initially founded as the *R.K. Bouwblad* this was followed by a second phase, in which the letters R.C. were omitted in an attempt to not only serve Roman Catholic interests, but to more broadly heal architecture and the visual arts. [...] Currently in the third phase, we are again published as *Katholiek Bouwblad*. Our objective remains unwaveringly the same.
>
> *Editorial Board, 1946b*

The principal concern was to 'start with the recognition that every renewal can only start with Christ. For the arts this means that every rejuvenation and renovation can only come into being with an impulse from the sacred arts' (Editorial Board, 1946b). This proclamation emphasised the journal's credentials and left little room for dialogue.

With the relaunch of the *KB*, the field of professional journals oscillated from one moment to the other. An introductory article by Delft professor Granpré Molière (1883–1972) published in the first issue of the *KB* was symptomatic.

He reacted, in his in-depth and verbose response, to two articles on the Delft School: the first by J. Vriend, 'Dictatuur van het Delftsche bouwen' (Dictatorship of Delft Architecture), in *De Groene Amsterdammer*; and the second by J. J. P. Oud in *BW* 'De Delftsche school en de synthese in de architectuur' (The Delft school and synthesis in architecture). Vriend suggested that many cities were being rebuilt in a conservative manner, without taking into account new social developments. His criticism was directed at Granpré Molière and the urban planning of his traditionalist followers. Oud opposed any such synthesis, seeing it as weakening contemporary imperatives. Typically, he claimed an independent position and raised issues in various journals and newspapers, troubled by the idea that a pursuit of compromise would distract from what was essential: 'One must quietly concentrate on one's own goal: building well and pure in a form that could be expressed as beautifully as possible, focused on the essence of the

FIGURE 3.7   Portrait of M.J. Granpré Molière by Joan Colette 1941.
Source: Courtesy TU Delft Library.

present time' (Oud, 1946a, p. 222).[5] Granpré Molière immediately caused a controversy and launched a full attack against *Het Nieuwe Bouwen* (The New Architecture). He attacked those who over-emphasised technique: 'One sometimes has to move away from single-minded perfection for the sake of harmony especially when this is not identified with the correct measure of beauty, but rather prematurely determined', concluding:

> Some people refer to such ideas as reactionary. And they may be called that, insofar as they entail a certain resistance to the cultural movement, which, among others, unleashed two world wars [...]. There should be a response to every unilateral action. Modernism was also a response, indeed against the spirit of preserving the outdated forms; it was even reactionary in this sense. These notions are also referred to as dictatorial. This says too little and too much; because it is more than a dictatorship. Dictatorships collapse, but these insights are, I trust, not bound by time and place. They are in any case abstract thoughts. And I trust that people will also challenge and supplement these ideas; because, in doing so, they could be clarified and improved. A break has been made with the years behind us. Now is the time to rebuild. Tempus faciendi est.
>
> *Granpré Molière, 1946*

Any desire for unity had completely disappeared. Almost every sentence was a carefully formulated attack on the supporters of modernism. The disappointment of the younger generation was inevitable. Whether this was intentional remained unclear:

> Many people ask themselves [...] why, apart from *Forum*, the *Bouwblad* is still published, which they take to be a sign that another divisive and stifling fungus and divisive spirit have again appeared in this important part of cultural life in our country. Nothing is further from the truth. Whereas *Forum*, just like the association A. et A., aims to bundle all positive powers directed from within our – in many ways broken – society and thus perform a national task, it is also necessary for architecture to be viewed from a higher vantage point. [...] We believe that there is a place for the *Katholiek Bouwblad*, based on the position that it is not unbecoming to a Christian to profess his faith in the invisible

seclusion within the four walls of a church building, but that his Christian life should have consequences for every part of his existence, therefore also in the area of professional practice.

Editorial Board, 1946c

However, many did not share this opinion, viewing the article by Granpré Molière as a declaration of war. He could count on provoking a response, having also written an article in which he elucidated the difference between the Delft School and the new architecture. Granpré Molière was naturally upset by the manner in which the reconstruction plan for Middelburg was discussed in *Forum*. But he would certainly have noticed the winds of change in Delft, although he remained the most influential voice there. The technical college had to modernise. For Granpré Molière, Delft was 'the rich vein for technical progress', but he also expected that it would be in Delft that 'the broken harmony of technique and art [would] be restored'. Delft, therefore, besides being the focal point for technological development, should also 'possibly remain the focal point of anti-modernism'. In his eyes, it was the *Nieuwe Bouwen* that aimed to erase the boundaries between art, architecture and urban planning. In doing so, in Granpré Molière's view they went too far:

> I am not saying that Delft thinkers are dictators, but their [own] doctrine condemns this. Nor do I claim that the masters of the *Nieuwe Bouwen* are tyrants, but their doctrine commands them to be so. The uniformity, which is inherent to the *Nieuwe Bouwen*, should stringently impose this on architects; yet the doctrine of hierarchy and variety naturally should allow for freedom.
>
> *Granpré Molière, 1947*

In his long article, the Delft professor gave a sample of his scholastic reasoning based on numerous historical antecedents, which certainly irritated Bakema and Van den Broek. The latter, who would become a professor in 1947, responded laconically by publishing a paper 'Doel en wezen van de architectuur' (The objective and essence of architecture) that he had presented as a lecture in Amsterdam on 15 January 1947 (Van den Broek, 1947, pp. 69–70).[6] He had no need to indulge in rhetoric. Bakema was much more concrete – at least at the start of his article – 'Het nieuwe bouwen en verder' (The new architecture and beyond):

> Let us realise that Democracy is a societal form in which both religious dogmatists and humanitarian artists can work, provided they show a willingness to cooperate and create conditions in which every member of society has the biggest possible chance of being a complete human being or, stated differently, to in *his own* way aspire to harmony with the infinite. And that, in my opinion, is the purpose of freedom – and the reason that Oud reached for the pen even if he stated it [the argument] differently.

In fact, later on Bakema confronted Molière in the terms of his own line of reasoning:

> What is stronger than the primary Human–Cosmos relationship? What speaks more to our imagination, and even transcends time, than a silent starry night or a violent storm over far-away shores, or the eyes of children and sunflowers? What can integrate and inspire more? Christianity? After two world wars in a world full of Churches and

Church officials? There is but *one* spatial conception, that which remains untouchable. Our space can only be Cosmic.

Bakema, 1947

This could not have been stated more vaguely, suggesting that Bakema was consciously mocking his opponent. The battlefronts had hardened – and Van Embden wrote that the quarrel had resumed – but it did not have the same intensity as the 'Bauhaus debate' instigated in Germany by Rudolf Schwarz and others (van Embden, 1946b).[7] In the Netherlands, each exponent had his own domain and worked within it. Likewise, urban planners had their own responsibilities. In fact, there was only occasional disagreement. In 1952 Dudok became involved in a dispute with Bakema and Van den Broek about their design of a housing complex in IJmuiden. According to Dudok, the architects did not abide by the rules that he had prescribed as master planner.

The discussion unfolded in the professional journals. There was frequent friction between *Forum* and *BW*. *Forum*'s publisher regularly complained that the latter was increasingly encroaching on its terrain, while in the past their respective editorial limits were clearly established. Bakema held the opinion that *Forum* must not only document completed construction work, but also elucidate the background to the various tendencies in contemporary architecture. *Forum* gained a steady increase in subscribers, especially after the designer Friedrich Vordemberge-Gildewart was appointed in 1950 to give the journal a makeover. *BW* responded by printing vouchers to promote the advertising required to generate the income needed to compete. Differences re-emerged at a meeting of both parties on 27 June 1951, and the division of tasks was once again discussed. Komter suggested that *Forum* could not and should not pursue current topical issues:

> The difficulty for *Forum* is that the focus is on opinions, while architects really are not authors. Moreover, *Forum* misses someone who gives direction to the periodical, like Mr. Mieras at *Bouwkundig Weekblad*. The result of these difficulties is that *Forum* frequently appears late and that often a miscellany has had to be presented in the absence of general views.[8]

After the historian and critic R. Blijstra joined the editorial board of *Forum* in 1951, this dispute was alleviated and the journal continuously improved its position. From 1952 it would include English abstracts that increased its influence abroad. The most influential young architects featured in the journal eventually became involved in CIAM, where Bakema and Van Eyck would eventually gain an influential position within Team X.

In the case of Van den Broek, the reality of his position was more complex. He had multiple responsibilities and was active on many fronts: a member of various advisory committees, he was also active in the Union Internationale des Architectes, and had a significant role in establishing the *Bouwcentrum* (Building Centre) and the periodical *Bouw* (Building).

In addition, he was also involved with the *Consumentenstichting Goed Wonen* (Good Living Consumer Foundation) and its eponymous journal. This set out publicity and propaganda against poor-quality housing and was identified with attractive design in order to reach a larger public. It was illustrated with images of furniture and domestic interiors that exuded a contemporary lifestyle. In 1959, when it had 6,000 subscribers, the journal decided to change

FIGURE 3.8 Journal cover, *Bouw* (October, 1945).
Source: Courtesy Bouwcentrum.

its focus from advice on design and materials to a regard for general and specific housing strategies. Van den Broek was a crucial influence and occasionally wrote for the journal.[9]

He was without doubt one of the most influential figures in postwar architectural culture in the Netherlands. In addition, he was involved in numerous construction contracts and from 1948 collaborated with Bakema. Above all, they would together leave their mark on the Lijnbaan in Rotterdam, a project that would receive recognition from all over the world. By the early 1950s, however, Dutch modern architecture had lost much of its international appeal, yet individual foreign critics witnessed improvement and change. Sigfried Giedion wrote, less than impartially, that:

> The retrogressive movement which occurred in Holland during the late '30s and the '40s has been particularly astonishing, as during the '20s Holland undoubtedly played a leading role both in art and in architecture. This spirit has vanished from most of its rebuilding projects – from Middelburg to Rotterdam – that exhibit unscientific city planning or pseudo-romantic tendencies. But there are signs that the coming generation is reviving the pioneer spirit.
>
> *Giedion, 1951*[10]

It is not easy to determine which signs Giedion referred to. During this period, many architects were still preoccupied with the empirical problems of post-Second World War reconstruction and a pragmatic attitude was an absolute requirement. The Netherlands was still recovering from the war and the economy had yet to be revived. Reconstruction proper only started in

FIGURE 3.9   Photo of J.J. van den Broek.
Source: Courtesy TU Delft Library.

FIGURE 3.10   Photo of J. Bakema (date unknown).
Source: Courtesy TU Delft, Faculty of Architecture.

the 1950s. A. van Eyck believed that the well-worn battle between imagination and common sense had too often favoured the latter and argued that it was time for 'a new consciousness' (Giedion, 1951).

Nonetheless, in the 1950s, *Forum* remained a compliant journal, with neither contemporary currency nor polemical interest (Van Dijk, 1983). Once a year, an issue was published about CIAM and its activities, edited by Bakema and Van Eyck. Circulation predictably remained static in the late 1950s and there were once again meetings between *BW* and *Forum* about a possible merger; younger members were keen to breathe new life into the association's journal. In April 1959, the editor of *Forum*, Staal resigned, writing a bitter letter to the executive board:

> As there was no verbal support or potential criticism and disagreement detected from younger parties, I ask myself with great concern what after three issues by the new editors – who we strongly advised to take action, instead of forcing us to step aside – will be further accomplished. I am afraid that as 'arrivistes', we, the old members are no less part of architecture, and its newest supporters (minus one or two clearly 'irrationals')

FIGURE 3.11   Journal cover, *Goed Wonen* 1 (February 1948).
Source: © Het Nieuwe Instituut.

> have infected the entire problem. There is not much more to gain, and the consolidation and peaceful simplification and enrichment will not take place in the present time.
>
> *Staal, 1959*

Staal was wrong. It was time for a substantial change. Journals were compelled to revise their layouts and adapt to a new visual culture. *Goed Wonen* (Good Living) did so, while Joost Baljeu started his own international journal, *Structure*, in a new contemporary format; *Forum* could not allow itself to be left behind.

The new editors had completely different viewpoints from those they had replaced, and transformed the journal. They focused on obtaining a more sophisticated and dynamic combination of text and illustrations. Each issue's themes were to be communicated more forcefully. Van Eyck wanted fewer, more specific photographs of a certain expressive character. The publisher asked whether this would make the journal less 'professional', to which Van Eyck responded that it would, mostly, be more critical. He intended the content and layout to be better coordinated, and nominated J. Schrofer as the typographer.[11] The journal clearly positioned itself as an experimental cultural publication with the totality of the 'architectural environment' as its point of departure.[12]

Only one journal could maintain publication without difficulty in the first decade after the war: *Bouw* – since it was itself the product of the postwar reconstruction. The full title was the *Centraal Weekblad voor het Bouwwezen* (CWB; Central Weekly of the Building Industries), published in both the Netherlands and Belgium by *Stichting Bouw*. Numerous institutions, governmental and otherwise, provided their support, although it was not officially

FIGURE 3.12 Journal cover, *Structure* 1 (1958).
Source: Courtesy C. Baljeu.

a government publication. The Netherlands, rather than Belgium, was the main focus. There were four editorial boards concerned with: architecture and town planning; social problems; technical aspects; and economical-statistical issues. This determined the broad scope of the journal. It dealt with the influence of industrialisation, the publication of standard architectural plans, architectural-economic developments, and their sociological implications. The layout incorporated a characteristic logo designed by the famous designer and typographer Piet Zwart. He was retained almost throughout, until times changed and the journal took on a dated, old-fashioned image (Groenendijk, 2011, pp. 23–25).[13] The colour of the cover of each issue identified with its content. *Bouw* – more directly than the *Tijdschrift voor Volkshuisvesting* and *Stedenbouw*, which had already been relaunched during the war – actively guided postwar reconstruction in discussion of design, newly realised buildings, new production methods and insight into relevant typologies, not to mention other aspects of building.[14]

Van den Broek was one of the members of *Bouw*'s editorial board for architectural and urban issues and often set the tone of the journal. The journal was financially viable and fortunate in retaining numerous commercial sponsors for advertising. Municipalities and other institutions also placed announcements for new staff and tenders in the journal. In the first issue for October 1945, Zwiers wrote an article entitled: 'Not separated, but connected: towards a balance of material, social and cultural aspects', which argued that 'balance' as a form of synthesis had to work programmatically. In the following issue, published in the New Year 1946 issue, Van Embden proclaimed much the same message in 'Architect's dialogue', although he was not a proponent of synthesis. Later, the editorial board supported Vriend's contentions about the dictatorship of the Delft School. An important contribution to the first issue was a long article written by Van den Broek about 'Stroomingen en tendensen in de nieuwere Nederlandsche architectuur' (Trends and tendencies in the newer Dutch architecture). In an attempt at reconciliation, he wrote:

> The scope of the building programs to be executed during the next few decades is so enormous, that all resources will be required to realise it. This applies not only to the material, but especially to spiritual realisation, that is the form, in which the totality will reveal itself and what we imagine will be a dignified expression of our cultural life. All the work will therefore need to be built on the basis of a solid, balanced design of the architects.
>
> *Van den Broek, 1946*

This will-to-form was to lead to industrialisation and the use of new materials. Despite all controversies, the peace had to be kept.

Van den Broek evidently enjoyed writing this type of article, in which the history of architecture in the twentieth century was discussed point by point in order to justify a certain trajectory. He also liked to write articles about general solutions for the problems of his time; one of the last Dutch architects to value history, but only in terms of modern architecture. Concerned with emphasising a distinctive type of continuity, he argued that architecture necessarily remained a skill or craft that combined various technical disciplines. Consequently, he strongly focused on practice and, given his responsibilities in the building of the *Technische Hogeschool* (predecessor to TU Delft), there was rarely time to write about anything else. By the end of the 1950s his exploratory, contemplative and reflective stance was no longer appreciated as, by then, history was looked at in a different, more engaged and active manner. Applicability to the future had become important. A new generation within both architecture and the visual arts, who expressed their ideas in new ways, had arrived. The second phase of the postwar restructuring was less focused on architecture than on architecture's position within society.[15] Politics was not the driving force; instead an emphasis on the 'poetic' from a cultural or anthropological viewpoint prevailed. *Forum* offered the opportunity to manifest this, although the young editorial board sometimes had difficulty publishing promptly. Their verbal and visual rhetoric questioned not only architecture, but also other cultural phenomena. This changed the character of the publication, which many now saw as a cultural journal rather than a professional journal, and one actively promoting the ideas of Team X.[16]

The editorial board, of which Herman Hertzberger was the secretary, had an innovative message and used the journal to enthusiastically support their ideas. This polemic was published in both Dutch and English with a predilection for poetic metaphors. The 'prison house' of national language had to be torn down. Fermentation was required to induce a focus of attention towards sociological issues. This completely changed the character of the journal. Instead of an informative, reflective and tolerant publication, it served as the pamphlet for an anti-intellectual direction in Dutch architecture which privileged associated subjective visions. There was much focus on archaic societies and the 'meaning' that could be attributed to elemental form. The journal no longer had any room for architects who promoted an alternative approach, nor did it pay much attention to new buildings.

A new generation stepped forward and Van den Broek, who had been an overarching figure in the Dutch architectural debate for so long (Taverne, 1990), stood down. But he remained a central figure at the architecture school in Delft, taking over the pivotal role of Granpré

Molière and engaging students with his 'peer comment lectures'. Under his guidance, students also published their own low-cost journal, *Delftse School*, stencilled and typically unillustrated. It was neither visually nor theoretically rigorous, offering only comment. Nonetheless, the student journal provided a stark departure from the graphic indulgence of the 'official or professional' journals, which would eventually face a series of identity crises. These were reflected in successive changes of name and in content: *KB* became *Tijdschrift voor Architectuur en Beeldende Kunsten*, then *Wonen TA/BK*, later *Archis*, and eventually much later *Volume*. In this fashion an important trade journal developed a new impulse of its own, acting as a cultural seismograph. This constant renewal, according to changing circumstances, became habitual in the experience of Dutch architecture journals. But that is a different story with its own curious history.

Notes

This chapter was translated from Dutch by Wolfestone, with kind financial support from the University of Liverpool, School of the Arts. All illustrations, unless otherwise indicated, derive from the collections of the TU Delft.

 1 There was very little interest in the Netherlands for architecture journals after 1945 in comparison to other countries. In the US and the UK, for example, two UK journals were discussed in dissertations. See Erten (2004) and Parnell (2011).
 2 See Wendt (2008, p. 96). An interesting image of the social reality in the Netherlands in 1950 was illustrated in Schuyt and Taverne (2000).
 3 On the association, see Schilt and van der Werf (1992). On art journals during the interbellum, see Freijser (1990, pp. 173–191, 219–222).
 4 See letters in: The New Institute, Archive of the Association Architectura et Amicitia, ARAM 180.
 5 This contribution is dated July 1946. Also see: J. J. P. Oud (1946b, pp. 613–614, 620). The reaction of Van den Broek was to write that it is not the architect but the commissioner who have to dare or not (Van den Broek, 1946, p. 615).
 6 Also see what he wants to do in Delft: 'Professor Van den Broek gaat het anders doen', *Het Vrije Volk*, 4 maart 1948, p. 1. From this newspaper article it appears that Van den Broek recently returned from the US.
 7 Refer to Conrads (1994) for the situation in Germany in 1953.
 8 See minutes in: Het Nieuwe Instituut, Archief van het Genootschap Architectura et Amicitia, ARAM 179.
 9 See the documents in the archives of the Foundation in: Het Nieuwe Instituut, Archief (Goed) Wonen, SGWO 8.
10 Also refer to Hilkmann (2011).
11 See the minutes of the meeting of the board and the new editors on 13 July 1959, in: Het Nieuwe Instituut, ARAM 180. On Schrofer, see Huygen (2013).
12 Two broadly cultural magazines from after the war were the *De Vrije Katheder* and *Kroniek van Kunst en Kultuur*. Both sporadically gave attention to architecture (Bavelaar, 1998; Van den Burg, 1983).
13 Architectural critic A. Buffinga was appointed as permanent editor in 1957.
14 The magazine *The Way Ahead: Quarterly Economic Review* was also issued by the Building Centre and the *Stichting Bouw* in the years 1947–1962. This colourful magazine should have put the prosperous Netherlands on the map abroad (Garcia, 2011, pp. 141–149).
15 Kennedy specifically focused on the Dutch fear of being considered old-fashioned. For this reason, words such as 'progressive', 'renewal' and 'new' are used extensively (Kennedy, 1995).
16 It is no wonder that we see that Van Eyck, with his 'poetic naivety', distanced himself from the negativity of the Italian architectural historian Manfredo Tafuri and others. He could also not identify with the manner in which a poet like Lucebert emphasised the negative sides of the city (van Bergeijk, 2014).

References

Bavelaar, H. (1998). *Kroniek van Kunst en Kultuur, geschiedenis van een tijdschrift 1935–1965*. Leiden: Primavera.

Bakema, J. B. (1947). Het nieuwe bouwen en verder. *Forum*, 2 (3/4), pp. 66–68.

Conrads, U. (Ed.) (1994). *Die Bauhaus-Debatte 1953: Dokumente einer verdrängten Kontroverse*. Braunschweig/ Wiesbaden:Vieweg+Teubner.

Editorial Board (1946a). Preface. *Bouwkundig Weekblad*, 1 (1), p. 1.

—— (1946b). Het Bouwblad herrezen. *Katholiek Bouwblad*, 1 (1/2), p. 1.

—— (1946c). Onze plaats te midden van de vakbladen. *Katholiek Bouwblad*, 1, (1/2), p. 0.

Erten, E. (2004). Shaping 'The Second Half Century': the Architectural Review, 1947–1971. PhD dissertation, Cambridge, MA, MIT.

Forum (1947). Jongeren en nieuwe architectuur. Forum, 2 (4), p. 103.

Freijser, V. (1990). De kunsttijdschriften en de receptie van de moderne kunst 1945–1951. In Willemijn Stokvis (Ed.), *De doorbraak van de moderne kunst in Nederland. Vernieuwingen na 1945*. Amsterdam: Meulenhoff.

García, R. (2011). The Way Ahead. De weg naar de naoorlogse industriële wederopbouw in Nederland. *Erfgoed van Industrie en Techniek*, 3 (4), pp. 141–149.

Giedion, S. (Ed.) (1951). *A Decade of New Architecture*. Zurich: Edition Girsberger.

Granpré Molière, M. J. (1946). *Ter inleiding. Katholiek Bouwblad*, 1 (1/2), p. 8.

—— (1947). *Delft en het nieuwe bouwen. Katholiek Bouwblad*, 14 (4), p. 156

Groenendijk, P. (2011). 65 jaar BOUW. Van Centraal Weekblad voor het bouwwezen tot Architectuur NL. *ArchitectuurNL*, 66 (7), pp. 23–25.

Hilkmann, N. (2011). Het begrip kitsch in goed wonen. www.designhistory.nl/2011/het-begrip-kitsch-in-goed-wonen/

Huygen, F. (2013). *Jurriaan Schrofer: grafisch ontwerper, fotoboekenpionier, artdirector, docent, kunstbestuurder, omgevingskunstenaar*. Amsterdam: Valiz.

Kennedy, J. C. (1995). *Nieuw Babylon in aanbouw. Nederland in de Jaren zestig*, Amsterdam/Meppel: Boom.

Mieras, J. P. (1946a). Naschrift. *Bouwkundig Weekblad*, 64 (6), p. 69.

—— (1946b). Het Pentagon-gebouw te Arlington bij Washington. *Bouwkundig Weekblad*, 64(4), p. 45.

—— (1947a). Een nieuw tijdschrift. *Bouwkundig Weekblad*, 65 (7), p. 57.

—— (1947b). Progressief. *Bouwkundig Weekblad*, 65 (16), p. 127.

Neuburg-Coray, H. (1943). Die ausländischen Fachzeitungen vom Gesichtspunkt des Grafikers aus betrachtet. *Das Werk*, 30 (8), p. 13.

Oud, J. J. P. (1946a). *De Delftsche school en synthese in de architectuur. Bouwkundig Weekblad*, 64 (24), p. 222.

—— (1946b). Durven en niet durven in de architectuur. *Bouw*, 1 (29), p. 615.

Parnell, S. (2011). Architectural Design 1954–1972. Unpublished PhD thesis, Sheffield University.

Schilt, J. and van der Werf, J. (1992). *Genootschap Architectura et Amicitia 1855–1990*. Rotterdam: 010 Publishers.

Schuyt, K. and Taverne, E. (2000). *1950: Wealth in Black and White. Dutch Culture in European Context*. Den Haag: SDU.

Staal, A. (1959). Letter of Arthur Staal to the the board of A et A, dated 27 April 1959. Het Nieuwe Instituut, Rotterdam, Association Architectura et Amicitia, Archive ARAM 180.

Taverne, E. (1990). Towards an Open Aesthetic. Ambities in de Nederlandse architectuur 1948–1959. In W. Deen, C. Grafe, B. Leupen (Eds), *Hoe modern is de Nederlandse architectuur?* Rotterdam: 010 Publishers.

van Bergeijk, H. (2014). Moeilijke liefdes. Lucebert. Forum en de stad. *Eigenbouwer*, 3, pp. 64–79.

Van den Broek, J. H. (1946a). Durven en niet durven in de Magistratuur. *Bouw*, 1 (29), p. 615.

—— (1946b). Stroomingen en tendenties in de nieuwe Nederlandsche architectuur. *Bouw*, 1(1), p. 4.

—— (1947). Doel en wezen van de architectuur. *Forum*, 2 (2/3), pp. 69–70.

—— (1958). *De artistieke en sociale positie van de architect.* In J. P. Mieras, *Liber Amicorum J. P. Mieras.* Amsterdam: B. N. A.

Van den Burg, F. (1983). *De Vrije Katheder, 1945–1950: Een platvorm van communisten en niet-communisten.* Amsterdam: Van Gennep.

Van Dijk, H. (1983). Forum. In S. U. Barbieri (Ed.), *Architectuur en planning. Nederland 1940–1980.* Rotterdam: 010 Publishers.

Van Embden, S. J. (1946a), *Wanordelijk artikel bij Rotterdam's stadsplan. Forum,* 2, pp. 33–47.

—— (1946b). IJdel dispuut: De oorlog is voorbij: het krakeel herleeft. *Bouw,* 1 (29), pp. 617–621.

Vestdijk, S. (1958). *De vrije vogel en zijn kooien (The free bird and its cages).* Gravenhage: Nijgh & Van Ditmar.

Wendt, D. (2008). *Academie van Bouwkunst Amsterdam 1908–2008,* Rotterdam: 010 Publishers.

4

NATION BUILDING

Sweden's modernisation and the autonomy of the profession

Claes Caldenby

The first postwar decades were a Golden Age for the Nordic countries. It saw the development of the Nordic model of the welfare state. The *Nordic Council* was founded in 1952, introducing passport-free travel and a common labour market. Collaboration between Nordic countries flourished. Scandinavian design became a buzzword with the exhibition *Design in Scandinavia* that toured the US and Canada in 1954–1957. In *Sweden Builds* (Kidder Smith, 1950), Sweden was considered to have the highest average standard of architecture in the world. Finnish architecture was widely exhibited internationally, thereby 'Constructing a Legend', as it was later referred to.[1] Architecture was clearly seen as a means of nation building, both literally and symbolically, and the architectural journal was part of that. This was by no means without its contradictions.

All four Nordic countries (here excluding Iceland) have one main journal of architecture, each one having long been affiliated with the architects' association of their respective countries. The oldest one is the Danish *Architekten* (later *Arkitekten*), which was first published in 1898. From 1957, *Arkitektur DK* has been the journal publishing architectural projects, whereas *Arkitekten* is primarily concerned with professional issues. The Swedish *Arkitektur och dekorativ konst* (Architecture and applied arts) was first published in 1901; it was renamed *Arkitektur* in 1909 and in 1922 became *Byggmästaren* (The Master Builder). In 1959 it was, for reasons that we will come back to, once again renamed *Arkitektur*.

The Finnish *Arkitekten* was first published in Swedish in 1903. From 1921 it was published in Finnish as *Arkkitehti* and was affiliated with SAFA, the Finnish association of architects. The youngest journal is the Norwegian *Byggekunst* (The Art of Building), published from 1919, till 2007. It is now titled *Arkitektur N* and closely related to the NAL, the national association of Norwegian architects.

The focus of this chapter is Sweden, as Sweden during the postwar period was, for better or worse, leading developments in the Nordic countries. The years 1945–1965 are known as the 'record years' of modernisation, and the contradictions inherent in this development are most clearly visible in Sweden. Kidder Smith, with remarkable foresight, not only praised the 'civilised' architecture of Sweden as the physical manifestation of the welfare state, but also

FIGURE 4.1   *Byggmästaren* 17 (1947) in which Asger Jorn's second article in the Apollo
and Dionysus debate was published. Cover design by Jorn.
Source: Courtesy of Arkitektur/Swedish Review of Architecture.

warned of the 'timidity' of Swedish architects and the risk of the bureaucratisation of planning
and building.

Apollo and Dionysus

One of the few heated architectural disputes in the otherwise predominantly pragmatic
Byggmästaren was the so-called 'Apollo and Dionysus' debate of 1946–1948. It concerned the
opportunities and threats of the imminent modernisation of society as well as architecture's
need for theoretical foundations. The debate naturally aroused strong feelings, but it was also
questioned for being unintelligible.

The controversy started somewhat unexpectedly with a review of a book on architectural history. The book was the first of ten volumes of the Swedish architect and architectural historian Erik Lundberg's oeuvre *Arkitekturens Formspråk* (The Formal Language of
Architecture). The review was written by the Danish painter Asger Jorn, later to become
famous as a member of the COBRA group. It was published under the title 'Formspråkets
livsinnehåll' (The live content of formal language). Jorn was enthusiastic but also free in his
interpretation of the book. He saw Lundberg's publication as 'a turning point in our relations
to the basic values of art history'.

Jorn did not mention Apollo and Dionysus but discussed, without making much reference
to Lundberg's text, the opposition between Greek classicism and barbarian spontaneity, clearly

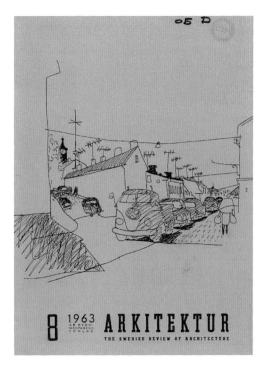

FIGURE 4.2 From 1959 the Swedish review of architecture was renamed *Arkitektur* (its name before 1922). This issue on Enköping argued for the value of its historic structure. Cover design by Stig Claesson.
Source: Courtesy of Arkitektur/Swedish Review of Architecture.

stating his preference for the spontaneous where 'the mystic gets meaning and purpose and the purely logical seems cold and empty'. Stating that 'only the young' could understand the book, Jorn concluded:

> Swedish architecture is superior to that of the other Scandinavian countries both theoretically and practically, and it has a leading position in the international development of the arts. It is therefore most important that it accepts the consequences this position brings with it. Its uniqueness is that it has admitted the artistic as something essential and innovatory.
>
> *Jorn, 1946*

The first response to Jorn came from Torbjörn Olsson (1947), a young architect who in 1950 started the practice AOS (Ahlgren Olsson Silow). Olsson was the first to make reference to Apollo and Dionysus.[2] He had studied art history before training as an architect and used his art historical knowledge to suggest that Jorn's text was uninformed, and written as if in a Dionysian delirium. Spontaneity to Olsson was synonymous with the quest for the new and thus the art of the rejected lonely genius. He referred to a classic tendency in contemporary literature, which demanded universality, precise concepts and strict composition: 'The architecture of the future must be built on a realistic basis and in a classical spirit in the sense of expressing clarity and calm control'.

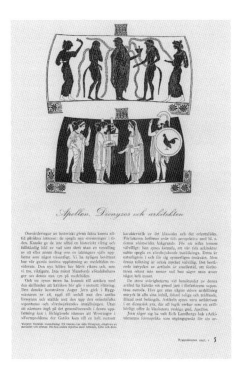

FIGURE 4.3 Torbjörn Olsson's article in *Byggmästaren* 1 (1947), the first to reply to Jorn, argued for the Apollonian stance and introduced the 'Apollo and Dionysus' title.
Source: Courtesy of Arkitektur/Swedish Review of Architecture.

Another long response came from Jorn (1947), interestingly enough this time published in its original Danish, perhaps as a sign of a mutual Nordic understanding.[3] A key issue for Jorn was that 'this is not about the opinion of authorities. It is about what is the truth. Is there a truth for us humans?'

Later in the same year there was another contribution, now under the established 'logo' of Apollo and Dionysus (Westerberg, 1947; Reinius, 1947). Eric Westerberg, in a satirical verse about a dialogue or polemic between Apollo and Dionysus, argued for a collaboration between the two gods, in order 'to keep the heart warm and the brain cool'. Leif Reinius, the editor of *Byggmästaren* from 1944 to 1949, and an important practising architect whose work showed influences of Frank Lloyd Wright, now entered the debate on the side of Dionysus. He claimed that Westerberg had interpreted the Dionysian too negatively. Modern society lacked a warm heart, argued Reinius.

In the first issue of 1948 he returned to the theme in his editorial titled 'Separate ways' in summarising the contents of issue 1/1948 (Reinius, 1948a). Mentioning Sigurd Lewerentz's own apartment in the attic of his factory in Eskilstuna, Reinius wrote that 'there is a richness and warmth in his architecture that we hope to see more of' (a hope that we will come back to). Commenting on Taliesin West, by his 'amply creative' favourite Frank Lloyd Wright, he enthused about Wright's 'fresh joy of building'. He concluded, with reference to Le Corbusier's Unité in Marseille: 'It shows that with a perfect organization you can also come to hell, if you don't have human feelings for humankind.'

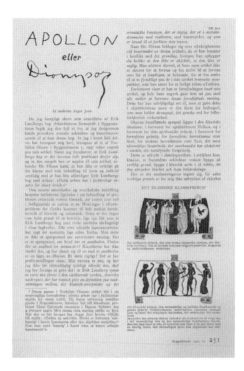

FIGURE 4.4 Asger Jorn's response in *Byggmästaren* 17 (1947) was published in Danish, typifying close Nordic relations. The title, now 'Apollo *or* Dionysus', polarised the debate. *Source*: Courtesy of Arkitektur/Swedish Review of Architecture.

Lennart Holm's long article in 1948 on ideology and form in postwar architectural debate is another argument pursuing the Apollonian stance. At the time Holm was still a student of architecture, extremely well-versed in contemporary literary and artistic debates and keen on sharp polemics; two characteristics that are unusual among Swedish architects (Holm, 1948).[4]

There followed a debate on Holm's article between the author and Reinius in which their positions became mutually exclusive (Reinius, 1948b; Holm and Reinius, 1948). Reinius argued that 'our lyrical need has terrible difficulties to be satisfied with an art on a basis of reason'. Holm accused Reinius of being 'against an ideological architectural debate' and declared the necessity of a 'continued critical debate concerning the direction of architecture based on a rationalist societal ethic'. Reinius, in his final reply, reacted against Holm's 'spasmodically dogmatic mentality'.

At the time Reinius' office (Backström and Reinius) was one of the leading Swedish housing practices, whose work had also been widely published internationally. But he had difficulties with the nature of the modernisation of planning and building that developed under the auspices of the 'strong society'. Holm, and others, were convinced that a democratic and egalitarian society must be built on rationalisation and standardisation. What is also evident here is a conflict between the view of the architect as artist, or at least an intuitive craftsman, against the need for rational and research-based design. The Apollonians were more convincing in debate and they would, in the years to come, gain the initiative.

From master builder to architect

The 1950s, as reflected in *Byggmästaren*, may be understood as a social imaginary: providing a somewhat idyllic, maybe naïve, if not desperate context for the role of architects in Sweden, who during this decade were under extraordinary pressure. There was an ongoing and dramatic shift, from architects to contractors, in responsibility for the building process. The latter were supported by a centralised state that was focused on solving the pressing housing crisis following rapid urbanisation and the legacy of one of the lowest housing standards in Europe. This marginalisation of architects was not countered and was hardly even discussed in *Byggmästaren*.

The long editorship of Leif Reinius during the 1940s was followed by an interlude of shorter editorships in the early 1950s. Folke Björck was the editor for one year in 1950 and Tore Virke for one and a half years until 1952. After Virke came Erik Thelaus, who stayed until 1960 and can be said to have shaped *Byggmästaren* in the 1950s.[5]

The first issue of 1950 was themed on Nordic relations, and connected to the conference *Nordisk Byggdag* (Nordic Building Day) held in Stockholm. *Nordisk Byggdag* was a tradition from the 1920s in which meetings between Nordic architects and builders were held in Stockholm (1927), Helsinki (1932), Oslo (1938) and, after a break during the war, in Copenhagen (1946). The associated editorial talked about the Nordic countries' 'common traits in climate, building traditions and mentality' (*Nordisk Byggdag*, 1950). But it also underlined the necessity for the building industry to adapt to 'new tendencies'.

The first article was written by professor Nils Ahrbom, who had been a young modernist in the 1930s, and was now one of the leading figures in Swedish architecture (Ahrbom, 1950). He looked back to the turn of the century, when he perceived the onset of modern Swedish architecture with its 'affirmation of architecture's natural conditions, climate, site, construction, function, social relations and a living sense for the environment'. He declared a belief in the programme of the 1930s, quoting the modernist manifesto of *Acceptera* from 1931. Mentioning in passing the confusion caused by 'the art-philosophical volubility, which during the 1940s has surged through the columns of *Byggmästaren* and other journals', he came to refer to the Apollo–Dionysus debate without being unduly explicit. Taking the position of an Apollonian, however, he warned of the risk of having too many regulations and ending up with 'the number of bureaucrats considerably exceeding the number of designers'. His ambition was for a free and responsible role for both designers and researchers.

After two years there was a brief return of the ideological debate in issue 4/1951, where a 'fragment' of Asger Jorn's article 'The poetic way' was published (Jorn, 1951). However, this was not without many ironic caveats and even incorporated the motif of a skull, as if handling a toxic substance (Virke, 1951).[6]

But otherwise the 1950s was a period of building when architects were very busy and there was much to publish, from large urban planning projects to exclusive villas. Usually the articles were written by the architects themselves, without any critical commentary or text. Sven Markelius, town planning director of Stockholm, for example, wrote about the structure of Stockholm and Vällingby centre in *Byggmästaren* 3/1956. This was probably the last internationally influential Swedish project for some time – a fact that was not lost on the journal – and to which it dedicated an entire issue, including a long summary in English, as well as another article in the following issue, 4/1956. Markelius' main argument against what he describes as a growing criticism of suburbanisation was to emphasise, as the only reasonable strategy, a decentralised expansion of Stockholm incorporating secondary suburban centres.

FIGURE 4.5 A brief return of 'the debate of ideas' appeared in *Byggmästaren* 4 (1951),
with editorial caveats attached and stamped with a skull warning of 'toxicity'.
Source: Courtesy of Arkitektur/Swedish Review of Architecture.

As was typical, another project which later and in other contexts was to be heavily criticised for being too large, was written about sympathetically by only a few external commentators. In this case it was the art historian Thomas Paulsson's 1955 article on the town plan of Täby northeast of Stockholm (Paulsson, 1955). He positively commented on the separation of low one-family houses and high multi-family dwellings 'for psychological reasons […] the inhabitants of the single-family houses wish to live among like-minded' and because of the 'unity and comfort of the cityscape'. In the 1950s there seems to have been a widespread understanding of what was perceived to be the right direction to follow.

One of the few external, and still fewer critical, commentaries can be found in art historian Elias Cornell's article on *H55*, an exhibition held in Helsingborg in 1955 (Cornell, 1955). Cornell's main argument was that exhibitions should be a field for experiment and that *H55* had missed this opportunity by aiming to be a complete work of architecture, 'an image of perfection'. 'The exhibition could have been a forerunner and a trigger for the discussion of some of the immense problems that are fermenting in our architectural world', he claimed. Nordic architecture students were considerably more critical in their journal *a5*, which was published in connection with *H55*, but instead explicitly and provocatively devoted itself to the twenty-fifth anniversary of the 1930 Stockholm exhibition: '25 years ago architecture was interesting, up to the point when even architects were having discussions', was the ironic verdict of the young on the architectural establishment.

FIGURE 4.6 In the 1950s projects were typically published only with the architect's description. Art historian Elias Cornell's critical review of the *H55* exhibition in Helsingborg in *Byggmästaren* 8 (1955) was an exception.
Source: Courtesy of Arkitektur/Swedish Review of Architecture.

Even if the 'new tendencies' and the 'immense problems' were surprisingly absent from the pages of the 1950s *Byggmästaren*, they can be said to have had a strong impact on the change of the title of the journal from 1959 (Redaktionen, 1958). The 1922 change of the name from *Arkitektur* to *Byggmästaren* (The Master Builder) was an expression of the modernist understanding of 'the built work as an indivisible synthesis of the contributions of several professionals' (with the architect as its coordinator, one might add). The change back to *Arkitektur* was explained in the last issue of 1958 as reflecting 'the ongoing specialisation among the practitioners of the art of building – a specialisation which might not be possible to stop, but which is wished for by no-one'. In a more hopeful spirit the editorial also talked about a growing public interest in architecture, which they hoped to influence with the journal's new format.

In the first issue of 1959 Thelaus wrote an editorial emphasising the importance of architectural criticism (Thelaus, 1959). His ambition for the journal was now to give more space to criticism, with the help of architectural journalists from the daily newspapers, while, he says 'The informative and documenting tasks of the review will be pursued more or less like before.' A series of articles published after 1960 illustrate this change. Art historian Thomas Paulsson, for example, commented on the architects' silence in the public debate. For nine years, he wrote, no other books on architecture of any note had been published, except that by Erik Thelaus on modern Swedish villas: 'How will the public dare to contact architects if architects don't want to contact the public?' (Paulsson, 1960). Architect Hans Erland Heineman complained that too many of his colleagues took the view that: 'No problems are solved by debating, our place is at the drawing board' (Heineman, 1960).

Art historian Göran Lindahl, writing on three new churches by Peter Celsing, argued that Celsing's 'fruitful and living relation to history is something of a new achievement in a time

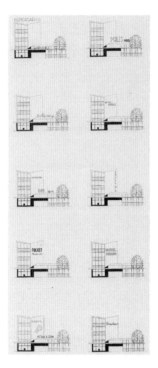

FIGURE 4.7 Hans Erland Heineman's article in *Arkitektur* 5 (1960) included this ironic comment on the standardised modernism of the late 1950s.
Source: Courtesy of Arkitektur/Swedish Review of Architecture.

which made the lack of history a routine convention' (Lindahl, 1960). In a debate taking place in a national newspaper in 1959 on Celsing's church in Vällingby, the same Göran Lindahl launched the concept of a 'haven of beauty' in church design, seen as the last resort in a pragmatic modern society for architects interested in the existential aspects of architecture.

Nonetheless, in an overview of the position of Swedish architecture in issue 9/1960, the architect Björn Linn saw a silver lining (Linn, 1960), noting that the June issue of *The Architectural Review* in 1960 had on its cover Anders Tengbom's *Skogshem*, a conference centre for the Swedish Employers' Association. This, according to Linn, was the first occasion in a long time that a Swedish building had received such international attention. This absence was indicative of a mutual lack of interest, he argued, adding that in Sweden 'we have been too content with the situation'. Further, he noted that while from abroad there was little to be found of interest in Sweden, a growing number of critical Swedish voices promised a re-awakening of the architectural debate, as well as an interest in research, and the history and theory of architecture. To support his case he mentioned a few important, carefully detailed and spatially sophisticated buildings (the Gävle crematorium chapel by ELLT; Lewerentz' St Mark's parish church; and the Ahlsén brothers' PUB shopping mall in central Stockholm), concluding that the high-quality output of 1960 made the future seem more hopeful.

But the mass production of housing was still a problem. One of the sharpest criticisms of its decreasing quality was interestingly enough written in 1960 by Lennart Holm, who later, as director of the National Board of Planning, was to be accused of being responsible for the so-called *Milijonprogrammet* or Million Programme (Holm, 1960). His article presented the introduction to an issue in which the best (model) multi-family dwellings were published: 'Still nobody shows the worst, or even the average or next best. This is probably lucky for those still living with the illusion that, step-by-step, we are approaching a higher level of housing.' Increasing costs led to both rationalisation *and* a reduction in quality: 'Production adapted design' became the motto. Holm argued that architects (dutifully) solved the tasks they were given:

> but sometimes it would perhaps be better to speak out and to state the obvious, namely that something is impossible, rather than leading the client to believe that it might be possible to make things a little thicker, higher or denser in the next project.

Disinterest in and lack of understanding architectural quality

In the late 1950s the shift of responsibilities within the building process in Sweden had clearly marginalised architects, leaving most of the control in the hands of the big contractors. The government was in favour of this in its attempt to solve the housing crisis by increasing production without increasing the workforce in the face of the postwar economic boom. Architects had good reasons to be critical, and this was fostered by the new editor Per-Olof Olsson, who was in charge of the journal from 1961 to 1967.

The novelty of the situation and the traditional responsibility of the architect as a professional was also addressed by Olsson in his comment in the journal on the new suburban commercial centre at Farsta in Stockholm, opened in 1960 as a southern counterpart to Vällingby. What was new to Sweden in this case was the explicitly commercial character of the centre, which was built by private investors. Backström and Reinius were the architects, and critics like Lindahl and Ahrbom perceived it, at long last, as a liberation from functionalism but also as a form of prostitution. Olsson took another perspective, seeing it as evidence of a potential breakthrough of democratic values within the mores of a modern consumer society, values that were never really achieved by 1930s modernism. At the same time he was well aware of potential problems:

> This type of commission – large areas to be developed very quickly – will most likely become more common. Architects must be prepared for these new commissions, which demand large offices with shock troops always ready to respond to the client's or developer's arbitrary planning decisions, or their wish to use cheap building components. The architects will in this new and ever more common situation, need to increase their knowledge and resources, and not forget their responsibility as professionals to be a trustee not only of the client but also of the general public. The architectonic expression of this new form of production has most certainly not yet been established.
>
> *Olsson, 1961*

According to Olsson, the modernisation of society had clarified these changes. The critical responses were often addressed to the general public, since clients and builders too often were not listening to the architect.

The threats to the role of the architect were also raised in a 25-year anniversary speech of the SAR, the Swedish Architects' Association, by Hakon Ahlberg, its founder and first chairman (Ahlberg, 1962): 'We have all reasons to believe that our current, and unfinished stage of history, will in the future be described as a transition to a completely new era.' As a 'builder of society' the architect had to be engaged in this, but at the same time was cut off from the building site and its economy, being seen only as a designer. This diminished any interest in influencing the work on site, as well as also constraining the builder's understanding of the architect's role. Ahlberg's hope was that 'the more complicated the technology gets', the more the architect would need to 'monitor human and aesthetic values'.

In an unusually outspoken political statement, Olsson, employing a materialistic credo, noted that the art of building had in any society been shaped by political and economic conditions. He described the contemporary Swedish society as a 'special structure: a meeting between a modified socialism and a modernised capitalism cooperating with socialism'. While reform of society had consequently been very successful, Olsson also referred to a growing Social-Democratic opposition, in accusing that party of being opportunistic and incestuous. The opposition proposed the introduction of a more overtly planned economy, but the dominating faction of the party was more conservative in collaborating with the bourgeois parties. A lack of engaged civil servants and professionals had led to a centralisation of political power: 'bureaucracy has increased and been given directly militant characteristics', Olsson claimed, noting that 'The material conditions for creating architecture are thus more than favourable. But the ideological, spiritual climate is not very inspiring.' According to him, everything was possible in architecture 'today', from abstract glass grids to bunker-like religious buildings, and in town planning the predicament was still worse:

> The situation is complicated by the lack of professional planners with authority and a surprising weakness – even among Social-Democratic politicians – to accept without caveats private companies' demands for central sites containing [servicing] infrastructure.
>
> *Olsson, 1962*

The work of the architect, Olsson argued, was not just to deliver drawings but also 'something of a democratic mission in contributing to an on-going discussion concerning the form of society and the conditions of its citizens'.

In 1962 the new centre of Stockholm had been completed with its 'landmark' five high-rise office buildings and a plan was presented for further renewal. A whole issue, 11/1962, was devoted to the latter, including texts of presentations made by the planners responsible. At the same time criticism was growing, which eventually, some years later, led to a change of direction, jettisoning ideas of wholesale renewal. One unusual example of this criticism was a complete 1962 issue given over to three young architects who, according to Olsson, were aware of the architect's responsibility for the renewal of the art of urban planning.

Under the headline 'Towards a new environment' they protested against a planning system which made:

> a mockery of man's needs for immaterial values and which in no way fulfils the ambitions of our democratic society […] which fosters a development where existing values are destroyed without new being created […] which in a one-sided way satisfies the demands of car-traffic, real-estate owners and commerce [and] which is directed by decision-making authorities ruled by short-sighted economic interests and not whole-heartedly using the enormous resources of our society.
>
> *Edblom et al., 1962*

MOT EN NY MILJÖ

Detta nummer är en protest mot den utformning som ges våra städer och dess ytterområden.
Vi kan ej acceptera en planering
— som medför att vår yttre miljö — bostadsområden och arbetsplatser — i sin avsaknad av medveten
gestaltning utgör ett hån mot människans behov av immateriella värden och som på intet sätt mot-
svarar vårt demokratiska samhälles ambitioner
— som ej på ett tillfredsställande sätt förmår ge arkitektonisk form åt valda förutsättningar
— som främjar en utveckling där befintliga värden förstörs utan att nya tillskapas
— som ensidigt tillgodoser biltrafikens, fastighetsägarnas och handelns funktionskrav
— som topprids av beslutande organ vilkas avgöranden ytterst bestäms av kortsiktiga ekonomiska
intressen, och som ej helhjärtat utnyttjar vårt samhälles väldiga resurser.

Mänsklighetens historia är kampen mellan enande och
upplösande krafter. De enande och försonande, de goda
krafterna, de som är villiga att försaka egen vinning till
förmån för gemensamma ideal. De upplösande och de-
struktiva krafterna — de onda — ovilliga till förståelse och
samarbete.
Det anses att vi trots allt lever i en relativt fredlig tid. Att
de ytterlighetshandlingar som vi dagligen upprörs över i
det stora hela är obetydliga. Men denna fred är skenbar och
upprätthålls av en makt- och terrorbalans som helt saknar
motstycke. Det arbete för större internationell förståelse
och samarbete som bedrivs inom FN, och som indikeras
av de överallt pågående handelspolitiska förhandlingarna,

utförs i skuggan av ett hot och en splittring som kan leda
till våldshandlingar, vilket omedelbart skulle betyda total
förstörelse och katastrof.
Denna förvirrande och egentligen outhärdliga situation
speglas i nästan all mänsklig verksamhet. De stora och om-
välvande tekniska förändringarna, de allt mer omfattande
kommunikationerna, såväl geografiskt som kulturellt, har
gett en förändring och förnyelse av våra värderingar och
denna omställning upplevs som svår och smärtsam. Vårt
gamla statiska samhälle har ersatts av ett nytt och dyna-
miskt spännande kanske och fyllt av möjligheter, men
krävande och hänsynslöst.
Ett samhälle får sitt förnämsta uttryck i staden, och tyd-

FIGURE 4.8 Three young architects edited *Arkitektur* 8 (1962), presenting 'Towards a new environment', an alternative proposal for the renewal of central Stockholm, arguing for its historic value.
Source: Courtesy of Arkitektur/Swedish Review of Architecture.

Their critique was followed by a proposal for an incremental renewal of Stockholm city centre, keeping the existing urban pattern and concentrating car traffic to a few streets within a larger-scale grid. As an alternative to a wholesale renewal of a suburban area of old timber houses with high-rise blocks, they proposed a more compact grid of the same density, preserving parts of the existing structure.

This polemic clearly resonated with the public. The architect Sune Lindström, professor of town planning at Chalmers university of technology in Gothenburg agreed that the planning of Stockholm seemed to have got out of hand (Lindström, 1962). In response, Stockholm planners questioned matters of detail and insisted that functional demands must be met (Nordberg, 1962; Sidenbladh, 1962). The young architects had the last word, however, questioning the emphasis on logistics, as well as the principle that traffic was the main feature of the modern city. They maintained that the existing city had much more to offer and that it must be given a flexible structure (Edblom et al., 1963).

The sentiment that things were going wrong, and that something had to be done, was ever-present in the early 1960s. The presentation of Lewerentz's St. Mark's Church was followed by a lengthy article on his whole body of work by Hakon Ahlberg. His final words summarised a certain unease:

His, [Lewerentz's] in many ways fragmentary work, is a testimony to the hard conditions, under which an architect with the ambition and character of Lewerentz has had to work in a country in a time of so little general interest and understanding of architectural quality.
Ahlberg, 1963

FIGURE 4.9   Lewerentz in his 'black box'. In *Arkitektur* 9 (1963), an issue completely devoted to the work of Sigurd Lewerentz, Hakon Ahlberg complained about a 'country in a time of so little general interest and understanding of architectural quality'.
Source: Courtesy of Arkitektur/Swedish Review of Architecture.

In a discussion of the ever more popular turnkey contracts, Per-Olof Olsson claimed that their weakest point was an inability to respect the interests of the consumer and those of society (Olsson, 1964): 'All sorts of building […] is a much too serious thing to be put in the hands of builders.'

The arguments of the young architects against the simplistic functional thinking inherent in the planning of Stockholm's city centre were, in an article by the architectural historian Göran Lindahl, extended to the dramatic changes that had become evident in the centres of mid-sized Swedish towns:

> The 1950s were caught unprepared, and counter arguments were mobilised much too late. There was also a commitment to functional studies and a rationale that left few avenues open for objections. The changes must be accepted it was argued, and the city needed to be formed into a functional tool.
>
> *Lindahl, 1965*

In one of the last issues of 1965, *Arkitektur* invited selected authors to air their critical views on developments. The first issue of 1966 continued this theme, where the journalist Olle Bengtzon – who in his daily newspaper in the same year described the first Million Programme housing projects as 'newly built slums' – introduced nine authors who wrote about the 'new city' of the city centres and of the suburbs (Bengtzon, 1966). Bengtzon quoted the author Pär Rådström, who in his short story had his protagonist, on hearing the song 'Row without oars', reflect that rowing without oars is what all powerless people have to learn.

The architect Sven Thiberg, who would later become a professor in building function analysis, gave a witty reply, defending functional thinking (Thiberg, 1966): 'There is a permanent [Kevin] Lynch rule hanging over the housing debate – a drive towards formal problems that relegates the social content to the background, that makes the debate superficial and unproductive when we really need a constructive in-depth analysis'. Thiberg saw the 'hesitant unease' of Bengtzon's authors as 'truly a row [quarrel] without oars'.

The antagonism between hard and soft values of the Apollo and Dionysus debate were repeated 20 years later, on the other side of the 'record years'. The Apollonians had won, but not altogether in the way they had hoped.

The field of architecture

One way of understanding this antagonism is to relate it to Pierre Bourdieu's theory of cultural fields adapted to architecture in a way that may be useful for a discussion here (Albertsen, 1998).

Bourdieu's four poles of his concept of field are 'autonomy', 'heteronomy', and high and low 'consecration'. Adapting Albertsen's version of Bourdieu to Swedish postwar architecture, the pole of autonomy can be associated with architects like Sigurd Lewerentz and Peter Celsing, and with church building as 'a haven of beauty'. This is very much architecture as art. The second pole could be called 'production adapted design' with the million programme of housing as its paradigm. It is heterogenic in being governed by the state and by builders' economic and technical imperatives. Within the wider field, architects tend to think about church architecture as identified with 'high consecration' (not just because of its religious function) and mass-produced housing as bread-and-butter jobs with 'low consecration'.

Albertsen also introduces a third 'sub-field' which he calls 'professional'. Applied to Swedish architecture this would identify with architects trying to defend their professional autonomy while at the same time working with the important, broader task of building a modern society. It is a position that most architects would accept, and probably what Kidder Smith referred to in 1950 by calling Swedish architecture 'civilised'.

If the theory is valid this could be used to describe all fields of culture, as well as architecture in a global context. There is always a polarisation between a more autonomous and a more heterogenic way of working as an architect. What might be said about Swedish architecture as it developed during the 1950s is that this polarisation was exceptionally pronounced. The reason for this could be that the heterogenic, state-governed 'pole' was unusually dominant and successful, thereby 'setting the rules' in a very literal sense. At the same time the autonomous 'pole' was also unusually strong (which is evidenced today by the international interest in an architect like Sigurd Lewerentz). The reason for this arguably lies within the tradition of (modern) Swedish architecture, beginning at the turn of the nineteenth century, with masters like Ragnar Östberg and Carl Westman.

We have seen how the thorough modernisation of the Swedish building industry during the 1950s passed seemingly unnoticed in the professional journals. The profession turned inwards, given the numerous and well-paid opportunities to build despite the surrounding turmoil. When the resulting consequences of this became all too obvious around 1960, architects started to protest. The outcome of this protest can be said to have arrived in the late 1960s when the 'record years' lost their momentum due to external economic pressures.

The role of the architect in the building process became marginalised in Sweden. For some time this could be compensated for by a general public interest in architecture. But architects in Sweden are still struggling today with the shift of power over the building process that happened during the 1950s and early 1960s.

The Nordic connection

In a Nordic context Sweden was leading developments postwar, for better and worse. In the beginning of the period this development could be seen as 'superior to the other Scandinavian countries both theoretically and practically' (Jorn, 1946). The modernisation of Sweden also took place earlier and was faster than in the other countries, which had been held back by the war. This meant that the consequences described above were less pronounced or arrived later in the other Nordic countries, and the polarisation between autonomy and heteronomy (according to Bourdieu's 'field') was less obvious there than in Sweden.

In his book on Nordic architecture the Danish architect Nils-Ole Lund makes a similar comparison between Sweden and Denmark, noting a 'gap' between architecture as art and architecture as construction:

> Foreign architects who worked in Sweden in the 1950s clearly saw how the Swedish architects lost control of the construction process, and how the Asplund ideal came into conflict with Swedish reality. The result was a kind of architectural schizophrenia that pointed towards what was to come everywhere in the Nordic countries in the 1970s and 1980s.
>
> *Lund, 2008, p. 174*

At the same time it is worth underlining that, despite these problems, Swedish and Nordic architecture have a long common tradition in the loyalty of their architects to the building of a welfare state, where architecture is a common good in a relatively egalitarian society. In his foreword, Lund mentions that he wrote the Danish edition of the book in 1993 in order to try to 'safeguard' a Nordic version of modernism in an era of European integration:

> In Scandinavia international modernism was translated into a pragmatic, socially aware architecture, which was also nuanced and 'human' in its formal expression. One can speak of an architecture for the welfare state.
>
> *Lund, 2008, p. 5*

As an example of this role of architecture, Lund discusses Nordic housing in one chapter, claiming that 'it is a characteristic feature of the Nordic countries that one can get a picture of the whole architectural development since World War II solely by using examples from this building sector' (Lund, 2008, p. 245).

As a final part of the analysis of Swedish architecture journals, it might be of interest to see what role housing projects played in the material presented. Of the 951 projects published in *Byggmästaren* and *Arkitektur* from 1945 to 1965, 302 were housing. Of these 302, 124 were multi-family dwellings and 178 were single-family houses. Considering that just over half of the buildings constructed were for the housing sector, and that two-thirds of the housing were in multi-family houses, it is obvious that housing, and especially multi-family dwellings, were under-represented in the material published. An explanation of this is, naturally, a low priority within the field of architecture given to the 'production adapted design' of housing. Although an unusually large proportion of housing is of high quality in the Nordic countries, this does not apply to all housing. Whether this under-representation also occurs in professional journals in other countries is an interesting question which would be a test of Lund's hypothesis concerning the outstanding characteristics of the Nordic welfare state.

Notes

1 Ceferin (2003) describes how the Finnish Museum of Architecture, by sending exhibitions abroad from the 1950s, helped to create the image of Finland as a modern country close to nature.
2 Apollo and Dionysus is used in the title, but not mentioned in the 1947 text by Olsson, suggesting that it might have been introduced by the editors.
3 Jorn's first article had been translated into Swedish and Olsson had pointed to some possible mistakes in the translation. It is also worth noting that Jorn's title is 'Apollo *or* Dionysus'.
4 Later he would complete one of the first Swedish PhDs in architecture with a dissertation on functional studies of housing, and become a strong proponent of architectural research with close connections to the governing Social-Democratic party. He ended his career being the top executive of the Swedish planning authority for almost 20 years.
5 All three were practising architects, but Björck mainly worked as a town planner.
6 Later on, another of the leading figures of Swedish architecture, Sven Ivar Lind, was to refer to this as 'the notorious issue with the skull' (Lind, 1952).

References

Ahlberg, H. (1962). Arkitekten i det moderna samhället. *Arkitektur*, 5, pp. 121–128.
—— (1963). Sigurd Lewerentz. *Arkitektur*, 9, pp. 201–244.
Ahrbom, N. (1950). Vi passera ett halvsekel. *Byggmästaren*, 1, pp. 2–5.
Albertsen, N. (1998). Arkitekturens fält. In D. Broady (Ed.), *Kulturens fält*. Göteborg: Daidalos.
Bengtzon, O. (1966). Ny vind i slaka segel. *Arkitektur*, 1, pp. 1–12.
Ceferin, P. (2003). *Constructing a Legend: The International Exhibitions of Finnish Architecture 1957–1967*. Helsinki: Suomalaisen Kirjallisuuden Seura.
Cornell, E. (1955). H55 och utställningsarkitekturens möjligheter. *Byggmästaren*, 8, pp. 205–211.
Edblom, M., Strömdahl, J. and Westerman, A. (1962). Mot en ny miljö. *Arkitektur*, 8, pp. 205–224.
—— (1963). Kejsarens nya kläder. *Arkitektur*, 1, p. 32.
Heineman, H. E. (1960). I går i dag i morgon. *Arkitektur*, 5, pp. 115–116.
Holm, L. (1948). Ideologi och form i efterkrigstidens arkitekturdebatt. *Byggmästaren*, 15, pp. 264–270.
—— (1960). Flerfamiljshus idag. *Arkitektur*, 11, pp. 221–222.
Holm, L. and Reinius, L. (Eds) (1948). *Byggmästaren* 20, p. 368.
Jorn, A. (1946). Formspråkets livsinnehåll. *Byggmästaren*, 18, pp. 317–326.
—— (1947). Apollon eller Dionysos. *Byggmästaren*, 17, pp. 251–256.
—— (1951). Poesiens väg. Fragment ur en artikel. *Byggmästaren*, 4, pp. 54–62.
Kidder Smith, G. E. (1950). *Sweden Builds*. London: Architectural Press.
Lind, S. I. (1952). Två inlägg med anledning av Lennart Holms artikel 'Två ämbetsbyggnader'. *Byggmästaren*, 3, p. 84.
Lindahl, G. (1960). Tre nya kyrkor. *Arkitektur*, 7, pp. 133–134.
—— (1965). Omvandlingen i städernas mitt. *Arkitektur*, 5, pp. 152–159.

Lindström, S. (1962). Reflektioner till en protest. *Arkitektur*, 10, pp. 270–272.

Linn, B. (1960). Den svenska arkitekturens ställning. *Arkitektur*, 9, pp. 169–171.

Lund, N.-O. (2008). *Nordic Architecture*. Copenhagen: Arkitektens Forlag.

Nordberg, A. (1962). För en funktionsduglig stad. *Arkitektur*, 11, pp. 319–320.

Nordisk Byggdag. (1950). Nordisk Byggdag 1950. *Byggmästaren*, 1, p. 1.

Olsson, P.-O. (1961). Acceptera Farsta? *Arkitektur*, 3, pp. 66–68.

—— (1962). Arkitekturen inför 60-talet. *Arkitektur*, 7, pp. 173–177.

—— (1964). Totalentreprenad: framtidens byggeri. *Arkitektur*, 6, p. 125.

Olsson, T. (1947). Apollon, Dionysos och arkitekten. *Byggmästaren*, 1, pp. 5–7.

Paulsson, T. (1955). Stadsplan för Täby. *Byggmästaren*, 6, pp. 169–172.

—— (1960). Miljöplanering och miljöforskning. *Arkitektur*, 3, pp. 70–71.

Redaktionen. (1958). Byggmästaren A + B i ny utgivningsform. *Byggmästaren*, 10, p. 201.

Reinius, L. (1947). Apollon och Dionysos. *Byggmästaren*, 24, p. 341.

—— (1948a). Skilda vägar. *Byggmästaren*, 1, p. 1.

—— (1948b). Undergångssymbol hos Joyce. *Byggmästaren*, 17, p. 316.

Sidenbladh, G. (1962). För en ny miljö. *Arkitektur*, 11, p. 198.

Thelaus, E. (1959). Arkitektur 1959. *Arkitektur*, 1, p. 1.

Thiberg, S. (1966). Oro utan åror. *Arkitektur*, 5, pp. 201–244.

Virke, T. (1951). Idédebatten. *Byggmästaren*, 4, p. 53.

Westerberg, E. (1947). Apollon och Dionysos. *Byggmästaren*, 24, p. 341.

5

VISUAL SENSIBILITY AND THE SEARCH FOR FORM

The Architectural Review in postwar Britain

Andrew Higgott

> Far too often in recent years the progressive architect's attention has been directed to the big idea, the town plan, the national plan, the cosmic pattern, to the exclusion of more local and particular interests. The result has been that he has begun to lose his ability to see other than with his mind's eye.
>
> *The Architectural Review, January 1950, p. 45*

The Architectural Review (*AR*)[1] had become firmly established as the voice of authority in British architecture in the years before the Second World War. Its role in shaping the development of a modernist culture in British architecture in the 1930s was crucial, and provided an interpretation of modernism that shaped its translation into the making of buildings in the years that followed. Its role was far from being simply a journal that reflected the work of the architectural profession, and the specifics of its approach were to relate to deeply felt cultural and artistic qualities that shaped its content and critical position, as well as its graphic form being more extraordinary than most.[2] Hubert de Cronin Hastings was its proprietor and editor from 1927, and with James Richards who was appointed assistant editor in 1935, had effectively established a personally inflected British modernism that mirrored the politically progressive spirit of the age. It was attuned to advanced social thinking of the times, and embodied an aesthetic that served to reflect it; the white walls, flat roofs and lack of decoration which were to become the signifiers of international modernism. That this position was a simplification and reduction of the complex interweaving of different strands of thought that formed modern architecture was perhaps already problematic: its universality, unleavened utopianism and predilection for an anonymous, generic approach set the scene for an architecture that was compromised by its limitations. But after the Second World War, when this approach had been embodied in official plans and policies, its serious shortcomings, paradoxically given the *AR*'s own involvement, were to create a fundamental shift in the journal's thinking.

Visual culture and 'Townscape'

The *AR*'s consistent articulation of a number of critical terms which expressed fundamentally different ideas as correctives to prevailing practice and which were developed through the period of the late 1940s and 1950s, was of the greatest significance. 'The Functional Tradition', 'Townscape' and 'Outrage' were among terms reiterated throughout the decade and beyond. De Cronin Hastings, who along with James Richards continued to lead the *AR*'s editorial policy, was the main source of these radical but conservative ideas: an issue for the fiftieth anniversary of the journal in January 1947 made clear the editorial programme for the next decades under what was described as a collective editorship comprising Hastings, Richards, Nikolaus Pevsner and Osbert Lancaster. Its general aim was 'to pursue the cause of visual culture', described as a unique role for an architectural journal to pursue, beyond its 'first function' of recording for posterity the significant buildings of its time. In particular it aimed to 're-educate the eye: that is the special need of the next decade'; the architect, it was said, needs to 'learn from the painter how to see' and to apply a sense of the visual to the architectural forms produced by the science-based processes of planning. The historical sense, it asserts, can be used constructively, rather than as an escape from contemporary realities. The issue also introduced the *AR*'s specific preoccupations, such as the interest in Townscape, which were to become long-term issues in its editorial position; this developed out of the Picturesque and became, along with the reappraisal of the Functional Tradition, its most important shaping factor in the 20 years after the Second World War.

The *AR* had first promoted an interpretation of the Picturesque in an issue of January 1944 with an unsigned article entitled 'Exterior furnishing or sharawaggi: the art of making urban landscape'.[3] Initiated by Hastings and developed with Pevsner, this argument appropriated the idea of the Picturesque in the design of British landscapes introduced in an earlier book by Christopher Hussey (1927). It expanded the *AR*'s existing concerns by bringing to light an anonymous urban tradition which, in localities as different as Oxford or the Midland town of Shrewsbury, made places that worked in a scenographic sense, satisfying to those that passed through them, even if perhaps they did not know why.

Its principles of variety, intricacy and contrast, in contradiction to the clarity and geometry maintained by a modernist position, were seen to be relevant and applicable to current issues. In this debate, the composition of three-dimensional space in city streets corresponding to that in landscape design gave an aesthetic that transcended the orthogonal as an alternative system of ordering. That this historical practice, rooted in eighteenth-century British landscape-making, could form the basis, not for an historicist revival, but for a new way of developing a modern urbanism, was central to the *AR*'s new strategy. Its editors – certainly including Pevsner who had done so much to introduce European modern architecture in Britain, and Richards, who had taken the leading role in arguing for it in the journal in the 1930s – were at pains to argue that modernism – in some form – was the only way forward. Writing in *AR* April 1954 on 'C20 Picturesque', Pevsner argued that the aesthetic qualities of such paradigmatic modernist buildings as Le Corbusier's Stuttgart villas and Centrosoyus in Moscow corresponded to those of the Picturesque in their free grouping and combination of materials, and as the expression of their designer's imagination, and also asserted that the principle had particular relevance in the planning of towns.

Townscape as a polemic term was introduced in December 1949 with a special issue of *AR*, written by Hastings under the pseudonym of Ivor de Wolfe (de Wolfe 1949). Described as 'a plea for an English visual philosophy' (see Erten, 2015),[4] its argument is rooted in a horror of the degradation of the environment that has been allowed, quite disregarded, to take place. 'We foul our nest […] the contemporary world is a kind of visual refuse heap', as Hastings wrote. Its argument is also for a specifically British means of rectifying these problems: the

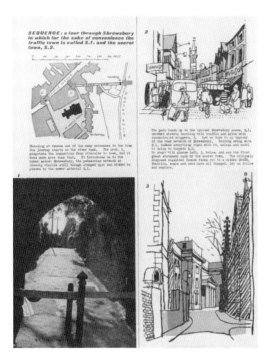

FIGURE 5.1 Townscape analysis, Shrewsbury: from 'Midland Experiment', Gordon Cullen.
The Architectural Review (May 1954).
Source: *The Architectural Review*.

urban effects of the age of mechanisation can be mediated by the making of 'pictures', of compositions of disparate elements that were no doubt unconventional but visually pleasing. As the campaign developed, the valuing of the Picturesque tradition, melded with a deeply rooted appreciation of the historical fabric of British towns, saw the existing visual urban landscape as a given: architecturally impure, and certainly never 'planned', the town or city was to continue to be experienced through changing spatial incidents and the way objects were perceived, rather than the totalising view implied by modernism. A polemic was developed that expressed a reaction to the axial planning and uniform street line of both the Beaux Arts tradition and of modernist urbanism. Elements of surprise and the conjunction of disparate built objects were valued: their detail and their materiality were to be appreciated. Towns were also seen as specific, as if there were a quality in each place, the *genius loci*, which could be teased out and enhanced. A series of analyses of Midland towns appeared later, which provided a key example of the understanding and application of these new principles (Cullen, 1953a–d, 1954). That this was a critique of the current practice of planning operations goes without saying: and the *AR* proposed a number of models for the modification of streets and towns, starting with Lyme Regis in the January 1950 issue, which set out many of its concerns.

Hastings' initial argument is presented also, and persuasively, through the collection of images, combining drawings and photographs, in the 'Townscape Casebook' edited by Gordon Cullen (1949), initially the assistant art editor on *AR* from 1946. Cullen's Townscape drawings, both of existing urban sequences and of possible improvements to scenes of civic failure, were

FIGURE 5.2 Lyme Square, Lyme Regis re-planned: Townscape drawing by Gordon Cullen.
The Architectural Review (May 1950).
Source: *The Architectural Review*.

persuasive evidence of the campaign to revalue the juxtaposition of buildings and the spaces between them.

Cullen's imagery was a pervasive part of the *AR*'s aesthetic as it developed through the 1950s and beyond. The streets of still-austere Britain were pictured as full of leisured, comfortably-off people: there was bunting, the planting of trees and café tables. While such a scene may have been glimpsed in the microcosm of the Festival of Britain site on the London South Bank, Cullen's depiction of life in British towns of the 1950s was of a different kind of utopia. His descriptions of the visual subtleties of passing through streets, squares and alleys gave an immediacy to the campaign for visual education, and the accompanying vivid sketches have perhaps come to supplant Hastings' fervent campaigning and obscure Pevsner's historical understanding of the Picturesque as a principle of design (see Aitchison, 2010). Cullen was to appear to be the originator of the idea to a later generation, through the publication of the book *Townscape* in 1961 which was a compilation of text and images published in *AR* over the previous 13 years. In one example, his Townscape analyses served to accompany J. M. Richards' July 1953 article on the 'Failure of the new towns' with a text on the towns' 'prairie planning'. Demonstrating its failures, Cullen wrote 'Even a small congregation of buildings can produce drama and spatial stimulation', but in the absence of any of the coherence of Townscape design: 'if buildings are the letters of the alphabet they are not used to make coherent words but to utter the desolate cries of AAAAA! or OOOOOO!' (Cullen, 1953, p. 33)

The 'Functional Tradition'

A wider criticism of modernism as it had developed until then formed the January 1950 issue of *AR* – the mid-century issue (quoted at the head of this chapter) which took as its theme what was termed the Functional Tradition. Its judgement was based on what it argued was the mistaken scale of the object of the architect's attention, that of the town plan or larger dimension, rather than the tangible processes of building at a human scale (see Higgott 2007b). Very little rebuilding had taken place by then, but the plans that were in place for reconstructing almost every British city took a strategic view, concerned with overall principles of organisation, practical issues such as road building, and the urgent issues of replacing poor housing, not on how these buildings would look or feel. The editorial continued with a criticism of the underlying basis of this approach, identified as concerned with the analysis of issues of fact and evidence as well as incorporating an overweening social commitment:

> One might say that the more sensitive architect today staggers under the weight of his realisation of the facts of life. The burden of technical awareness hangs heavily on the student and practising architect alike and the sense of social responsibility often assumes the proportions and character of an incubus as well as a stimulant.

Instead, it argues, the architect's thought should be elsewhere and at a very different level of attention, on the qualities of the materials used in making buildings, and further, on the overall visual effect of what is designed:

> Let the modern architect then drop his mental gaze from the great distances, suffi-cient to notice the qualities of the ordinary things around him. […] Let him study the surface of a rock, for instance, and experience afresh the sudden realisation of how the values inherent in its textural qualities have re-occurred in walls, buildings, roads, giving them a complexity and vitality which are completely passed by in the present-day Townscape.
>
> *The Architectural Review, January 1950, p. 45*

Thus, it declares, the architect should work with the immediate visceral sense of material, and (not least) value what is already there, appreciating the manifold qualities of the architecture created outside modernist discourse. Most significantly, the 'eye' – the concern with aes-thetics – was to redeem the modern architect's error: it is the visual qualities of architecture that are presented as the most important, overtaking all other attributes such as spatial conditions, functionality or the expression of architecture's socially effective role. This interpretation fun-damentally shaped the editorial position of *AR*, and it extended into its campaigns about the visual qualities of the environment, on Townscape and Subtopia which were to be developed through the 1950s, as well as an ongoing series on the visually extraordinary, 'the exploring eye'.[5] And, while many aspects of international modernism were represented in its pages, the overarching concern was with a culture that was local rather than universal, and in this sense was a repudiation of the strictures of CIAM[6] or of Walter Gropius,[7] which had figured so large in the discourse of the pre-war period.

A September 1947 *AR* article by the artist John Piper, 'Pleasing Decay' formed a reappraisal of vernacular structures: 'an ancient building has as much individuality as a human being […] not to be "restored" by a general policy […]. In the restoration of "ruins" it [is] clear that the artist's view had lost out to the archeologist's.' Such an attitude seems tinged with nostalgia at a time when architects were involved with overwhelming urgent and practical issues, but may also be interpreted as an artist's view of the meaning of artefacts: that they communicate on a level other than the pragmatic in creating meaning and resonance. This contributed to the view that was to be consistently expressed by the *Review*'s editors that much was missed from the architectural position that they earlier had done so much to shape.

The key example in the 1950 *AR* on the Functional Tradition was the Cobb, the sea wall at Lyme Regis in Dorset:

In plan it has what appears to be a free form, full of interesting sweeps and curves, which at closer inspection are seen to be dictated by the position of the reef on which it is built, and the need for a seaward face that will carry the force of the sea away from its entrance. Seen in section, this curve is repeated in the manner of a glacis to seaward, and cut off abruptly within the arc, so that an oblique view provides a most interesting exercise in masses. On still closer inspection, what in cold fact is literally no more than a half mile of stone sea wall, reveals such a wealth of detail and such a variety of surface and pattern that almost every yard of it becomes an object lesson in surface treatment [...] it is a unique example, on a magnificent scale, of form conditioned by the strict discipline of function, yet so remarkably virile and expressive as to deserve the title of the Parthenon of the functional movement of the twentieth century.

The Architectural Review, January 1950, p. 9

Eric De Maré (later known primarily as an architectural photographer; see Higgott, 2016), who had earlier been a writer on the *AR* and editor of the *Architect's Journal*, had made these observations in an earlier January 1949 *AR* issue on canals, which he wrote and illustrated with his own photographs.

Throughout the history of English – or for that matter of any other – architecture, there is a continuous thread running parallel with the historical styles but owing little or nothing to them. It might be called a timeless tradition of functionalism if the term had not become confused by being used to define a far more sophisticated phase of contemporary architecture. For its constituent elements are geometry unadorned, and it owes its effects to the forthright, spare and logical use of materials. To this extent it has affinities with the architectural effects sought by the modern architects of today, which no doubt explains why, looking back over the centuries, our own eyes are especially apt at picking out structures that owe their charm and quality to this tradition of functionalism.

De Maré, 1949, p. 19

FIGURE 5.3   The Cobb sea wall, Lyme Regis, illustrating 'The Functional Tradition' issue.
The Architectural Review (January 1950).
Source: RIBA Collections.

De Maré (1950) outlined the history of canals and documented canal life as well as such architectural concerns as bridges and locks; and the quality of these structures was communicated by the strength of his photographs – even more so than by his text. Buildings which do not rely on the aesthetic language of the historical styles of architecture should be valued and understood, for architects may then learn from simple forms and the natural qualities of material.

In an extension of this work, de Maré was commissioned in 1956 by J. M. Richards to travel throughout England on the trail of early industrial buildings. He photographed the whole range of surviving industrial architecture from the late eighteenth and nineteenth centuries: images of all kinds of structures are included in this body of work, which are effectively architectural but built without architects. They range in scale from the bollard and brick wall to the largest, vast and highly engineered bridge projects such as the Forth rail bridge, through warehouses, dock buildings, breweries, mills, maltings and windmills. The end result was a powerful body of photographs, published as a special issue of the *AR* in July 1957. The buildings' effectiveness and success as objects of fascination to architects lay in their unselfconscious, unaestheticised use of materials, the scale and power of such large structures as dock and railway warehouses, as well as the simplicity and clear fitness for purpose which could be seen throughout.

Buildings invariably embodied a clarity of function and directness of form: constituent elements, such as staircases built outside a main structure, formed their own defined volumes: many successfully combined iron and masonry construction. The built forms collected were uncompromised and strong – and to many appeared to be more successful as architecture than the work currently being designed and constructed (see, for example, Stirling, 1960). Richards' intention, in assembling the material for this issue consistent with the principles outlined in earlier *AR* issues, was similarly to reconstruct a history:

> [bringing] into focus another episode in our architectural history when the functional values that we look up to now were dominant [...] may serve to put our own age in its proper perspective (and thus to allay the feeling that there is anything alarming or subversive in our preoccupation with functionalism) and at the same time, perhaps, furnish some useful lessons about the range and subtlety of the aesthetic effects of which an architecture dominated by functionalism is capable.

FIGURE 5.4   Stanley Textile Mill (1813): Eric de Maré photograph from 'The Functional Tradition in early industrial buildings' special issue. *The Architectural Review* (July 1957).
Source: Architectural Association.

FIGURE 5.5   Chemists shop in Kelso: 'the street scene' – illustrating the importance
of lettering. Journal cover, *The Architectural Review* (March 1953).
Source: The Architectural Review.

Richards' aim was to provide a useful source of reference, and the journal was published as a
book the following year (Richards, 1958).

'Subtopia' and the degraded environment

Emerging from the same impassioned root referred to by Hastings, that 'we foul our nest' in
degrading the environment, in his 1949 article introducing Townscape, was the vehement
Outrage campaign begun in June 1955 (Nairn 1955a, 1995b). Led by Ian Nairn, who had
joined the *AR* staff in 1954, it reflected the manifold failures of the ad hoc modernisation of
postwar Britain. Nairn made the campaign his own and, it appears, coined the term Outrage,
which was to become a national battle with a huge and widely acknowledged influence (on
Nairn, see Darley and McKie, 2013). Reacting to such objects as ugly street furniture and a
mass of traffic signage in cities and towns, these visible scars on the urban fabric were seen
collectively as destroying Britain's townscapes. A large element of the issue is the account of
a journey across the middle of England, from Southampton to Carlisle, through the edges of
Birmingham and other larger cities, illustrated by Nairn's bleak photography and impassioned
accounts of dreary speculative housing, endless wire fences, signs and posts making up the
Subtopia of an unnoticed despoiling of the environment, everywhere and always the same,
that was too urgent and too dreadful to ignore.

Architects were not those under attack here, but rather public authorities, whether town
councils, suppliers of utilities, the army or simply those insensitive to environmental degradation
who allowed this visual pollution to happen. Thus it was again a fight on behalf of an acute visual
sensibility; but it also implied a plea for a different, denser urbanism that allied the campaign both
to Townscape issues and to its criticism of suburban development. Outrage and Subtopia were to

FIGURE 5.6   'Leaving Southampton arriving at Carlisle' in 'Outrage' special issue
edited by Ian Nairn. *The Architectural Review* (June 1955).
Source: *The Architectural Review*.

become recurrent themes in the journal after this, and in their wide popularity crystallised the long-running attention to larger questions of the environment that had been part of the *AR*'s approach for two decades. A further and far more extensive special issue, 'Counter-Attack' in December 1956, edited by Nairn, made a more positive argument for a 'Visual ABC', a casebook of principles that would allow for the needs of modern life – housing development, road traffic, signage and much else to be accommodated in more aesthetically pleasing ways to begin to heal the damage done to rural and urban landscapes. The counterpart of the Townscape campaign, but its negative shadow, Subtopia, was to become a widely understood term and the theme of far wider debates, both in local communities and in Parliament.

New modernisms

With the argument for the acceptance of modern architecture won by its near-universal adoption by government bodies and city authorities, the *AR* developed its further series of critiques of what had been achieved at exactly the same time as Britain's buildings and cities were transformed in the image of modernism. Alongside these campaigns, an approach sympathetic to the modern and innovative current work in Britain and abroad was comprehensively documented: Le Corbusier's Unité d'Habitation in Marseilles in May 1951, for example, and much work from Sweden and Brazil. But its commitment to the progressive continued to be leavened by the very particular visual sensibility that manifested in a modernist mining of history that shaped its ongoing search for meaningful form.

The *AR* promoted the 'New Empiricism' in Swedish architecture in the later 1940s: the term, invented by Hastings, effectively redefined functionalism to include that which had earlier been excluded, described as the 'psychology' of the users of the new architecture

FIGURE 5.7   Imperator project, São Paulo, Oscar Niemeyer, illustrating 'Brazilian Preview'. Journal cover, *The Architectural Review* (July 1953).
Source: The Architectural Review.

(*The Architectural Review*, June 1947). This was explored more fully in an influential article by de Maré, 'The new empiricism: the antecedents and origins of Sweden's latest style' (*The Architectural Review*, January 1948). Informality of plan and fenestration, the use of traditional materials often in combination, attention to landscaping and site relationships – as seen in the public and private work of contemporary Swedish architects including Sven Backström and Sune Lindström. Though this work was not intended as a return to the traditional, it might have appeared to be, as de Maré wrote:

> The justification that in their architectural tradition are many still relevant solutions to contemporary problems is well founded [...] it would be disastrous if those members of the public who but dimly understand the meaning of the great aesthetic revolution (and still they are legion) should get the idea that the new architecture has abdicated in favour of just one more traditional revival.
>
> *de Maré, 1948, p. 10*

But this revised interpretation of modernism certainly became established, and as modern development began in Britain, the brick wall and pitched roof suggested by these Swedish models were often to appear, with a dilution of the modernist aesthetic.

> The new objectivity was not always so objective, the houses did not function as well as had been expected [...]. The new human beings were not so different from the older ones. Man and his habits, recreations and needs are the focus of interest as never before.
>
> *de Maré, 1948, p. 10*

FIGURE 5.8   The Machine Aesthetic from J. M. Richards' 'The Next Step?'.
The Architectural Review (March 1950).
Source: *The Architectural Review*.

A wider critique was advanced in 'The next step?' an *AR* article of 1950 (Richards, 1950) illustrated with varied examples of recent work; here, Richards outlined the situation of younger architects for whom the modern architecture already established was not enough. After the vanquishing of stylistic historical revivals it was necessary to develop an equivalent of their aesthetic strengths within the language of modernism. 'Literal' functionalism, he argues, 'never could and never did exist', but the work of those who simply followed that of the architects who originated modernism was lacking in real architectural qualities and had, he admitted, been subject to no real criticism in the pre-war period. As well as the 'empirical' tendency, Richards identifies the alternative directions of the 'machine aesthetic', 'post-cubist', 'diagrammatic' and 'regional organic', illustrated with built examples from the late 1940s.

He writes that the former (in itself a precursor of so-called 'High Tech') has an unwelcome neutrality devoid of human qualities, while the 'organic', expressing aspects of the familiar, represents the repudiation of modernist rigour in favour of creating visual effects, and the 'new empiricism' may move into the sentimental. He concludes with the assertion that architecture's primary responsibility is to accurately represent the social meaning of its time, and that anything else is simply rhetoric: but rather than simple functionalism, what is needed is a direct expression of the particular, in its 'time, place and purpose'. He seems reluctant to agree with, for example, the enthusiasm of Sigfried Giedion on Alvar Aalto, published in *AR* the previous month (Giedion, 1950), that the individual might develop their own expressive architecture within modernist practice: instead, a more finely tuned rational approach should triumph.

The New Town building programme[8] was generally seen as one of the great and unambiguous achievements in postwar Britain, but it was comprehensively condemned at an early stage of its realisation in an article by Richards, who described its failure in social and economic as well as architectural terms (Richards, 1953). While their scale dwarfed the achievement in new building elsewhere in Britain, for Richards the New Towns represented a travesty of the possibilities of a new urbanism: the creation of vast low-density estates on a garden city model made for meaningless space and an acute lack of identity. And, he concluded, was a 'failure of modern architecture itself'. Accompanied by a visual study of the towns' urban deficiencies by Gordon Cullen, it was one of the most controversial of Richards' texts but underlined the journal's consistency in arguing for a specifically British modern architecture that could engage and enrich society, which the massive missed opportunity of the New Town building programme emphatically did not: a second wave of New Town building including the unbuilt Hook (London County Council, 1962) were to address the specific concerns that Richards raised.

Seen more positively were two major projects of the early 1950s, the building of the Festival of Britain, a celebratory national cultural exhibition on the London South Bank and the subject of a special issue in August 1951, preceded by an issue on the permanent structure of the Royal Festival Hall in June 1951. The Hall is discussed in a critical essay by Richards, who is impressed by a building that is truly modern but is also monumental. Its highly inventive section, where the auditorium is raised above ground level as an 'egg in a box' with circulation spaces all around it, its careful materiality and detailing, its variations on symmetry, are approved of more than the composition of the river facade, but it is described as 'without precedent in this country' as a successful modern public building. The overall planning of the site of the Festival, with its irregularity, contrasts of scale, and elements of sur-prise is seen as an example of

FIGURE 5.9 'Failure of the New Towns' drawing by Gordon Cullen.
The Architectural Review (July 1953).
Source: The Architectural Review.

the Picturesque theory [that] has been followed with triumphant results. That is the great contribution of the exhibition to contemporary architecture; it demonstrates how successfully the informal principle of town-planning, so well rooted in the English countryside, can be transplanted to the English urban landscape.

Richards, 1951, p. 75

The site, broken up into a sequence of enclosed spaces, and with its appropriation both of the adjacent Thames and distant views of such buildings as the Houses of Parliament, is described as modelled on the design of eighteenth-century landscapes. The buildings are described in terms that reflect *AR*'s contemporary preoccupations, in the attention to street furniture and lettering, and as embodying aspects of the Functional Tradition and 'nautical style', and overall certainly not conforming to the idea of a modern architecture that was dull and restrained. The Festival was a popular success, although criticised elsewhere as lacking in seriousness but – and the *AR* was partially responsible – it shaped much architecture and design in the following decade.

The Coventry Cathedral competition was also a major event in British architecture in the postwar years and the debates over both the competition brief and its assessment were particularly contentious: for the editors of *AR* it presented a prime opportunity to demonstrate that, against voluble opposition, modern architecture could become both admired and meaningful in such a symbolically loaded situation, replacing a cathedral destroyed in war. The winning entry by Basil Spence was greeted by Richards (1952) with the faintest of praise: while Spence had avoided a pastiche of the Gothic style, the inconsistent relationship of visible interior structure with the exterior wall along with other aspects of the design were summed up as 'arbitrary and capricious'. By the time it was completed it appeared anachronistic – for 1962, certainly not modern enough – but a critical account by Furneaux Jordan (1962) was at pains to point out its fulfilment of a profound symbolic brief of Christian resurrection, and at least allow for its expression of a coming together of form and feeling. But Coventry may also be

FIGURE 5.10   Festival of Britain, South Bank, London: view across site to the Transport Pavilion. *The Architectural Review* (August 1951).
Source: RIBA Collections.

seen as highly representative of the *AR*'s desire for a modern architecture that was, in the end, neither doctrinaire nor unpopular.

Banham: the rigour of the new avant-garde

As the 1950s developed, the *AR* was increasingly open to new cultural directions, and a greater plurality can be seen emerging from the editorial interventions of Nairn, Ian McCallum and, in particular, Reyner Banham, on the staff as an assistant editor from 1952 (see Whiteley, 2002). His unambiguous but nuanced conviction that modernism was essential in the modern world characterised his contributions from the beginning, and certainly distinguished his work from the more opaque and mannered writing of his senior colleagues. His early articles on recent building – 'Italian eclectic' (1952a) and 'The Voysey inheritance' (1952b) – were his first in a very long and illustrious career devoted to iconoclastic architectural criticism, while he later contributed important and original texts on modernist architectural history that related to his concurrent PhD studies (later a book, Banham, 1960a), producing work on Mendelsohn in 1954, Sant'Elia in 1955, and Loos' theory in 1957.

But Banham's 1955 article on the 'The New Brutalism' went very far beyond the *AR*'s usual concerns: it was a highly perceptive discussion that introduced his definition of the neologism: 'Memorability as image, clear exhibition of structure, valuation of materials as found.' He begins by discussing the term itself, which is both a campaigning banner and a historian's label: the use of 'new' opens up a historical perspective (as well as being a response to the 'new empiricism'). The echoes of both 'béton brut' and 'art brut' are contained in 'Brutalism' which for him essentially is about 'image': the building as an 'immediately apprehensible visual identity… confirmed by experience of the building in use', which is holistically the product of its functions and materials (Banham 1955b, pp. 355–361). The contemporary art work of Jackson Pollock, Eduardo Paolozzi and Nigel Henderson is seen as expressing a new material aesthetic: their relationship to processes of building remains somewhat tentative, but Louis Kahn's Yale Gallery, as well as the Smithsons' work, including the Hunstanton School and projects for Soho and Sheffield are seen as embodying a quite new approach and aesthetic.

The introduction through Banham of the characters of a new avant-garde seems utterly different from the discussion of Townscape, the Picturesque, or the poor design of housing estates: but perhaps the buildings presented by the *AR* as expressive of the Functional Tradition may be seen also as quite closely related to the new sense of materiality and developing aesthetic of Brutalism: a 'memorability of image, clear exhibition of structure, valuation of materials as found' was equally true of de Maré's images of old industrial structures. Banham later wrote critically about the apparent 'picturesque' aesthetic in Smithson projects: 'it is difficult to see how the Smithsons' insistence on "accepting the realities of the situation" as put into effect in their Berlin project [Haupstadt, 1957], really differed from the Picturesque injunction to "consult the genius of the place in all"' (Banham, 1966, p. 74). The Smithsons indeed used Cullen, the visualiser of Townscape, for drawings of their built Economist project (Cullen, 1965, p. 115), perhaps proving Banham's point.

Reyner Banham, writing in *AR* in 1960, makes a fitting coda to this discussion, and a demonstration of a shift which had certainly not been prefigured in the issue of January 1950, marking the beginning of the previous decade. In a text 'Stocktaking: tradition and technology', he introduced a strict new interpretation of functionalism:

FIGURE 5.11   From 'The New Brutalism', Reyner Banham. *The Architectural Review*
(December 1955).
Source: The Architectural Review.

Architecture, as a service to human societies, can only be defined as the provision of fit environments for human activities. The word 'fit' may be defined in the most generous terms imaginable, but it still does not necessarily imply the erection of buildings. Environments may be made fit for human beings by any number of means […]. Architecture, indeed, began with the first furs worn by our earliest ancestors, or with the discovery of fire – it shows a narrowly professional frame of mind to refer its beginnings solely to the cave or primitive hut.

Banham, 1960b, p. 93

Banham's article expressed the real possibility of starting afresh with the eternal problems of building houses and creating cities. For him and for many of his contemporaries, this exciting potential was the result of transformations in technology, enabling the making of structures in ways inconceivable even in the recent past. The article, remarkably written as two parallel texts – 'tradition' and 'technology' – presents on the one hand the way that the tradition of architecture has recently developed, with such tendencies as the revivals of classical geometries, neo-expressionism and even neo-modernism. In the parallel text he puts forward the alternative – the radical material and structural advances of the time. Concrete shells, fibreglass and lightweight space frames have, as yet, he admits, hardly effected any change in the practice of architecture. For him the provocation of technology demands a response from architecture: Banham warns that existing ways of working in architecture cannot accommodate the changes in environmental servicing and building construction. Architecture was on the threshold of something entirely new, not at all dependent on tradition: an architecture based on serving the needs of human activities, in fact the *opposite* of architecture as it had

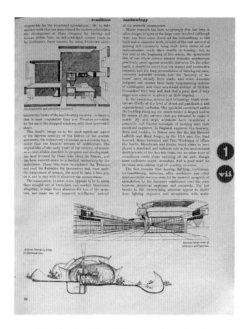

FIGURE 5.12   From 'Stocktaking' Tradition and Technology, Reyner Banham.
The Architectural Review (February 1960).
Source: *The Architectural Review.*

been practised. He admonishes architects in a manner reminiscent of Le Corbusier's polemic in *L'Esprit Nouveau* 40 years earlier, for their overindulgent concerns with style and their blindness to the technological transformations around them.

After leaving the *AR* staff in 1964, Banham argued against the journal and its reiterated concerns that their position seemed to 'justify, even sanctify, a willingness to compromise every "real" architectural value, to surrender to all that was most provincial and second rate in British social and intellectual life' (Banham, 1966, p. 13). A critique by Joseph Rykwert was published in 1959 of the planning strategy advocated by the *AR*, in other words Townscape:

> the weakness at the foundations of the *Review* is a concern for surface and a neglect for structure. This is true at every level: in the matter of town planning, to take the salient instance, the *Review* is concerned with traffic signs, the pattern of advertising, street furniture […] street surfacing, all the paraphernalia of Townscape occupy infinitely more space than the […] speculative or even strictly technical aspects of the subject.
>
> *Rykwert, 1959, p. 13*

Putting both the credit and blame for this in the hands of the 'visualisations' by Gordon Cullen, he says that these vociferous campaigns actually had little effect on the contemporary development of British towns and cities, the 'failure to register an influence on the bulk of current architecture'.

Taking a contrary view, Banham wrote, looking back at the period, of the 'revenge of the Picturesque' (Banham, 1968), as if to say that despite its deficiencies as a programme for modern architecture, it had been ultimately successful and the growth of building conservation, the valuing of mediocre historic buildings and the design of neo-vernacular housing estates at a high density would seem to prove his point. But his own influence as the theoretical precursor of 'High Tech' architecture – architecture that was meant to efface form and primarily provide enhanced servicing for human activities – was soon to develop beyond the imagination of Banham and his initial followers. And the *AR* itself lost its role as the primary British architectural journal during the 1960s, to be supplanted by a revived *Architectural Design*,[9] which had a currency and relevance for a younger generation; here, technologically inflected and certainly un-picturesque work would be reflected and would thrive at the *AR*'s expense. James Richards, who had fought so hard for the development of British modern architecture through his editorship of the journal from the 1930s to the early 1970s was to shock his RIBA audience with an admission of its failure in *The Hollow Victory*, at the 'Annual Discourse' of 1972, and its inability to achieve its ideals, concluding that 'the environment is too important to be left at the mercy of architects' (Richards, 1972).

Notes

1   *The Architectural Review* was founded as *The Architectural Review: a Magazine for the Artist, Archaeologist, Designer and Craftsman* in London in 1896 and soon replaced *The Builder*, founded in 1843, which had dominated the professional architectural press through the Victorian period as the leading journal in Great Britain.
2   See Higgott (2007a, pp. 33–57) on *AR* in the 1930s.
3   'Sharawaggi' is a term inspired by the informal qualities of Chinese landscape design, and used in the eighteenth century.
4   The author argues that Hastings was influenced by T.S. Eliot's 1948 essay 'Notes towards the definition of culture'.
5   The 'Exploring Eye' is a short section published in many *AR* issues of the period, two contrasting 1959 examples being February (p. 105) on Charles Eames' toy-machine for ALCOA and June (p. 415) on vernacular tower buildings in southern Arabia.
6   The MARS group was founded in 1933 as the British counterpart of CIAM to further the modernist cause, and is reflected in the approach of the 1930s *AR*.
7   Walter Gropius was a major influence on *AR* in the later 1930s. His book *The New Architecture and the Bauhaus* was published in London in 1935 and became the most read book on modern architecture in Britain in that period.
8   The 'New Town' building programme was instituted by the British government in 1946 to build new autonomous communities outside London and other cities: Harlow, Stevenage and Crawley are early examples.
9   *Architectural Design* published in London, and edited by Monica Pigeon, was primarily shaped by its so-called technical editors from 1954, successively Theo Crosby, Kenneth Frampton and Robin Middleton.

Bibliography

Aitchison, M. (Ed.) (2010). *Visual Planning and the Picturesque: Nikolaus Pevsner.* Los Angeles: Getty.
The Architectural Review (1944). Exterior furnishing or *Sharawaggi*: the art of making urban landscape. *The Architectural Review*, January, pp. 6–7.
—— (1947). The second half century. *The Architectural Review*, January, pp. 21–36.
—— (1947). New empiricism. *The Architectural Review*, June, pp. 199–204.
—— (1950). The Functional Tradition. *The Architectural Review*, January, pp. 1–66.
—— (1951a). Le Corbusier's Unité d'Habitation. *The Architectural Review*, May, pp. 292–300.
—— (1951b). South Bank Exhibition. *The Architectural Review*, August, pp. 71–138.

Architect's Journal (1964). New Building for the Economist. Architect's Journal, 16 December, pp. 193–196.

Banham, R. (1952a). Italian Eclectic. *The Architectural Review*, October, pp. 215–217.

—— (1952b). Voysey Inheritance. *The Architectural Review*, December, pp. 366–371.

—— (1954; 1955a; 1957). Mendelsohn; Sant' Elia; Loos. *The Architectural Review*, August, pp. 84–93; May, pp. 295–301; February, pp. 85–88.

—— (1955b). The New Brutalism. *The Architectural Review*, December, pp. 355–361.

—— (1960a). *Theory and Design in the First Machine Age*. London: Architectural Press.

—— (1960b). Stocktaking: Tradition and Technology. *The Architectural Review*, February, pp. 93–100.

—— (1965). The Economist buildings, St. James's. *The Architectural Review*, February, pp. 115–124.

—— (1966). *The New Brutalism: Ethic or Aesthetic?* London: Architectural Press.

—— (1968). Revenge of the picturesque: English architectural polemics 1945–65. In, J. Summerson (Ed.), *Concerning Architecture*. London: Penguin Press, pp. 265–273.

Cullen, G. (1949). Townscape Casebook. *The Architectural Review*, December, pp. 363–374.

—— (1953a). Prairie Planning in the New Towns. *The Architectural Review*, July, pp. 33–36.

—— (1953b). 'Midland Experiment' Ludlow. *The Architectural Review*, September, pp. 169–175.

—— (1953c). Bewdley (by D Dewar Mills). *The Architectural Review*, November, pp. 319–324.

—— (1953d). Evesham. *The Architectural Review*, February, pp. 127–131.

—— (1954). Shrewsbury. *The Architectural Review*, May, pp. 322–330.

—— (1961). *Townscape*. London: Architectural Press.

Darley, G. and McKie, D. (2013). *Ian Nairn: Words in Place*. Nottingham: Five Leaves Publications.

De Maré, E. (1948). New Empiricism. *The Architectural Review*, January, pp. 9–22.

—— (1949). Canals. *The Architectural Review*, July, pp. 1–64.

—— (1950). *The Canals of England*. London: Architectural Press.

De Wolfe, I. (1949). Townscape. *The Architectural Review*, December, pp. 355–362.

Erten, E. (2010). The 'hollow victory' of modern architecture and the quest for the vernacular. In P. Guillery (Ed.), *Built from Below: British Architecture and the Vernacular*. Abingdon: Routledge.

—— (2004). Shaping 'The Second Half Century': the Architectural Review, 1947–1971. PhD dissertation, Cambridge, MA, MIT.

—— (2015). Townscape as a project and strategy of cultural continuity. In J. Pendlebury, E. Erten and J. Larkham (Eds), *Alternative Visions of Postwar Reconstruction* (pp. 35–53). London: Routledge.

Giedion, S. (1950). Alvar Aalto. *The Architectural Review*, February, pp. 77–84.

Gosling, D. (1996). *Gordon Cullen: Visions of Urban Design*. London: Academy Editions.

Higgott, A. (2007a). The Mission of Modernism. In A. Higgott, *Mediating Modernism: Architectural Cultures in Britain*. London: Routledge, pp. 33–57.

—— (2007b). The shift to the specific. In A. Higgott, *Mediating Modernism: Architectural Cultures in Britain* (pp. 86–116). London: Routledge.

—— (2016). Eric de Maré: Between the Functional and the Beautiful. *The Journal of Architecture*, 21 (6) pp. 873–889.

Hussey, C. (1927). *The Picturesque: Studies in a Point of View*. London: Putnam.

Jordan, R. F. (1962). Cathedral Church of St Michael Coventry. *The Architectural Review*, July, pp. 24–42.

London County Council (1962). *The Planning of a New Town*. London: LCC.

Macarthur, J. (2007). *The Picturesque: Architecture, Disgust and Other Irregularities*. London: Routledge.

Nairn, I. (Ed.) (1955a). Outrage. *The Architectural Review*, June.

—— (Ed.) (1955b). *Outrage*. London: Architectural Press.

—— (1956). Counter-attack. *The Architectural Review*, December, pp. 354–438.

Parnell, S. (2011). *Architectural Design 1954–1972*. Unpublished PhD thesis, Sheffield University.

Pevsner, N. (1944). Genesis of the Picturesque. *The Architectural Review*, November, pp. 139–146.

—— (1954). C20 Picturesque. *The Architectural Review*, April, pp. 227–229.

Piper, J. (1947). Pleasing Decay. *The Architectural Review*, September, pp. 85–94.

Richards, J. M. (1950). The Next Step. *The Architectural Review*, March, pp. 165–181.

—— (1951). The Royal Festival Hall. *The Architectural Review*, June, pp. 335–394.

—— (1952). Coventry. *The Architectural Review*, January, pp. 3–7.

—— (1953). Failure of the New Towns. *The Architectural Review*, July, pp. 28–32.

—— (1957). The Functional Tradition as Shown in Early Industrial Buildings. *The Architectural Review*, August, pp. 3–73.

—— (1958). *The Functional Tradition in Early Industrial Buildings*. London: Architectural Press.

—— (1972). The Hollow Victory: 1932–1972. *RIBA Journal*, May, pp. 192–197.

Rykwert, J. (1959). Review of a Review. *Zodiac*, 4, pp. 13–14.

Stirling, J. (1960). The Functional Tradition and Expression. *Perspecta*, 6, pp. 88–97.

Whiteley, N. (2002). *Reyner Banham: Historian of the Immediate Future*. Cambridge, MA: MIT Press.

6

AXE OR MIRROR?

Architectural journals in postwar Hungary

András Ferkai

At a decisive moment in the history of *Magyar Építőművészet* (*MÉ*; Hungarian Architecture), the official journal of the Association of Hungarian Architects, the editor-in-chief stunned the audience of a conference with the following metaphor:

> In the movie *The Rainmaker*, a spinsterish woman character is told: 'You will be beautiful, whenever you see yourself as beautiful in the eyes of a man'. We hoped that, if the Hungarian architecture sees itself as beautiful in the mirror of our journal, this would be beneficial to its development.
>
> *Bonta, 1961*

These sentences shed light on a position hardly known in the West, where architectural journals have their own editorial policies, that is, with an individual character in the international marketplace. In contrast, journals of the former Eastern Bloc had acquired the lone role of representing the whole architectural production of a country. Even if published by a professional institution, they had to exceed partisan interest. Another peculiarity of the quotation is the belief that the task of a journal is to change architecture instead of presenting or analysing it objectively. Of course, most editors have an idea of good architecture or promote some tendencies, but this degree of solicitude is something more, the operative attitude of a Marxist theorist. Postwar reconstruction had been intertwined with politics and ideology everywhere in Europe, yet, it is impossible to discuss, in the satellite states of the former Soviet Bloc, reconstruction strategies and their reflection in the architectural press itself. Planning and architecture were an integral part of the state-orchestrated modernisation programmes, but professionals could affect these only to various degrees in different periods. In the same way, editors of architectural journals were given different grades of independence. While they were hopelessly subordinated to the political establishment in the Stalinist era, it seems more useful to focus on the preceding and succeeding periods of transition. In the first (1945–1949), several concepts would compete within the ever-narrowing battlefield of the coalition years, while de-Stalinisation gave architects relative autonomy again in the second (1956–1963). Complete dismissal of the period in between, however, would be misleading since the totalitarian model was, after all, one option among different postwar strategies of reconstruction. This chapter will examine the issue of modernisation through scrutiny of Hungarian architectural journals: three from the first period and one that bridged the second and the third periods.

Reconstruction and engagement: journals and party struggles (1945–1949)

The first phase of postwar reconstruction in Hungary occurred under the direction of coalition governments and the circumstances of a capitalism gradually restricted by waves of nationalisation. As in other Eastern European countries that had fallen under the Soviet sphere of influence after the war, democratic rules prevailed until the outbreak of the Cold War. Once Cominform was established and began to tighten the bonds between these countries and the USSR, a rapid Sovietisation commenced which radically changed political conditions. The small Hungarian Communist Party (HCP)[1] strengthened its position and, step by step, ground down the opposition parties and even its coalition partners. The method of discrediting leaders of rival parties as 'reactionaries', forcing their resignation from the government and, if necessary, prompting their arrest by the security police, was a Soviet practice. The Independent Smallholders' Party, a leading force of the first coalition that had attained an absolute majority at the first free election was, together with other bourgeois parties, expelled from the parliament by the end of 1947. The last step for assuming full control was the enforced merging of the Social Democratic Party (SDP) with the HCP in June 1948, forming the Hungarian Workers' Party (HWP). In the summer of 1949, the ratification of a Soviet-style constitution consecrated the one-party system with a central command economy promoted by large-scale nationalisation.

This period strongly affected the practice of architecture and encouraged for the first time the ambition that architects could participate in reshaping the totality of the built environment. Since severe war damage, shortage of materials and hyperinflation did not favour private practices, many migrated to the political parties as well as to the state and municipal administration. Along with the ministries, the Budapest Municipal Board of Public Works (FKT)[2] offered architects the opportunity to influence the work of reconstruction. A leading figure of modern architecture in the interwar years, József Fischer (1901–1995) was appointed chair of FKT and the government commissioner for reconstruction. Fischer, the former 'second' delegate of the Hungarian CIAM section and an established member of the SDP, was a nominee of his party to these key positions. The role of FKT was limited to the capital city and its agglomeration but, as a commissioner, Fischer could lay claim to affect reconstruction policies nation-wide. While keeping the majority of the staff at FKT, he employed new planners and architects who could counterbalance the conservativism of the former by their commitment to hardline functionalism and the Athens Charter. The first visions of postwar reconstructions were forged in and around CIAM. The reason we are rather well informed about these visions is due to the first postwar architectural journal *Tér és Forma* (*TF*; Space and Form) being published by FKT and edited by Fischer.[3]

TF was not new, but the continuation of an internationally significant avant-garde journal of the interwar years. The founding editor Virgil Bierbauer (1893–1956) was responsible from 1928 to 1942 until drafted into military service, when he passed on his post to Fischer and an editorial board who would work until October 1944.

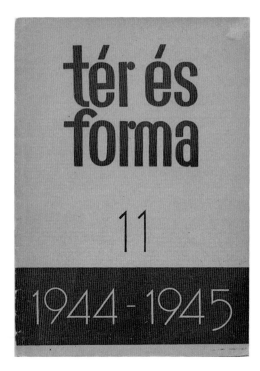

FIGURE 6.1   Journal cover, *Tér és Forma* 11 (1944–1945).

Issue 11, which had been ready to print, could not come out because of the Nazi-sponsored military coup and the subsequent siege of Budapest. It was eventually published in October 1945 with both years, 1944 and 1945, listed on the cover. This issue contained a programme that the editors had formulated during the war about future tasks that Hungarian architects would need to accomplish in the course of postwar reconstruction. The signees represented the most significant modernists of the pre-war architectural elite. Fischer and Máté Major (1904– 1986) belonged to the Hungarian CIAM section whose activity was temporarily suspended in 1938.[4] Pál Rihmer-Granasztói (1908–1985), a specialist in urbanism and a prolific writer; Jenő Kismarty-Lechner Jr (1908–1992) and János Weltzl (1912–1945) had all contributed articles to maintain the momentum of modern architecture in a hostile atmosphere. The declaration outlined tasks that modern and socially committed architects opposed to the previous regime would expect of 'a new, more progressive societal and economical system'. A prerequisite was, in their view, a comprehensive national office for the field of building and architecture that had the necessary entitlement, and would act 'without bias, political affiliations, according to purely professional considerations' (Fischer et al. 1944–1945). With the 'twin-institute' headed by Fischer, the latter condition was met. The photographs with which the declaration was illustrated revealed what kind of architecture was imagined as the basis for reconstruction.[5]

Postwar conditions precluded other than a low-cost journal. Fischer, as the editor, was aided by only two people: a technical editor inherited from the previous publisher and an acting editor.[6] The new *TF* could not compete with its prestigious earlier volumes. A slender monthly journal wrapped in brown paper with an unimpressive printed-text cover reported on the redevelopment of bombed out cities all over Europe (including the County of London Plan; Forshaw and Abercrombie, 1943), industrialisation of the building process and examples

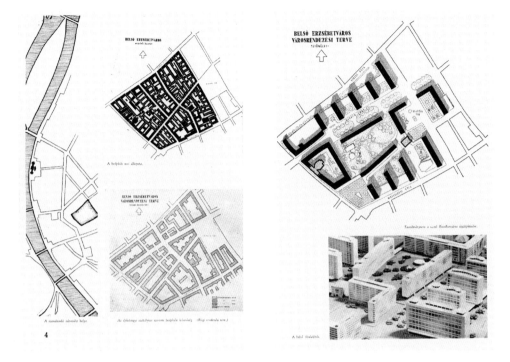

FIGURE 6.2   Reconstruction plans for the inner Elisabeth Town district
of Budapest. *Tér és Forma* 1–3 (1946).

of prefabricated houses. Given lack of construction,[7] the Hungarian section consisted mostly
of urban plans and winning entries of architectural competitions together with several theoretical essays.

The primary focus of the journal stemmed from the obligation of FKT to prepare the general plan of Greater Budapest with the revision of the 1940 development plan. The planners
and architects gathered around Fischer could rightfully feel that the devastation of the war
provided, if not a tabula rasa, then fundamentally changed physical and social conditions for
a large-scale reshaping of the urban structure of the city. Earlier in 1945, entries for an ideas
competition proposed, for instance, the transformation of Budapest into a linear city or a
'city of four angles' with four sub-centres 'discharging' the central core (Vadas, 1985). The
new master plan more moderately envisaged changes in functional zoning and traffic regu-
lation, and local interventions such as the redevelopment of the riversides; transformation of
Marguerite Island into a spa and hotel area; and the slum clearance of some inner districts.
The pre-war perimeter block system was rejected in favour of freestanding slabs adrift in a
continuous green landscape.

The plan of the inner Elisabeth Town district, fundamentally changing the townscape and
street pattern of the former Jewish quarter, was apparently inspired by Le Corbusier's *ilot
insalubre* and the Civic Centre of the Future project by F. R. S. Yorke and Marcel Breuer.
However, the urgent task of simply providing citizens with shelter hampered the realisation
of these plans.

It is somewhat surprising that in these lean years another architectural journal was launched.
The first issue of *Új Építészet* (*ÚÉ*; New Architecture) was published in September 1946 by the

Free Trade Union of Engineers and Technicians, as a supplement to an existing technical journal. The reason why this second periodical was needed is revealed in retrospect by one of the editors:

> We older and neophyte communists, did not feel [it] acceptable that the only professional journal of the new country was edited by Social-Democrats[8] and, in that journal we could not be more than co-participants.
>
> *Major, 2001, p. 141*

The author, Máté Major, was one of the signatories of the 1944 declaration, having returned from the Soviet Union in November 1945. His editor-companion, Imre Perényi (1913–2002), returned earlier in August 1945.[9] Both joined the HCP on their return. They prepared the first issue in secret because Fischer was their employer as well as president of the trade union. To make the new journal more acceptable, Major and Perényi invited a renowned architect of the older generation, Lajos Kozma (1884–1948), who also worked in the modernist idiom though never belonged to the avant-garde,[10] to join the editorial board. The list of editors thus included three names, and Perényi acted as editor-in-chief.

The editorial note written for the first issue, entitled 'To the architects of Hungary!' and signed by Major, clarified the policy of *ÚÉ*. It is impossible to cope with the complex task of reconstruction, he declared, unless we 'liberate the field of building from the economic and legal constraints of a narrow private interest and architects from the intellectual prison of a disappearing society that they take for an ivory tower' (Major, 1946). The overt attack on capitalism and the faith that politics must pervade everything was consonant with the programme of the HCP, and imbued the activity of the Circle of New Architecture[11] that before long formed around the journal. The militant standpoint provoked a prompt answer in *TF*, where Granasztói expressed his disagreement. He refuted the argument that 'ideologies and doctrines' should determine the work of an architect and lacked the use of the terms 'professionalism and realism' in Major's text (Granasztói, 1946). Given the indignation that Major provoked in the profession, his reply to the 'devotees of anti-political professionalism' was conciliatory in tone (Major, 1947), and affirmed that a new journal might help illuminate important issues for discussion. Indeed, the two journals did not differ much in their commitment to modern architecture. Although the HCP and SDP were allies, the former strove to gain ground at the latter's expense,[12] which had its consequences for the journal's prospects. While Fischer edited *TF* under deteriorating circumstances, the trade union generously financed the journal of the communist architects. *ÚÉ* had an editorial board of six people from November 1947 onwards,[13] although members of the Circle also contributed.

The elaborate colourful cover, with a full-size picture fitted into a Constructivist frame[14] and its considered typography, combined to make *ÚÉ* an attractive journal. Despite publishing articles on urban and large-scale planning, construction and organisational matters, it was definitely architecture that dominated the initial issues. They offered the reader a valuable repository of the architectural ideas and production envisaged in the first three-year plan (1947–1949). Along with projects for individual public buildings such as polyclinics, trade union headquarters, schools or the grand national stadium, they published the first projects for the standardisation of housing prepared by the employees of a new (private) 'scientific' centre (ÉTK) founded by Imre Perényi in 1947.[15] The following year, when this centre was transformed into the first state architectural planning office, systematic work began to provide series of standard projects to be used in national economic plans.[16] Reference is generally made today to spectacular individual examples where it is easy to demonstrate direct influences of Le Corbusier or Brazilian architecture, while other modest structures that the architects managed to adapt to the landscape and rural traditions of the countryside are usually overlooked.[17] Both domains were represented in the journal, and revealingly two thematic issues were devoted to urban and rural reconstruction. The first was related to the exhibition of 'Housing in the City and the Village' (1947) initiated by the Arts Council and supported by the Ministry of Building and Public Works, while the other, 'New Csepel, the City of the Workers' (1948), was jointly executed by the Circle and ÉTK.

The first exhibition offered various solutions for housing provision in urban and rural contexts. The urban part, 60 posters from a total of 100, was prepared by Jenő Kismarty-Lechner, who published a handsome booklet on urban flat types (Kismarty-Lechner, 1947), together with 40 posters on rural proposals by Lajos Kozma,[18] editor of ÚÉ. His influence might be the reason for the exclusive review in the rural section of the journal where – after an introduction by Péter Veres, head of the Ministry of Building and Public Works and Under Secretary Virgil Bierbauer,[19] both members of the National Peasant Party – a series by communist architects followed. They elaborated all aspects of the topic, from village regulations and the functional analysis of ground plans, to furniture and the most appropriate building materials (Moravánszky, 2012; Perczel, 1947).[20] Though most projects followed traditional site planning and building form, the architects insisted on the difference that separated these unadorned and functional buildings from the romantic, neo-vernacular types built in

FIGURE 6.3 Journal cover, *Új Építészet*, 5 (1948).

the 1940s. The press roundup contrasted modern French and American agricultural colonies with the architecture of the Soviet *kolkhoz*, suggesting that the reworking of traditional house-types of the latter were closer to their aspirations. Many themes of the postwar reconstruction were already in fact published during or before the war. The ONCSA programme for housing large families in 1940–1944 used a set of standard projects and normalised building elements, utilising a methodology identified with the activity of the postwar housing cooperative OHÉSZ, who employed the same architects.

The other exhibition presented an ambitious project to reconstruct Csepel, an industrial town in the agglomeration of the capital city, soon to be incorporated into Greater Budapest. Dissatisfied with the piecemeal interventions within the master plan proposed by FKT, the communist architects traced the vision of a new socialist city. The team analysed traffic connections, functional zones, a possible schedule for realisation, and also prepared the design of virtually every necessary residential, communal and public building type. A revived version by Major of the 1931 CIAM collective house was also included.

Most projects represented full-blooded modernism, while some combined hardline functionalism with a visual language intended to dissolve the rigidity of the so-called International Style. Since this vision might seem a utopia to most people, Perényi hastened to note in his preface that New Csepel *is* a realistic project since 'the required economic and social conditions are partly given and partly coming into existence in the people's democracy of Hungary to warrant the reconstruction of Csepel' (Perényi, 1948a). And he was completely correct in this regard.

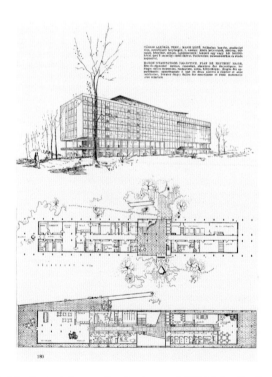

FIGURE 6.4 Project for a collective house, Máté Major for the Csepel redevelopment. *Új Építészet* 5 (1948).

As we have seen, the 'year of the turning' (1947–1948) reconstituted the political map of Hungary. As a consequence of these drastic measures, many politicians, intellectuals and architects left the country.[21] The FKT was disbanded by the communist mayor in February 1948 and, with Fischer's demise as chair, publication of *TF* also ceased with the second issue of that year.[22] In contrast, *ÚÉ* continued, moreover, obtaining state financial support. All the more surprising, then, that it could not escape the same fate a year later.[23] Anecdotes suggest that the real reason was the double issue dedicated to the deceased fellow editor Lajos Kozma, which was held by party leaders to epitomise the 'personal cult' of 'an architect of the capitalists' (Major, 2001, p. 141). The real motive was obviously different. The show-trials in progress during spring 1949 included the Circle of New Architecture; two members were sentenced to imprisonment.[24] On the other hand, the process of Sovietisation had progressed to the field of culture, and the new cultural policy required a break with 'cosmopolitan and decadent' modernism. Perényi forecasted these changes in 1948, with his afterword to the Csepel exhibition, and he was the first to pronounce that 'our art must stand on the theoretical base of the so-called Socialist Realism' (Perényi, 1948b). The editors and contributors of *ÚÉ* found themselves in a schizophrenic situation, where their professional judgement was confronted with stalwart political conviction.

The Stalinist dictatorship: interlude (1949–1956)

Postwar reconstruction was to become definitively detached from modern architecture, and the profession lost all its potency to influence planning throughout the Rákosi era. If we dwell on this transitory period it is first necessary to emphasise the critique of modernism that aspired to a healthy revisionism, and second to stress the fact that, while modern architecture could not survive in stylistic terms during the Stalinist period, modernisation as the principal aim behind forced industrialisation remained inherent in the process of reconstruction.

The third journal published postwar, *Építészet – Építés* (Architecture – Building), in contrast to the intellectual nature of *ÚÉ*, was conceived in a corporative spirit. Once reconstruction became equated with 'planning', visions were replaced by compliance to work plans and efficiency ruled; and the inclusion of engineers and construction workers in the editorial team was not so strange.[25] The reduction of building costs and the role of architecture as monumental propaganda are but two sides of the same coin. Despite the overt campaign in favour of Socialist Realism, buildings published in the first and second volumes of the journal remained modern.

Since criticism was deemed to be inefficient, the editor-in-chief (Major once again) initiated a series of articles on 'formalism' in architecture, a concept that in the hands of the party served to label someone as an agent of the enemy. Most texts were no more than indoctrinations (which did not apply to the illustrations and captions). It is revealing to discover fashionable, arbitrary or irrational details in interwar and early postwar architecture. This criticism, offered in a more democratic context, could have paved the way for a 'situated' modern architecture. The desire for this evolutionary path characterises the press reviews edited by Virgil Borbíró. No matter what source he selected for his examples (from mostly Western journals, sometimes Czech and Soviet ones), he could draw a lesson for Hungarian conditions. Czech housing projects prompted him to explain to the authorities the importance of analysing data before large-scale housing construction. Commenting on recent Western architecture, he warned Hungarians against copying idiosyncratic artistic forms, and expressed doubts about

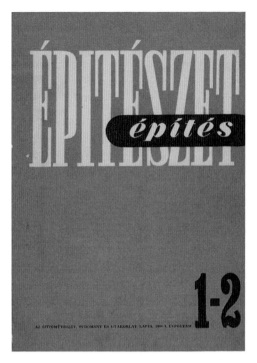

FIGURE 6.5   Journal cover, *Építészet Építés* 1–2 (1949).

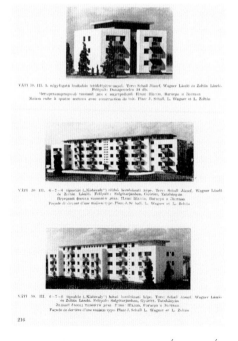

FIGURE 6.6   Models of 1950 housing types, *Építészet Építés* 4 (1951).

FIGURE 6.7   Cartoon for the debate on formalism, *Építészet Építés* 5 (1949).

the acrobatic structures of, for example, the Festival of Britain. He sympathised, in turn, with Scandinavian architects whose sober and humanistic way of building was considered a possible model for Hungarian reconstruction.[26]

The reluctance of Hungarian architects to practise Socialist Realism was broken by the so-called 'Great Architectural Debate' in the spring of 1951, with Imre Perényi cast in the role of the accuser and Máté Major, who still defended modern architecture, as the accused.[27] Subsequently the culture minister and notorieties such as the philosopher György Lukács declared themselves in favour of the new style and it became virtually impossible to resist. The Association of Hungarian Architects (MÉSZ) was established as a sign of unanimity and their new journal became a megaphone for official views. Since the building industry was identified with a separate journal, the album-like *MÉ* could deal exclusively with 'architectural art'. Its editor-in-chief between 1952 and 1956 was Tibor Weiner (1906–1965), a trustworthy communist[28] who assiduously mediated Stalinist theories and Soviet models. The aim of the reconstruction in this period was to transform a basically agrarian society into an industrial one with an emphasis on heavy and military industry. Consequently, investments were concentrated in industrial centres and those sectors that principally served the working class (or to a lesser extent collectivised agriculture). The journal published redevelopment plans for industrial towns (giving a high priority to the first socialist new town, Sztálinváros); housing in these centres using standard projects; industrial plants; vocational schools; technical universities and culture houses; all conceived primarily in a neoclassical style. Without wishing to reinterpret the Socialist Realist period, it is worth noting that along with the monumental axial compositions of Soviet town planning, Swedish neighbourhood units of the 1940s and the picturesque city planning theory of Sitte also served as a model. One even encounters some ideas close to the British Townscape movement. Industrial architecture, beyond serving as a refuge for those trying to escape Socialist Realism, became a laboratory for new structures and technologies. The ingenious on-site pre-casting system of the 1950s industrial plants contributed to the award of the Perret Prize to the Iparterv Planning Office in 1961 (Haba, 2012).

Return to the abandoned path or a new start? 1956–1963

The totalitarian regime of Rákosi was swept away by the October uprising and, though the revolution was crushed, his rule was not restored. The new Kádár regime has been typically interpreted in historiography as a version of state socialism with a human face, approaching the characteristic identity of Western welfare states. Recent studies argue that Kádárism was not an ideology in its own right, but only a shift within the system (Majtényi, 2013), since the 'base' (state property, centrally planned economy) and the power structure remained the same. Retribution and consolidation liquidated the workers' councils characteristic of a Yugoslavian form of self-management, together with other modes of direct democracy. Meanwhile, the compromise between the political power and popular opinion produced a more humane system for a large proportion of the population, with more freedom, new opportunities and rising living standards, but it also created a characteristic peaceful opportunism in Hungary.

In May 1956, the general assembly of MÉSZ dismissed most communist members of the management and opened up a new era for *MÉ* in electing fresh editorial staff. Jenő Juhász (1918–1999), the new editor-in-chief, was a celebrated architect from the state planning office for industrial buildings (Iparterv), who could keep both politics and Socialist Realism at a certain distance. His editorial programme underscored what he wanted to retain, and what to remove, noting: 'The journal strives after a modern, *real, socialist* and specifically Hungarian architecture' (Juhász, 1956). Notably his witty quibbling with the term *socialist realism* transformed it into a notion admissible in the new era, declaring consequently that the relation of the journal to the profession should be modified as well as its spirit, tone and format. This meant the refusal of dogmatic theories and the 'aristocratic character' of the previous volumes, in favour of a democratic attitude that paid respect to the voice of architects and the people. The journal pledged the contribution of architects to surveying needs and developing briefs,

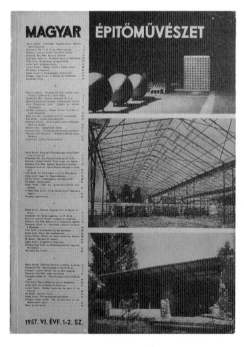

FIGURE 6.8   Journal cover, Magyar *Építőművészet* 1–2 (1957).
Source: Association of Hungarian Architects (MÉSZ).

before embarking on large-scale building programmes. The break with the past was manifest in the 'modern', colourful cover and in the revised content of the journal. A fresh and vivid tone continued in the next two years to promote a public openness towards various opinions and attitudes. The editor gave prominence to those marginalised in the Stalinist era, publishing the first buildings realised in modern spirit (from 1954–1955), as also inventive contemporary projects. Several ideas effaced in the Rákosi era were revived, such as the innovative light-weight building system of Béla Sámsondi-Kiss, developed from the late 1930s, that could have been a local and ingenious alternative to imported industrialised technologies (Sámsondi-Kiss, 1957; Sámsondi-Kiss and Farkas, 1950).[29]

Apparently the government counted on the proficiency of architects, given the evidence of the large number of competitions which were organised and new programmes launched, all of which the journal assiduously reported. Since housing was an effective way to increase living standards and thereby win over the wider population, the Kádár regime in 1958 ordered the drafting of a 15-year plan for building one million dwellings. To prepare a large-scale housing construction programme associated with industrial methods, a series of competitions were organised to procure design proposals for building and flat types, standardised furniture and building technologies.[30] The government also considered possibilities of supporting the construction of private houses and condominiums, including the residential infilling of vacant inner city bombsites. The latter task was a real challenge for architects to reconcile the vocabulary of modernism with existing urban neighbourhoods. To comply with the newfound desire of the population to spend leisure time privately, another 1958 competition offered schemes for small summer and weekend houses, meant to be produced as prefabricated structures

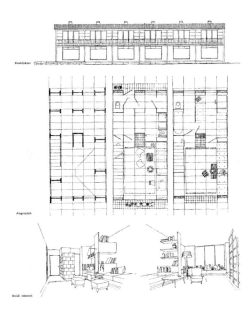

FIGURE 6.9   Project of an experimental terraced house, Béla Sámsondi-Kiss and
Tibor Farkas. *Magyar Építőművészet* 1–2 (1957).
Source: Association of Hungarian Architects (MÉSZ).

or proposed as an economic model for self-build. These years saw the implementation of the internationally renowned Balaton Lake Regional Plan (1957–1963)[31] that was awarded the Abercrombie Prize (of the UIA) in 1965. The journal also reported the first Hungarian attempts to export architectural expertise to the Third World,[32] and attempted to reframe the contested practice of designing generic projects for housing and communal buildings. Architects enthusiastically joined in this work and the experiments produced exceptional projects and realisations until around 1963.

The apparently positive changes at the journal had been overshadowed by publication difficulties. In 1957 only three double issues could be realised and, while 12 issues were envisaged for the next volume, only half were in fact published in the three issues contracted. The delay was due partly to financial problems, partly to an overburdened editorial team that consisted of only one full-time and one part-time position. Without a full editorial board, Juhász occasionally involved fellow architects to contribute. These deficiencies led to his stepping down in 1959. Máté Major was appointed as the president of a renewed editorial board, in which architects who opposed the Stalinist regime featured along with longstanding communists such as János Bonta, Imre Perényi and Tibor Weiner. Coinciding with the final year of retributions, there is a tendency to regard these changes as a restoration of sorts, not least that of party control.

In 1960, when Bonta (1921–) replaced Juhász, the financing and publication problems were resolved and *MÉ* continued as a bi-monthly journal. With the return of Major and Bonta, however, the Marxist viewpoint was revived and leading articles contradicted the professed modernisation of the journal. Nevertheless, *MÉ* and its mediated image of Hungarian architecture played a considerable part in the election of Hungary as a voting member of the council of the UIA (1959) and Major's role on the jury of the newly founded Perret and Abercrombie Prizes (1960) (Major, 1960). Despite this, the account Bonta gave to the general assembly of MÉSZ in 1961 was self-critical and full of doubts. He explained the metaphor of the beautifying mirror that opened this chapter: 'We do not promote the case of Hungarian architecture since if the journal pictures it as more beautiful than it actually is, this will tend to play down errors. Yet a periodical cannot be critical unless the critical spirit flourishes in the larger context, too' (Bonta, 1961). Nonetheless he saw no sign of this within the confines of professional life. In fact, debates did take place in the daily or weekly papers or monthly journals of the cultural media (Simon, 2013a, 2013b) rather than *MÉ*, which was slow to respond. The voice of popular opinion or of lay intellectuals consequently did not appear in the journal, and sporadic disputes remained esoteric. Bonta, who at the time saw contemporary Hungarian architecture as 'chaotic' and 'provincial' (Bonta, 1961), did in fact make an attempt at a debate. Instead of starting from local circumstances, he analysed modern Western architecture on a purely theoretical level, aiming for a Marxist interpretation. Despite some intelligent critical remarks, his conclusion that the modern movement had lost its 'progressive' face – arguing that the Seagram Building and the Chapel at Ronchamp were but extreme manifestations of the contradictory nature of capitalism – is quite weak. Apart from two invited and one voluntary contributors, nobody joined the debate in the *MÉ* .

This was regrettable since 'the return of modern architecture and technology raised a number of questions: about the relationship between capitalist and socialist modern architecture, about that between modern architecture and national traditions, and about the relative position of architecture between the sciences and the arts'[33] (Simon, 2013a). Bonta tried to resolve the controversial resemblance of new Hungarian architecture to modern Western tendencies in emphasising 'social content' – the first criterion of Socialist Realism – while replacing the second, 'national form', with 'mass-production'. His younger colleague, Elemér Nagy, also found technology decisive, but only when based 'on the grounds of our own conditions' (Nagy, 1960). Unlike many of his contemporaries, Nagy did not mean local or national traditions in that regard, but an alternative to industrialisation. The 'new craft' he proposed speculatively was an alloy of engineering, technology and art, to be found in the works of Charles Eames, Tapio Wirkkala and Konrad Wachsmann.

When a considerable proportion of Hungarian architects drew inspiration from Scandinavian, Japanese or English modern architecture, some inevitably raised the issue of national character. It is strange that this eminently contemporary problem was first raised in articles that tried to reinterpret, sometimes actualise, Art Nouveau and National Romanticism – past tendencies rejected by modernism. Imre Kathy, an admirer of the latter style, was convinced that any internationally significant novelty could only be based on tradition (Kathy, 1960).[34] He propounded the example of Japan, where modern architecture imported from Europe was soon transformed into a particular 'style' meeting the physical and spiritual needs of the Japanese (Kathy, 1963). Vernacular building, he claimed, should not be considered a source of borrowing forms but a model for adapting to the ever-changing needs and possibilities (Kathy, 1961). This down-to-earth mentality reverberated from several articles and a good many buildings realised in the 1960s.

A new era of the journal began in 1962 with Elemér Nagy (1928–1985), who initially contributed to the journal as a graphic editor and to whom the *MÉ* logo, a permanent element of the cover from 1960, is also credited. He aspired to fall into line with illustrious

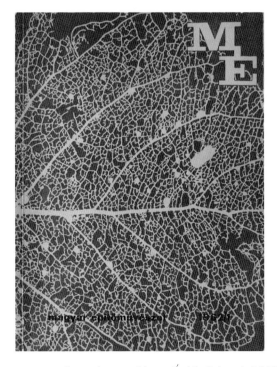

FIGURE 6.10   Journal cover, *Magyar Építőművészet* 1 (1962).
Source: Association of Hungarian Architects (MÉSZ).

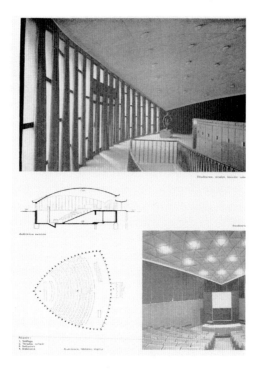

journals like *The Architectural Review, Architectural Design* and *L'Architecture d'Aujourdhui*, but the logo also hid the previous epithet 'építőművészet' (architectural art), rendered obsolete against the terms of industrialisation. Nagy completely restructured the journal by separating the core material arranged under permanent headings from the complementary part printed on colour paper. Best-quality projects were selected, with mostly informative and sometimes analytical writing.

Reviews of international architecture took the shape of personal accounts and translations from original texts. From 1962 onwards, full-size photographs appeared on the cover. The image of a leaf, a curtain wall, scaffolding, floating logs or stacked brick blocks, all represented a structure or texture instead of forms and well expressed the new perspective of the editor and his young collaborators. Nagy was enamoured of Finnish architecture, Charles Polónyi belonged to Team 10[35] and Károly Jurcsik, who reviewed Louis Kahn in *MÉ* (issue 5/1963), was soon to join Ernö Goldfinger's studio in London. Their sensitivity to structuralist and phenomenological approaches marked a shift from mainstream modernism, which nevertheless was not a proclaimed programme. Nagy never presented his editorial policy explicitly, theorising being the privilege of Major, who still acted as the president of the editorial board. As an *eminence grise* Nagy defined the character of the journal with his good taste and broad horizon of interest.[36]

Major and the leadership of MÉSZ were content with the changes and, indeed, *MÉ* became a forum able to represent Hungarian architecture at home and abroad, even if the lack of full translations was only partially compensated by summaries and the graphic editing of illustrations and visual content. The circulation of the journal increased from 4,000 (1960) to 5,000 (1964) copies, one-fifth of which went abroad. The general assembly of MÉSZ stated in 1964 that the journal had reached such a high standard that it could arouse even the interest of the general public. This optimistic view was opposed by remarks at meetings on *MÉ* organised by MÉSZ during 1964 and 1965. Many lamented the lack of a critical editorial policy, and the name of Bierbauer came up as a model of the militant, clear-sighted editor. One member of the presidency even disputed whether the editorial board had a consistent position towards current problems, largely absent from the journal: 'It has a registering nature – he summarized – impersonal in its statements, does not publish critiques and polemics, hardly deals with topicalities and does not comprise the totality of our architecture' (Brenner, 1966). The individual concerned reproached the editors for not writing on urban and architectural problems of general interest to people, and for not taking on board their personal viewpoint. He missed criticism and lay reactions as useful feedback for architects. Brenner believed that, without appropriate presentation of the architects' thoughts and work, they would never be acknowledged as artists. He mentioned Elemér Zalotay in particular since this visionary architect, who fought desperately with authorities to realise his gigantic strip building between 1958 and 1966, was passed over in *MÉ* without a word (Simon and Haba, 2013). Similarly, the editors failed to address the metabolist megastructural projects by László E. Kiss,[37] as was also the case with the later works of Imre Makovecz and the organic movement, in mutual revolt against faceless and inhuman mass-production architecture. Virtually no mention was made of controversies about tower buildings, mass housing or demolition of old town centres in favour of new schemes, and private house construction in the countryside (beyond 60 per cent of the total housing production) was neglected. Thus the elegant visual perfection affected by the journal at the beginning of the decade began to be distorted by the mid-1960s. This is no surprise given the political background of the period.

Following the consolidation of the Kádár regime (1957–1962), where the 'foundations of socialism had been laid', conditions for architecture abruptly changed. The long-term building programme of the next five-year plans could not be fulfilled without large-scale prefabrication, favouring the construction sector against the designers, whose workplace was transformed within increasingly bureaucratic and profit-oriented companies. Architects who stuck firmly to their professional authority, in the full sense of the word, were likely to come into conflict with the establishment. Creativity and invention became suspicious, and the bureaucrats did their best to wreck 'Difficult People' as a documentary of 1964 had it. In an 'uncivil society', to use Stephen Kotkin's term, that lacked both autonomy and solidarity, neither architects nor editors could be expected to defy the system for long. The power structure of the state planning offices, labelled a little later 'project factories', filtered out every beneficial market-style reform until the early 1980s. *MÉ* thus had to publish an increasing number of buildings of an ever decreasing quality. It is the misfortune of Nagy that, remaining the editor of *MÉ* until 1982, in tandem with the increasingly dogmatic modernist Máté Major, he had to participate in the entropy of the flagship of the Hungarian architectural media.

Notes

1 HCP received 17 per cent of the votes at the first free elections in November 1945.
2 FKT was founded in 1870 to coordinate the unification of the three towns from which the new capital city was formed and to manage and regulate its development. Consequently its relationship with the municipal council remained controversial.

3 This is also the reason for the lack of knowledge about the reconstruction concepts of more conservative professionals.

4 Though Fischer and Granasztói, together with László Málnai, attended the Bridgewater congress in 1947, the Hungarian group as such was not reactivated.

5 The range went far beyond Gropius and Le Corbusier, and included Aalto, Neutra, Lubetkin, BBPR and several less well-known Swiss, Danish and Swedish buildings.

6 The acting editor, Dr István Gyöngyösi, was a jurist, acquainted with Fischer from the milieu of the Social Democratic party, who headed the presidential office of the FKT from 1945 to 1948.

7 The immense task of renovating damaged buildings proved insufficiently photogenic to be published in the journal.

8 Fischer was a member of the Social Democratic party from 1932, while Granasztói joined in 1945.

9 Having left for the USSR in his childhood, he graduated from the Moscow Architectural Institute as an architect. After losing his whole family in 1943 he decided to repatriate.

10 Kozma was appointed the director of the Academy of Applied Arts in 1946 as a recompense for the disadvantages he suffered during the inter-war period because of his Jewish origin and leftist stance. According to Major's memoire, he was a member of the Social Democratic Party during 1946–1947.

11 The memorandum was signed in November 1946, and the Circle was officially registered one year later with the goal of 'fostering the case of new, progressive architecture imbued with social spirit'. Informally, they spoke about themselves as 'communist architects and those sympathizing with them'.

12 The omnipotence of the social democrat Fischer was abridged when his commissariat of reconstruction was merged in October 1946 to become a new ministry. Reconstruction and housing affairs were no longer FKT's responsibility and one-third of its staff were cut. A serious reduction of its budget followed.

13 Gyula Kaesz, József Körner, László Málnai, Gábor Preisich, Gyula Sebestyén and Iván Tabéry. Lajos Gádoros joined in August 1949 together with Ágost Benkhard and Andor Lévai in January 1949.

14 There are no records of the cover's designer but the authorship of Gyula Kaesz is likely since he made similar designs for both *Tér és Forma* and *Magyar Építőművészet* in the early 1930s.

15 Several of these projects were realized (as one of the so-called point blocks proposed along the Budapest riverbank), some were limited to duplication in one area (slabs for shock-workers at Lehel Square, Budapest), while others became truly generic, like the miners' houses built in a number of country towns (see Gádoros, 1948).

16 The Építéstudományi Központ (ÉTK, Centre of Building Science) was first established within the FKT, but Fischer showed them the door when they started to coax the best staff with higher salaries. The State Institute of Design and Building Science (ÉTI) started to work in June 1948 and moved to the premises of FKT when the latter was closed down in 1948.

17 For miners' standard house types designed by Pál Németh, see Major (1948).

18 It seems surprising, at first glance, that an architect of eminently bourgeois character deals with rural issues, but he had already undertaken this task in his book *Das neue Haus* (Kozma, 1941).

19 Borbíró at that time.

20 Károly Perczel reported on French experiments with earth walls stabilized by cement for the reconstruction of farms. It is interesting that he refers to Jean Bossu, a disciple of Le Corbusier who managed to adapt the scheme 'la ferme radieuse' to the real needs of local agriculture. The pisé, a traditional construction technique for Hungarian peasant houses, had been considered outmoded and unhealthy, yet the French 'models' made it more acceptable to modern architects.

21 From the staff of FKT, among others, Péter Kaffka and Aladár Münnich emigrated to Canada, László Acsay, György Masirevich and the Olgyay twins to the USA, while Jenő Kismarty-Lechner left for Sweden.

22 Fischer worked subsequently on housing renovations in the municipal state planning office.

23 The last, No. 4/5, issue of *Új Építészet* came out in May 1949.

24 Málnai, who had worked for Le Corbusier in 1936–1937, was arrested for sabotage, and Perczel similarly for espionage. His case was attached to the trial of László Rajk, the former interior minister, and

he was sentenced to life imprisonment. He attracted suspicion for his stay in France during the war, being accused of disclosing state secrets. In fact, he guided the visiting communist architect André Lurçat (delegate of the French government) around several industrial plants in the summer of 1949.

25 The first double issue was published in August 1949. The title of the journal changed from the second issue by reversing the sequence of the two words, thus emphasising 'building' rather than 'architecture'.

26 Scandinavian New Empiricism attracted many Hungarians. Students of the Budapest TU were evacuated at the end of the war to Denmark and returned to model Hungarian socialism on the Nordic welfare state.

27 A 1951 special issue of the journal published papers of the debate. *Építés - Építészet* 3 (9–10).

28 Weiner was a pupil and colleague of Hannes Meyer at the Dessau Bauhaus and in the USSR, fleeing via France to Chile from where he returned to Hungary in 1948, to be commissioned to plan and design the first socialist new town, Sztálinváros.

29 For a 1946 apartment project prepared with the Olgyay brothers, see Weidlinger (1958).

30 The best projects representing various forms of occupation were realized at the Óbuda Experimental Housing Estate (1959–1964). See Branczik and Keller (2011).

31 This idea was first raised in 1946 (*Tér és Forma*) and subsequently in a thematic issue of *Magyar Építőművészet*, 8 (4) 1958. See Wettstein (2016).

32 A mixed team of the Lakóterv and KÖZTI state planning offices was commissioned in 1956 to prepare tender projects for hotels in Istanbul and Ankara. See *MÉ*, 6 (3–4) of 1957 and 7 (1–3) of 1958.

33 See, furthermore, Simon (2013b).

34 He referred to Ronchamp as inspired by North African vernacular building.

35 Charles Polónyi published four articles on recent work of Team 10 members in *Magyar Építőművészet*, 11 (4), 1962, pp. 38–43.

36 Retrospectively, he spoke about a published list of the aims the editorial board set out in 1962, but this is not to be found in issues of the journal. The four aims were: the publication of the best of recent work, its critique, the consequent development of Hungarian architecture, and coverage of the fine and applied arts.

37 László E. Kiss (1927-) emigrated to Britain in 1969 and Elemér Zalotay (1932-) to Switzerland in 1973.

References

Bonta, J. (1961). A 'Magyar Építőművészetről' és a magyar építészetről. *Magyar Építőművészet*, 10 (6), p. 59.

Branczik, M. and Keller, M. (2011). *Korszerű lakás 1960: Az óbudai kísérlet*. Budapest: Terc.

Brenner, J. (1966). A 'Magyar Építőművészet'-ről. *Magyar Építőművészet*, 14 (1), pp. 58–59.

Fischer, J., Granasztói, P., Kismarty-Lechner, J., Major, M. and Weltzl, J. (1944–1945). Az építészet háború utáni feladatai Magyarországon. *Tér és Forma*, 18 (11), pp. 158–159.

Forshaw, J. H. and Abercrombie, P. (1943). County of London Plan. London: Macmillan.

Gádoros, L. (1948). Lakásépítés a 3 éves terv keretében. *Új Építészet*, 3 (9) pp. 314–320.

Granasztói, P. (1946). Az építész és a dolgozók társadalma. *Tér és Forma*, 19 (7/9), pp. 79–80.

Haba, P. (2012). Responses to Socialist Realism: Form and Ideology in Hungarian Industrial Architecture 1950–1956. *Építés - Építészettudomány*, 40 (3/4), pp. 331–363.

Juhász, J. (1956). A Magyar Építőművészet új szerkesztőbizottságának programja. *Magyar Építőművészet*, 5 (9), p. 261.

Kathy, I. (1960). Korszerűség, szecesszió, hagyomány. *Magyar Építőművészet*, 10 (3), pp. 34–39.

—— (1961). Családiház: parasztház. *Magyar Építőművészet*, 10 (1), pp. 40–41.

——. (1963). Japán mai építészete. *Magyar Építőművészet*, 12 (1), pp. 54–56.

Kismarty-Lechner, J. (1947). *Városi háztípusok*. Budapest: Országos Építésügyi Kormánybiztosság.

Kozma, L. (1941). Das neue Haus. Zürich: Verlag Girsberger.

Major, M. (1946). A Magyar építészekhez! *Új Építészet*, 1 (1), p. 1.

—— (1947). Politika és építészet. *Új Építészet*, 2 (3), pp. 42–43.

—— (1948). Lakótelep Várpalotán. *Új Építészet*, 3 (11–12), pp. 4–14.

—— (1960). Év végi mérleg. *Magyar Építőművészet*, 9 (6), p. 3.

—— (2001). *Tizenkét nehéz esztendő (1945–1956)*. Budapest: Magyar Építészeti Múzeum.

Majtényi, Gy. (2013). What Made the Kádár Era? Two Books on Hungary's Recent Past. *Hungarian Historical Review*, 2 (3), pp. 667–675.

Moravánszky, Á. (2012). Peripheral Modernism: Charles Polónyi and the Lessons of the Village. *The Journal of Architecture*, 17 (3), pp. 333–359.

Nagy, E. (1960). A formálás szerepe az építészetben. *Magyar Építőművészet*, 9 (3), pp. 45–49.

Perczel, K. (1947). Vertföld-beton: A falu új építőanyaga. *Új Építészet*, 2 (7), pp. 157–158.

Perényi, I. (1948a). Bevezető. *Új Építészet* 3 (5), p. 160.

—— (1948b). Megjegyzések a kiállításhoz. *Új Építészet*, 3 (6), pp. 214–215.

Sámsondi-Kiss, B. (1957). Könnyű épületek. *Magyar Építőművészet*, 6 (1–2), pp. 13–17.

Sámsondi-Kiss, B. and Farkas, T. (1950). Vasbeton szövetház. *Építés - Építészet*, 2 (6).

Simon, M. (2013a). 'Taste Must Arise from the Doctrine' Architecture in the Hungarian Cultural Media in the 1960s. *Studii de Istoria si Teoria Architecturii*, 1 (1), pp. 30–44.

—— (2013b). Progressive, Forward-looking and Advanced: Hungarian Architecture and Modernity 1956–1962. *Architektúra & Urbanizmus*, 47 (1/2), pp. 20–33.

Simon, M. and Haba, P. (2013). A Difficult Person for Socialism. In I. Weizman (Ed.), *Architecture and the Paradox of Dissidence*. London: Routledge, pp. 45–58.

Vadas, F. (1985). Budapesti tervpályázatok 1945-ben II: Az újjáépítési ötletpályázat. *Magyar Építőművészet*, 34 (3) pp. 52–55.

Weidlinger, P. (1958). Partitions function as columns. In: *Apartments and Dormitories*. New York: Architectural Record, pp. 24–29.

Wettstein, D. (2016). The Balaton Region as an Experimental Territory. *Építés - Építészettudomány*, 44 (1/2), pp. 129–156.

7

PERIODICALS AND THE RETURN TO MODERNITY AFTER THE SPANISH CIVIL WAR

Arquitectura, Hogar y Arquitectura and Nueva Forma

Ana Esteban Maluenda

The Spanish Civil War (1936–1939) marked a definitive break in the cultural activity of the country. In terms of architecture, it would be more than two decades before the pulse of modernity would be recovered through the gradual restoration of contact with the outside. Throughout this time the information published in national journals supplemented the lack of travel, contacts, meetings, exhibitions and foreign publications which, although not entirely absent, but were at best scarce, especially in the years immediately after the war. The conflict had paralysed the production of all Spanish architecture journals, and once it was over different circumstances co-existed. The political, economic and social landscape of the country had changed radically, so that very few pre-war publications managed to resume their activity and most of them fell by the wayside. Undoubtedly the most common situation was the creation of new titles in keeping with the new context.

In April 1940, just one year after the war ended, the first issue of *Reconstrucción* appeared; this journal was created as a mouthpiece of the *Dirección General de Regiones Devastadas y Reparaciones*, a new state agency whose primary mission was to guide, facilitate and, in certain cases, directly execute the reconstruction of the towns and cities most affected by the war. The aim of this journal was merely propagandist, as illustrated by its issues full of images of ruins and subsequent repairs. The journal only existed for as long as it was thought necessary to publish the type of content to which it was dedicated. The last edition was released in summer 1953, just over three years before the final dissolution of the state agency for which it had been a voice.

Revista Nacional de Arquitectura (RNA) is a very different case: a publication that started up again after the war, but was heavily modified in content, name and editorship. The journal was inaugurated in 1918 under the title *Arquitectura* as the official organ of the *Sociedad Central de Arquitectos*, but in 1931, with the establishment of professional associations, it moved to being published by the *Colegio de Arquitectos de Madrid* (COAM). After the civil war, the newly created *Dirección General de Arquitectura* (DGA) began publishing *RNA*, which replaced the old *Arquitectura*, although now under the *Ministerio del Interior*. In 1946, *RNA* became dependent on the *Consejo Superior de Arquitectos*, where it remained until 1959, when the COAM recovered it as a means of dissemination, and reverted to its name from before the civil war, *Arquitectura*.

Despite this apparent discontinuity, *RNA* and *Arquitectura* were both published primarily within the auspices of the COAM and can really be considered as a single journal. Furthermore, Carlos de Miguel, who was the editor-in-chief for 25 years (1948–1973), added a sense of continuity. Before taking charge of the journal, Carlos de Miguel had edited two dependent publications identified with government agencies: *Boletín de Información de la Dirección General de Arquitectura* (published from 1946) and *Gran Madrid* (from January 1948), newsletter of the *Comisaría General para la Ordenación Urbana de Madrid y sus alrededores*. A man of the regime but, above all, a professional interested in the evolution and development of Spanish architecture, De Miguel was instrumental in the journal's evolution, which changed from being merely DGA propaganda to a more or less balanced circulation of both a national and international context.

Cuadernos de Arquitectura* was founded in 1944 by the *Colegio de Arquitectos de Cataluña y Baleares*. Similarly to its contemporaries, *Cuadernos de Arquitectura* was established as a journal that belonged to an organisation, although it was always much more focused on Catalonia and its particular interests. The publication continued under that name until 1971, when it was changed to *Cuadernos de Arquitectura y Urbanismo*. However, as the editors changed periodically, it did not retain the consistency that Carlos de Miguel brought to *Arquitectura*.

Launching into this market of publications sponsored by organisations and institutions, *Informes de la Construcción* appeared in 1948, linked to the *Instituto Técnico de la Construcción y del Cemento* and focused on the publication of the latest achievements in the field of construction. However, the first few pages of each issue were devoted to current architectural projects which – given the personal relationships of some individuals responsible for the institute, namely, Eduardo Torroja and Fernando Cassinello – included many examples from America.[1] This same influence on content from the organisation promoting a publication could also be seen in *Hogar y Arquitectura* (*HyA*), which appeared in 1955 as a means of publicising the organism that gave it its name: the *Obra Sindical del Hogar y la Arquitectura* (OSH), another national body dependent on the DGA. However, the influence of OSH on the content of the journal declined with the arrival of its charismatic editor-in-chief, Carlos Flores. In the 1960s he transformed the publication into a showcase of both national and international developments.

FIGURE 7.1 Covers of the main Spanish architecture journals after the Civil War (1936–1939).

The first issue of *Temas de Arquitectura* came out in October 1958. Being the first journal that was not dependent on any particular body, and that was distinct in approach from the journals that had appeared to date, it didn't receive the acclaim that it deserved. Possibly the independent character of its editor-in-chief, the multifaceted Miguel Durán-Loriga, had much to do with the creation of this niche product which, nevertheless, comprehensively covered current architectural trends.

So too did the well thought of *Nueva Forma* (*NF*), edited by Juan Daniel Fullaondo, which, unlike *Temas de Arquitectura*, however, did make a strong impression on the readers at the time, who subsequently viewed it as 'a very important platform for cultural formation, and a parallel forum for knowledge – not just architectural – that is of great significance to our general education' (Humanes, 1996, p. 36). Its independence from any government agency – it was funded by the construction group Huarte – provided Fullaondo with the opportunity to maintain the intense critical approach that characterises it. Despite its short life – it didn't last more than a decade – *NF* is one of the most notable publications practitioners recall when they are asked about architectural journals.

In the 1970s new titles came out that followed the paths travelled by those early publications, although now framed in an era in which the main concerns were no longer viewing Spanish architecture against the international scene, but in equal participation in the debates that were underway worldwide. Three Catalan publications stand out: *CAU. Construcción, Arquitectura, Urbanismo*; *2C. Construcción de la ciudad*; and *Arquitecturas bis*.

If we try to filter down this list of immediate post-civil war publications, leaving aside those that had less impact on the evolution of Spanish architecture, the first to disappear would be *Reconstrucción*, *Boletín de Información de la Dirección General de Arquitectura* and *Gran Madrid*, all voices of government agencies with clear propagandist purposes and short duration.

Despite the number of contemporary buildings published, *Informes de la Construcción* should be considered a special case as many architects saw it as a collection of 'postulates and technical developments' (Fernandez Alba, 2011, p. 60) and did not consult it much; or at least they looked at it much less frequently than the journals published by the institutes, which were essential for Spanish architects in the 1950s. '*Arquitectura* was the most widely read', recalled José Antonio Corrales (2011, p. 52) without hesitation. Oriol Bohigas agreed:

> I think one of the most influential, though not the best, or even near, was the journal *Arquitectura*, from Madrid. Not so much for the journal, but because of that special personality that was Carlos de Miguel, a unifying force of the whole architectural cultural life of Madrid.
>
> *Coddou et al., 2011*

Cuadernos de Arquitectura was also widely available in Catalonia, but less so on a national level and was certainly in no way comparable to *RNA* when it was an organ of the DGA. In addition, the difference in frequency between the monthly *RNA* and the quarterly *Cuadernos de Arquitectura* marks a notable difference between the two, which were both probably the best reflection of architectural culture of the time (Bernal, 2011).

'The truth is that in my student days, the most read journals from Madrid were *Hogar y Arquitectura* and *Arquitectura*', noted Rafael Moneo (2011, p. 71), and until the appearance of *NF*, they divided, or more precisely, shared, the journal market. '*Temas de Arquitectura* was consulted much less' (Corrales, 2011, p. 52) because, as explained, it was driven by the particular and resolute journalistic vocation of Miguel Durán-Loriga, the editor-in-chief, who later shifted its focus towards design.

The strength and innovation with which *NF* arrived was one thing, but it was also the publication that heralded a new era in which the desperate search for modernity of the previous decades was coming to an end. If the publications that had appeared in the 1970s are discarded, only a trio survives from the initial list – *Arquitectura, HyA* and *NF* – curiously a trio that Oriol Bohigas had already proposed in 1978.

In an article published in a special issue of *Arquitecturas bis* dedicated to Madrid, Bohigas remembered – at some remove – the 'three journals' which, in his opinion, were those that most clearly addressed the task of reviving the architectural culture in Madrid in the 1950s and 1960s: *Arquitectura, Hogar y Arquitectura* and *Nueva Forma*.

> While the Barcelona journal of the time (*Cuadernos de Arquitectura*) explains only in part the cultural base of Catalan architecture […] in Madrid, referring to the journals of De Miguel, Flores and Fullaondo remains one of the more direct ways of understanding what was happening there.
>
> *Bohigas, 1978, p. 60*

And he refers to them as the 'journals of' because really the three were a direct result of the nature of those who were in charge of them: the balanced Carlos de Miguel, the methodical Carlos Flores and the vehement Juan Daniel Fullaondo. In fact, Bohigas restates in his text that his 'most persistent memory is the personality of their editors-in-chief'. For him, 'the qualities that marked the three journals respectively were: in one, the effort to promote and bring together; in another, the support of those who, from the outside or from the inside, were trying to challenge the local conformism; and in the third, the analytical discovery of our hidden realities'. And those same qualities 'could often mark their corresponding defects: excessive a-critical enthusiasm, astonishing arrogance and touching chauvinism' (Bohigas, 1978, p. 60).

But the designation of these 'three journals' as fundamental during the post-civil war period is not just supported by Bohigas. Years later, in line with her conversations with Juan Daniel Fullaondo about the decisive role that journals played in the renewal of the professional

FIGURE 7.2 Covers of the 'three journals': *Arquitectura, Hogar y Arquitectura* and *Nueva Forma*.

atmosphere of the time, María Teresa Muñoz selected them (again), affirming that '*Revista Nacional de Arquitectura*, *Hogar y Arquitectura* and then *Nueva Forma* had made the only valid history and critique of our recent history' (Fullaondo and Muñoz, 1997, p. 109). Not much earlier, Antón Capitel had referred to them in very similar terms:

> Fundamentally in Madrid – as Barcelona fed a little more of international publications – these three journals occupied a basic information role that was practically unique and that should now be recognised. Their archives help us understand the era in all of its aspects, with no limitations.
>
> *Capitel, 1996, p. 478*

In fact, a review of their archives probably provides the best testimony to the interests of a group of architects who, above all, maintained a constant struggle to be included in international circles (Esteban Maluenda, 2008).

Revista Nacional de Arquitectura and *Arquitectura*: chronicles of an era

> *Arquitectura* by Carlos de Miguel was […] 'more than a journal'. It was the promotional organ, the operative push of the new Spanish architecture […]. The punctuality, the precision, the eclecticism, the a-critical information were qualities of incalculable value, much more than the dissatisfied purists suspected – even though their dissatisfaction was at times justified. From the side lines, those purists proposed an architecture that was only led by ethical and social positioning, without any professional framework.
>
> *Bohigas, 1978, p. 60*

It would be difficult to come up with a more accurate description of the era in which *Arquitectura* was led by Carlos de Miguel: 25 years that were fundamental to the evolution and reactivation of Spanish architecture, which dawned after the break caused by the recent civil war and its consequences.

As already mentioned, Carlos de Miguel began his management duties at *RNA* in 1948. Years later, De Miguel (1978, p. 63), remembered what his intentions were in those first moments:

> I proposed two things. Rigorousness in the punctuality of the publication of the journal […] and […] dispassionate selection of the material to be published.

This dispassion, which at first glance might seem negative, was one of the greatest virtues of his work as De Miguel managed to adapt to the reality and context of the time, without becoming entrapped by architectural trends. Nevertheless, Carlos de Miguel was more interested in what was happening inside than outside the country, in particular in the updating of Spanish architecture.

Some of the most interesting experiences that the journal organised were the *Sesiones de Crítica de Arquitectura* (SCA), meetings between architects to discuss issues of shared interest that were held periodically for more than two decades. The structure was always the same: a guest speaker presented a topic and then opened the floor to others. Thus, each session generated a round table debate. Subsequently, most of the SCA were reproduced in *RNA*. The proposed topics were very varied, but often more focused towards the analysis of Spanish production, although some of the SCA were concerned with foreign architecture.

After the first session, dedicated to the UN building in New York (Moya, 1951), came some of the most memorable meetings: the heated discussion about the *Ministerio del Aire* between Francisco Javier Sáenz de Oíza and its architect, Luis Gutiérrez Soto (1951); those given by the Finn Alvar Aalto (1952) in 1951 during his tour of Spain; the meeting at the Alhambra which would lead to the important *Manifiesto* (Chueca et al., 1953); the successful visit to the school in Herrera de Pisuerga by José Antonio Corrales and Ramón Vázquez Molezún (1958); or the session dedicated to Le Corbusier (1958), when Miguel Fisac proclaimed Corbusier's work 'absolute poison for people like us, who are impressionable, impulsive' (Corrales and Vázquez Molezún, 1958, p. 34).

The journal's 'return' to the *Colegio de Arquitectos* in 1959 did not involve a radical change of line, although the format and cover were refreshed. Among other changes, Carlos de Miguel wanted to install Francisco Javier Sáenz de Oíza as editor, but he would never assume the post, held by Luis Moya in 1960. That same year, Curro Inza began his duties as deputy editor, a position in which he continued until the end of Carlos de Miguel's 25 years of management in 1973.

Among the elements that continued from its previous incarnation were the SCA sessions, although there was a break between 1960 and 1963, which were saved by the collaboration of several members of the *Colegio de Arquitectos* who, encouraged by Carlos de Miguel, donated sufficient funds to revive the meetings. This second round of interesting events included a

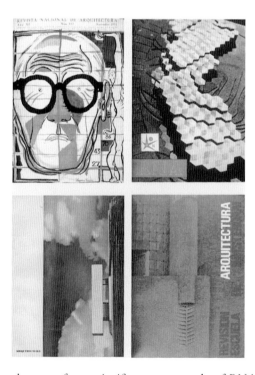

FIGURE 7.3 Journal covers of some significant monographs of *RNA* and *Arquitectura*.

meeting dedicated to current architecture (Casariego, 1964); Camilo José Cela's presentation on 'Madrid, architects and chance' (Cela, 1967); and presentations of the Girasol building, (Coderch, 1967), the Torres Blancas (Fernández-Longoria Pinazo, 1968) and the Huarte House (Corrales and Vázquez Molezún, 1966). And, of course, the debate between Juan Daniel Fullaondo and Oriol Bohigas around the schools of architecture in Madrid and Barcelona (Fullaondo and Bohigas, 1968). The last of the SCA on record took place in the early 1970s, close to the time when Carlos de Miguel bade farewell to the management of *Arquitectura*. It is unclear if this was what led to their demise – as seemed to be the case with the first cycle – or if the decline was caused by the scarcity or lack of interest of the audience. The differences of opinion that were beginning to become apparent between the different generations of architects attending the meetings should also not be underestimated. In any case, however, for two decades the SCA undoubtedly created one of the best places for communication among peers and a true stage for what was of interest to Spanish architects, and not just to those who attended the sessions but also to subscribers through the published transcripts.

Beyond the SCA, *RNA* and *Arquitectura* published some of the most important monographs of the time on Spanish and foreign architecture, which became a regular feature in their pages. Under the direction of Luis Moya as editor, *Arquitectura* published the most informatively on the culture of architecture outside Spain; and for five consecutive years it was the only journal that featured a permanent section devoted to international architecture: '30 d a' by Mariano Bayón.

Arquitectura was thus not only important as an organ expressing the interests of Madrid architects, but equally for the dissemination of Spanish contemporary architecture. It did not always maintain a clear critical position, but it managed to develop a strong chronological basis and served as a launching pad for young architects who found their best mentor in Carlos de Miguel.

Hogar y Arquitectura: Carlos Flores' hybrid

> *Hogar y Arquitectura* by Carlos Flores was only half a journal. The first pages devoted to the *Obra Sindical del Hogar* were redeemed by those that followed, which were truly controlled by Flores, and his aim to disseminate and update. There the information took on an air of amiable admonishment to the self-referential Spaniards whom he tried to enthuse with news from *Architectural Design* or examples highlighting the most international aspects of the national output. His dedication to everything systematic – which ranged from the ordered publication of foreign texts, to guides and monographs – fell clearly into this almost testimonial attitude, in which he was determined to remove himself from immediate influences, working on issues of a more general utility or postures that would 'pass into history'.
>
> *Bohigas, 1978, p. 60*

Only a few years before *RNA*'s return to COAM, in November 1955, the first issue of *HyA* was published. This bi-monthly journal emerged expressly as a communicator of the work of the *Obra Sindical del Hogar*. Therefore, in the first few issues their accomplishments filled all the pages of the publication, which barely had room for a series of brief reviews on the upcoming celebration of various international conferences specifically devoted to housing, the basic theme of the publication. At first the journal was led by Mariano García Benito, following the criteria set by the body that had created it. But from 1958, articles began to appear signed by the young architect Carlos Flores, who, at just 30 years old, would revolutionise the publication. His incorporation into the journal was progressive and exponential, until at the end of 1962 he was offered the position of editor-in-chief:

> The reason for my arrival at *Hogar y Arquitectura* was the publication in 1961 of my book of *Arquitectura española contemporánea* […]. [Francisco] Cabrero called me to replace the then editor-in-chief, Mariano García Benito, who didn't have the time to devote to the journal.
>
> *Esteban Maluenda, 2011, p. 69*

From the beginning, his main purpose was clear: to 'make it a [true] architecture journal' (Flores, 1978, p. 60), something that he undoubtedly succeeded in doing. To achieve this, he had to get approval for the content edition by edition from the administration board, 'which not only dealt with financial matters but exercised a double control – before and after – on the content of each issue. In theory, the relevant summaries had to be submitted to the deliberations of the board and only after approval could the printing of the journal begin' (Flores, 1978, p. 60). However, putting this into practice was not so simple:

> This system, designed as a plan to work without exception, failed in many cases, at least during my time. Difficulties of various kinds prevented or delayed board meetings and so the summaries were often approved with the issue already on the streets.
>
> *Flores, 1978, p. 60*

Carlos Flores always intended that 'the journal maintained his own criteria. This meant creating a trail-blazing journal, nonetheless avoiding exclusive or closed-minded positions' (Flores, 1978, p. 60). In discussing its structure, he commented:

> My intention – after a few months of backwards and forwards – was to explore a central theme at some length in each issue and complete this monograph with articles, different sections, collaborations, etc., and while that expanded the scope and interest of the journal, it also kept it from attempting to become a book.
>
> *Flores, 1978, p. 61*

After the three or four articles related to the work of the OSH came the themes of real interest, not just to Carlos Flores, but also the readers of the journal. It is worth highlighting several examples, including English New Towns (*HyA* 38, 1962), the city of the future (*HyA* 38, 1965) and urban renewal (*HyA* 38, 1966). And immediately afterwards he launched the journal's sections 'Forum', 'Journal review', 'Obituaries', 'Informative summary' and 'An architect in a book'. These sections were mostly gathered and organised as independent parts that would eventually be called 'Supplement', which was a rather ingenious formula as it enabled variations to the structure, with sections appearing or not depending on the amount of information received during the preparation of the issue. As Flores noted:

> From the beginning, what I logically tried to do was make an architecture journal separating myself from the essentially propagandist line that marked the *Obra Sindical del Hogar*. I also took care that the content was didactic, to serve as an educational tool;

FIGURE 7.4 Journal covers of *HyA* 38, 60 and 63, dedicated to the English New Towns, the city of the future and urban renewal, respectively.

> I thought about all those students who hardly read books, some because they didn't want to and others because they couldn't. [...] Definitely, it was about opening up the field of vision.
>
> *Esteban Maluenda, 2011, p. 69*

In addition, Flores specialised in identifying less known but important documents released in the foreign media, principally in the US and the UK. One of the most important was a course on North American architecture directed by Henry-Russell Hitchcock, broadcast on the Voice of America, which was aired during the 1960–1961 season of the Forum Lectures. In addition to the themes that were discussed, the importance of the series lay in the famous names who gave the various classes, including Louis I. Kahn, Vincent Scully, Richard Buckminster Fuller, Paul Rudolph, Philip Johnson and Minoru Yamasaki. The 12 sessions were reproduced in *HyA* in four groups of three articles published in consecutive numbers between September 1961 and April 1962 (*HyA* 36–39). Similarly, 'A prueba', was a literal translation of the 'On trial' articles written by Reyner Banham in 1962 for *The Architectural Review* (*AR* 780–786). The impact of this content, apart from providing Spanish readers with up-to-date views of the international scene, was due to Carlos Flores 'translating' them immediately to *HyA*, with just a few months apart from the original broadcasts and publications (*HyA* 43–48, 1962–1963).

But he also discovered and cited, before other Spanish publications, emerging figures hitherto unknown in the country, such as Álvaro Siza Vieira, to whom he devoted a special edition in early 1967 (*HyA* 68). Special mention too goes to the adventurous report on the Archigram group (*HyA* 73, 1967), unknown beforehand. In fact, that publication caused tremendous controversy, among the Madrid architects, in particular. In his conversations with María Teresa Muñoz, Juan Daniel Fullaondo remembered the case of Carlos de Miguel, who could not understand how in the same issue Flores had mixed information on the 'unusual' British group with the 'balanced' Elviña housing intervention by José Antonio Corrales. 'The mixture was quite explosive', even for Fullaondo. According to the Bilbao architect, De Miguel 'bristled':

> He got a few of us together to prepare a kind of counterattack. How could he juxtapose Corrales's fantastic project with the delirious Archigram? etc. I advised a little caution

FIGURE 7.5 Translations in *HyA* of the series on North American architecture broadcast on the *Voice of America* during 1960–1961, and of the 'On trial' articles written by Reyner Banham in 1962 for *The Architectural Review*.

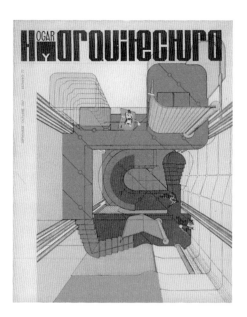

FIGURE 7.6 Journal cover, *HyA* 73, devoted to the Archigram group.

and that he reflected a bit. And that we all reflected a bit. We had a second meeting and I tried to talk to him – I do not know if with much success – about Reyner Banham, Brutalism, Team Ten, Utopia.

Fullaondo and Muñoz, 1997, p. 263

And that was not the only controversial issue. In the much discussed 'La arquitectura y el arquitecto' (*HyA* 79, 1968), Flores interviewed numerous professionals – mainly Spanish, but also many foreigners – about the roles that both sides of the equation, architecture and architects, should play in a society that was beginning to show significant signs of transformation. Initially, this issue was intended to serve as a tribute to Leopoldo Torres Balbás, but according to Carlos Flores that was forbidden, just as he was forbidden from using the cover that had been prepared. It was a cover that was very 'acidic', both in its colour and in its content: the issue was to begin with an article by Candilis and a harsh extract from that article was printed on the cover on a yellow background. Finally, the cover was changed to pinkish tones on which there was a background of buildings that were actually small cakes!

Carlos Flores remained in charge of *HyA* until the last issue of 1974, 'when I was forced to leave because of my absolute incompatibility with the guidelines and control established by the new head of the *Obra Sindical del Hogar*' (Flores, 1994, p. 15). Apparently, he had always expected that his relationship with the journal would finish in an 'inevitable and abrupt' manner, and after many years he had the impression that 'the wait had been longer than expected' (Flores, 1994, p. 17).

> The *Obra Sindical del Hogar* stopped counting on me in late 1974, after my many years of work and enthusiasm without even being on the payroll and with very low remuneration as a simple contributor. However, I must say that they always treated me with respect and gave me almost total freedom in terms of what was published. Everything would end, when at a certain time, they said, 'Carlos, this has to change: you cannot publish just one page on the *Obra Sindical* and the remaining ninety-nine on what you want. From now on it needs to be the other way around'. So I left, or they fired me, I still don't know which.
>
> *Esteban Maluenda, 2011, p. 70*

But it was that issue dedicated to Archigram that was the beginning of the end. In Fullaondo's words: 'it was extraordinarily provocative, symptomatic. But rather than reflecting, people prepared – as someone said – to charge [...]' (Fullaondo and Muñoz, 1997, p. 264). And charging head first is precisely what Fullaondo ended up doing, jumping into the ring from the platform of his own publication.

Nueva Forma: 'recreation and instruction'

> *Nueva Forma* was, in comparison, the sublimation of this native architectural work. A sublimation that magnified the incredible tumultuous vitality of Juan Daniel Fullaondo, a display of his broad vision and an almost indiscriminate capacity to put everything in one critical and controversial bag, that was both personalised and aggressive, to persuade us that we also had something to say and that we were also making history, although it was collecting together the crumbs that were left on the table of a battered country.
>
> *Bohigas, 1978, p. 60*

The adventure that was *NF* began in early 1966. In February of that year the first issue of *El Inmueble* was published:

> A trade journal for the construction world [...] in which there were texts and articles that related to the world of art and literary essays written by young architects, poets and writers.[2]
>
> *Fernandez Alba, 1996, p. 19*

However, soon it would change its name to *Forma Nueva – El Inmueble*, coinciding with the appointment of Juan Daniel Fullaondo, initially as an adviser and then later as the editor-in-chief. Together with the architect Santiago Amón, who was part of the editorial board from the early issues of 1968, and Juan Huarte, whose group funded the publication, it was Fullaondo who was the real agent of change, bringing to the journal his penetrating and original point of view. So, from September 1967, with the addition of Paloma Buigas as editor and Rafael Moneo and Francisco Javier Sáenz de Oíza as advisers, Fullaondo laid the foundation for this unique project.

The freedom of action enjoyed by those who created *NF* was in total contrast with the restrictions that Carlos de Miguel and Carlos Flores experienced during their time as editors-in-chief of *Arquitectura* and *HyA*, respectively. In this respect, Huarte played an exceptional role. A farsighted contributor who was receptive to the development of new techniques in architecture and engineering, he had already collaborated with José Luis Fernández del Amo in the initial phase of the Museo de Arte Contemporáneo in Madrid; with Camilo José Cela in creating the publishing house Alfaguara; and with Jorge de Oteiza, who he supported enthusiastically on his return from America.

From issue 20, the publication was renamed *Nueva Forma* and Juan Daniel Fullaondo definitively assumed leadership, replacing Gabino Alejandro Carriedo, who later joined the editorial board along with Rafael Moneo and Francisco Javier Sáenz de Oiza. In a bright red insert between the pages of this issue, the journal *Nueva Forma – El Inmueble* announced this development.

Antonio Fernandez Alba reminisced about the onset of the new journal:

> Above the bold heading a small Wrightian anagram was just visible, vaguely reminiscent of the endless museum, or a labyrinth open to infinity. As editor-in-chief, J. D. Fullaondo made the protest slogan of the time his own: 'I take my desires for reality because I believe in the reality of my desires', and based on these subjective principles he opened the pages of *Nueva Forma* up to that hidden arsenal of artistic avant-gardes, the emerging generations of architects, artists and art critics.
>
> *Fernandez Alba, 1996, p. 20*

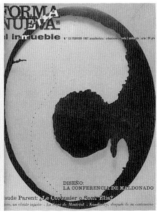

FIGURE 7.7 Journal covers of the consecutive stages of *Nueva Forma*: *El Inmueble* 2 (1966), *Forma Nueva* 13 (1967) and *Nueva Forma* 20 (1967).

From the very beginning, the differences with previous journals became patently obvious:

> Already in the first editions, having evolved beyond the initial outline of *El Inmueble*, the
> strong personality of its editorial team was evident and its desire to make an uncom-
> promising journal in which graphic images and feature articles were always balanced,
> and pedagogy always came before beauty. However, when comparing *Nueva Forma* with
> the official journal of the moment, *Arquitectura*, it is easy to see it was not an attempt
> to offer its readers a neutral overview of architecture and art, but to highlight and dis-
> seminate certain options, which could be broad and undogmatic, but they were always
> selective and freely chosen by its editorial team.
>
> *Martinez-Novillo, 1996, p. 27*

So, on one hand, the journal was devoted to selecting what the board considered most
interesting from the architectural and artistic milieu of the time – both national and international – and, on the other, to reviewing the groups or schools of the avant-gardes of the
modern movement. From the beginning, professionals and students eager for information
were attracted by this two-fold approach – both current and historiographical – which
was embodied in monographs about architects and artistic movements, and illustrated by
fragmented images.

Aimed at disseminating the current trends and personalities within the national panorama – nearly always showing a preference for more organic works – it is worth highlighting
the issues dedicated to the emerging architects.[3] However, there were some notable absences,
including any monograph dedicated to Francisco Javier Sáenz de Oiza, who was, after all,

FIGURE 7.8   Current trends and personalities, *Nueva Forma* covers.

a very present figure in the first stage of the journal (and in whose office Fullaondo had worked); or Álvaro Siza, whose work was already being published in *HγA*.

The issues dedicated to reviewing the modern movement were equally interesting, again in covering both Spain and abroad.[4] But the journal didn't only cover architecture. One of the greatest achievements of *NF*, which had not even been mentioned in previous journals, was the constant interaction between different artistic disciplines:

> It was produced in the projects that were covered in the journal and even in the same composition and typography of its pages in a continuous and natural way. Correlations between painting, sculpture and architecture were permanent in the issues of *Nueva Forma*, the influences were patently clear […]. This global vision of artistic reality would be completed with its relationship to literature. The permanent texts of those responsible for the journal […] and of their ideological mentors […] would be accompanied with one-off contributions from intellectuals […] and architects. […] In addition to the texts on architectural or sculptural images, on many occasions literary quotations enhanced the ensemble and became the trademark of the journal, often showing a surprising affiliation to particular artistic figures.
>
> *Humanes, 1996, p. 38*

Evidently this discourse was presented in a very specific manner, with a marked freedom in the graphic layout which acquired a power of expression far removed from that of other

FIGURE 7.9 Review of the modern movement, *Nueva Forma* covers.

journals. So impressive were these innovations that they were to become a reference for other publications such as *Poesía* by Gonzalo Armero, who years later would pay tribute to *NF* in curating an exhibition on the journal in 1996 (Fernandez Alba et al., 1996). Nevertheless, the potency of its pages was not only due to the overarching personality of its editor-in-chief, or indeed to chance, but to the attention paid to creating each issue. Images were carefully selected, cropped for emphasis and arranged on the page in a manner that supported conceptual explanation. Indeed there was always an underlying message, although at times it was not obvious or straightforward.

As more issues were published, they tested new ways of transmitting information: thick bands and white line drawings on a black background; variable typography adapted to each theme, and above all the meticulous care with which the covers were designed, selecting fragments of photographs and recomposing, reversing or colouring them (Pérez Moreno, 2015). They employed a variety of resources to create a powerful effect that invited the reader to open the journal and enjoy the content. This strategy did not limit the formative character of the journal, which went beyond the purely architectural to venture into other artistic disciplines, displaying them in an instructive and inspiring manner to a majority audience with cultural interests.

NF emerged as an endless interrogation of words and images, text and pretext, form and content, reference and historical data, compilation and testimony of what happened, photographic illustration and open chronicle. All this was a tribute to the memory of what was already history in the advancing century but a history and story unknown to most of those who attended the cultural lessons taught in the classrooms or who roamed the galleries and other cultural events (Fernandez Alba, 1996, p. 17).

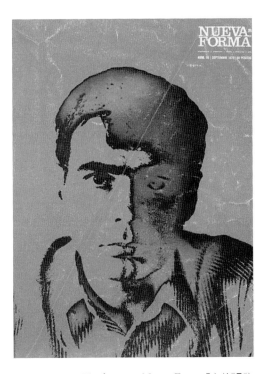

FIGURE 7.10   Final cover, *Nueva Forma* 56 (1970).

According to Javier Carvajal: 'Juan Daniel did everything. He personally made the journal, and you see that in how it was composed and how the articles were introduced and how each project was illustrated' (Anon., 1996b, p. 61). Fernando Higueras remembered him years later as 'a hugely gifted man, […], with a great passion for architecture' (Anon., 1996a, p. 61).

In May 1975, Juan Daniel Fullaondo, in an interview published in *NF*, ended his term as editor-in-chief of the journal with these words:

> What does it matter? I'm telling you that I'm used to abandoning definitively everything that, in one way or another, is over. I free myself from the memories accumulated there, those that try to perpetuate parasitically … Although it is within a precarious environment, the surprisingly 'optimistic hardship' of a renewed situation. I repeat that I don't like talking about myself. A final goodbye. Now there is a formidable backdrop.
>
> *Fullaondo, 1975, p. XXXII*

Indeed it was a formidable backdrop and on a stage that was unrecognisable from that at the inception of the journal.

A balanced content: the international in a local context

Despite being so different, all three publications discussed above serve to illustrate the same point: that Spanish periodicals provided significant support for architects and students of architecture during this period. Of course, we should also consider other channels of information. So, the architecture schools and professional bodies, and in particular their libraries, played a prominent role, especially as architects had a mandatory relationship with these institutions. However, architecture teaching was so anchored in the past that interest in what was happening outside the country did not usually come from teachers, but rather from students themselves, fuelled by their own curiosity. The professional bodies, though much more in contact with the outside world, were less interested in the development of architecture itself than in becoming part of the international architectural scene. The acquisition of foreign journals and books was typically affected by a restricted budget, both for libraries and individuals who often made the best possible use of opportunities like buying in instalments. There were few congresses or exhibitions specifically dedicated to foreign influences, but those that there were, were interesting and relatively well attended by the public.

In comparison, there was a plethora of information available through the journals. *Arquitectura* played a prominent role, with Mariano Bayón's regular feature '30 d a' featuring world architecture each month. *Arquitectura* also sought out and assessed, with only a few months' delay, important texts of the period.[5] *HyA* published 12 Forum Lectures coordinated by Henry-Russell Hitchcock on 'The Rise to World Prominence of American Architecture', broadcast on The Voice of America throughout 1960 and 1961 (*HyA* 36–39, 1962), and Banham's series of articles of 1962 and 1963 (*HyA* 43–48), first published in *The Architectural Review* under the title 'On trial'.

Beyond these examples, which came directly from foreign sources, the three journals devoted numerous pages to countries, cities, architects, architectural typologies and specific buildings. In general, except for typologies, we can see a more or less constant growth in all these issues over time, with an exponential growth after the first half of the 1960s. *Arquitectura* stands out from the other two journals in the number of articles published, although on occasion it was surpassed by *HyA*, and *NF* is notable for its dedication to certain architects.

While it is true that the coverage of competitions, meetings, conferences, exhibitions, even travel, was not comparable with the above, it is important to mention the work done by *Arquitectura* both in terms of the international competitions in which Spanish teams participated and by organising meetings and conferences.

The journals certainly contain more information than one might expect when first leafing through their pages. Indeed, compared to other ways in which modernity was having an impact in Spain, these three publications offered the easiest, cheapest and therefore most accessible way in which Spanish architects were informed about foreign architecture – not just regarding the quantity but also the quality of information.

But the importance of these journals should not be reduced to simply considering them as significant vehicles for the transmission of knowledge in the past. Their value increases when compared with other sources that chronicle information about the period, which in general are much less exhaustive. This leads us to the conclusion that the Spanish journals of the 1950s and 1960s acted as accessible sources that enabled Spanish architects to keep abreast of world architecture, and that the journals played the fundamental role that they have assumed today as a repository for knowledge, appreciation and the recovery of the architectural heritage of the twentieth century.

Notes

1 Along with the two journals from the institutes of architects in Madrid and Barcelona, it is the only other publication from the time that continues to be published to date.
2 These contributors included the architect Adolfo González Amezqueta, who coordinated some initial issues; Gabino Alejandro Carriedo, founder and first editor-in-chief of *El Inmueble*; Angel Crespo, Santiago Amón, Pilar Gómez-Bedate, and Germano Celant.
3 Antonio Fernández Alba (*NF* 15–16, 1967; *NF* 56, 1970); Fernando Higueras and Antonio Miró (*NF* 46–47, 1969; *NF* 49, 1970; *NF* 65, 1971); José Luis Íñiguez and Antonio Vázquez de Castro (*NF* 102–103, 1974); Martorell, Bohigas and Mackay (*NF* 83, 1972; *NF* 86, 1973); and Rafael Moneo (*NF* 108, 1975); and to the already well established José Antonio Corrales and Ramón Vázquez Molezún (*NF* 20–24, 1967; *NF* 25–26, 1968); Miguel Fisac (*NF* 39–41, 1969); Francisco Cabrero (*NF* 76, 1972); Julio Cano Lasso (*NF* 72–73, 1972); Rafael Aburto (*NF* 99, 1974); Javier Carvajal (*NF* 104, 1974); José Antonio Coderch (*NF* 106, 1974); and Alejandro de la Sota (*NF* 107, 1974). As for foreigners, Claude Parent (*NF* 13, 1967; *NF* 25–27, 1968; *NF* 50, 1970; *NF* 78–79, 1972); Robert Krier (*NF* 95, 1973), Robert Venturi (*NF* 81, 1972); and Bruno Zevi (*NF* 105, 1974), all shared the limelight with the works of Jorn Utzon (*NF* 96–97, 1974) and Max Bill (*NF* 92, 1973) which were still relatively unknown in Spanish circles.
4 Among the first, were issues devoted to Spanish Rationalism (*NF* 33, 1968), Eduardo Torroja (*NF* 32, 1968), José Manuel Aizpurúa (*NF* 40, 1969), Casto Fernández-Shaw (*NF* 45, 1969), Alberto del Palacio (*NF* 60–61, 1971), Martín Domínguez (*NF* 64, 1971), the Capitol building (*NF* 66–67, 1971), Víctor Eusa and Teodoro Anasagasti (*NF* 90–91, 1973), Spanish Expressionism (*NF* 68 and 70, 1971) and Fernando García Mercadal (*NF* 69, 1971). Later issues were dedicated to Constructivism and Futurism (*NF* 29, 1968; *NF* 38, 1969), De Stijl (NF 52, 57–58, 1970; *NF* 62, 1971), Gerrit Rietveld (*NF* 58, 1970) and Alberto Sartoris (*NF* 84–85, 1973).
5 For example: 'Stocktaking' by Reyner Banham, (Arquitectura, 1961b) previously published in *The Architectural Review* (Banham, 1960) and 'Balance 1960' (Arquitectura, 1961a), a review of 'Panorama 60' (L'Architecture d'Aujourd'hui, 1960), a special issue of *L'Architecture d'Aujourd'hui* dedicated to the early 1960s.

References

Aalto, A. (1952). El arquitecto Alvar Aalto en las Sesiones de Crítica de Arquitectura celebradas en el mes de noviembre en Madrid. *Revista Nacional de Arquitectura*, 124, pp. 19–36.

Anon. (1996a). Conversaciones sobre Nueva Forma: Con Fernando Higueras, arquitecto. In *Nueva Forma: Arquitectura, arte y cultura 1966–1978*. Madrid: Opponaox, pp. 60–61.

Anon. (1996b). Conversaciones sobre Nueva Forma: Con Javier Carvajal, arquitecto. In *Nueva Forma: Arquitectura, arte y cultura 1966–1975*. Madrid: Opponaox, p. 61.

Arquitectura (1961a). Balance 1960. La tradición, la tecnología, 26, pp. 2–18.

—— (1961b). Panorama de la Arquitectura en el 1960, 30, pp. 2–15.

Banham, R. (1960). Stocktaking of the Impact of Tradition and Technology on Architecture Today. *The Architectural Review*, 127 (756), pp. 93–100.

Bernal, A. (2011). Las revistas Arquitectura y Cuadernos de Arquitectura: 1960–1970. PhD thesis, Valladolid, Universidad de Valladolid.

Bohigas, O. (1978). Tres revistas. *Arquitecturas bis*, 23/24, pp. 59–60.

Capitel, A. (1996). Arquitectura española 1939–1992. In *Arquitectura española del siglo XX*. Madrid: Espasa Calpe.

Casariego, P. (1964). SCA: Sobre la arquitectura actual. *Arquitectura*, 66, pp. 34–45.

Cela, C. J. (1967). Madrid, los arquitectos y el azar. *Arquitectura*, 98, pp. 43–51.

Chueca, F., Aburto, R. and Fisac, M. (1953). *Manifiesto de la Alhambra*. Madrid: Dirección General de Arquitectura.

Coddou, F., Brito, A. and Correia, N. (2011). Oriol Bohigas. Entrevista. *Vitruvius*, 12. Retrieved 8 July 2016 from www.vitruvius.com.br/revistas/read/entrevista/11.048/4080?page=4.

Coderch, J. A. (1967). SCA: Edificio Girasol. *Arquitectura*, 107, pp. 29–37.

Corbusier, L. (1958). Le Corbusier. *Revista Nacional de Arquitectura*, 199, pp. 29–38.

Corrales, J. A. (2011). Cuestión de fe. In *España importa: La difusión de la arquitectura moderna extranjera (1949–1968)*. Madrid: Mairea libros, pp. 47–56.

Corrales, J. A. and Vázquez Molezún, R. (1958). Grupo escolar en Herrera de Pisuerga. *Revista Nacional de Arquitectura*, 203, pp. 11–22.

—— (1966). Casa Huarte en Madrid. *Arquitectura*, 94, pp. 1–10.

De Miguel, C. (1978). Revista Nacional de Arquitectura. *Arquitecturas bis*, 23/24, p. 63.

Esteban Maluenda, A. (2008). La modernidad importada. Madrid 1949–1968: cauces de difusión de la arquitectura extranjera. PhD thesis, Madrid, Universidad Politécnica de Madrid.

—— (2011). *España importa. La difusión de la arquitectura moderna extranjera (1949–1968)*. Madrid: Mairea Libros.

Fernandez Alba, A. (1996). Nueva Forma o la lucidez de la agonía. In *Nueva Forma: Arquitectura, arte y cultura 1966–1975*. Madrid: Opponax.

—— (2011). La crónica detallada. In *España importa: La difusión de la arquitectura moderna extranjera (1949–1968)*. Madrid: Mairea libros, pp. 57–62.

Fernandez Alba, A., Martinez-Novillo, A., Humanes Bustamente, A. and Gazapo de Aguilera, D. (1996). *Nueva Forma: Arquitectura, arte y cultura, 1966–1975*. Madrid: Opponaox.

Fernández-Longoria Pinazo, F. (1968). Contradicción y contrapunto en las Torres Blancas. *Arquitectura*, 120, pp. 3–20.

Flores, C. (1978). Hogar y Arquitectura. *Arquitecturas bis*, 23/24, pp. 60–61.

—— (1994). *Sobre arquitecturas y arquitectos*. Madrid: Colegio Oficial de Arquitectos de Madrid.

Fullaondo, J. D. (1975). Entrevista. *Nueva Forma*, 110, pp. I–XXXII.

Fullaondo, J. D. and Bohigas, O. (1968). Sesión de Crítica de Arquitectura: Las escuelas de Madrid y Barcelona. *Arquitectura*, 118, pp. 11–30.

Fullaondo, J. D. and Muñoz, M. T. (1997). *Y Orfeo desciende*. Madrid: Molly Editorial.

Gutiérrez Soto, L. (1951). Sesión de crítica de arquitectura: El Ministerio del Aire. *Revista Nacional de Arquitectura*, 112, pp. 28–43.

Humanes, A. (1996). Nueva Forma: Arte, Arquitectura y todo lo demás. In *Nueva Forma: Arquitectura, arte y cultura 1966–1975*. Madrid: Opponax, pp. 35–39.

L'Architecture d'Aujourd'hui (1960). Panorama. *L'Architecture d'Aujourd'hui*, 60 (91–92).

Martinez-Novillo, A. (1996). Un tiempo, unos hombres, una revista. In *Nueva Forma: Arquitectura, arte y cultura 1966–1975*. Madrid: Opponaox.

Moneo, R. (2011). La modernidad idealizada. In *España importa: La difusión de la arquitectura moderna extranjera (1949–1968)*. Madrid: Mairea libros, pp. 71–89.

Moya, L. (1951). Edificio de la ONU visto por arquitectos españoles. *Revista Nacional de Arquitectura*, 11(109), pp. 21–44.

Pérez Moreno, L. C. (2015). *Fullaondo y la revista Nueva Forma: Aportaciones a la construcción de una cultura arquitectónica en España (1966–1975)*. Alzuza (Navarra): Fundación Museo Jorge Oteiza.

Revista Nacional de Arquitectura (1953). Sesiones de crítica de arquitectura. Sesiones celebradas en la Alhambra durante los días 14 y 15 de octubre de 1952. *Revista Nacional de Arquitectura*, 136, pp. 13–50.

8

THE GREEK VISION OF POSTWAR MODERNITY

Panayotis Tournikiotis

Although Greece has exceptional neoclassical and modern architecture, there were no professional journals dedicated to architecture until the end of the 1950s. The reasons for this are mainly historical. Greece as an independent nation-state was founded in 1830 after centuries of Ottoman rule, in which culture there were neither architects nor architectural education, as they had been experienced in Western Europe. The construction of the new state and its public buildings was based on the work of European architects from Germany, France and Denmark, while the training of architects at the Polytechnic School, founded in Athens, started much later. As late as the end of the nineteenth century, architecture was only a specialisation at the School of Civil Engineering. The establishment of the School of Architecture in 1917 marked a new period and created an audience for the Greek, and the international, architectural press. However, the domestic audience was still limited since only 76 architects had graduated by 1930 (and only 142 more by 1940). At the same time, many Greeks were studying architecture in France and Germany, bringing together a creative nexus of Greek and international students, while in Greece a spirit of modernisation prevailed. The libraries of these architects included the typical manuals, avant-garde books and several contemporary journals.[1] Modernity was dominant in the interwar period, especially during the 1930s. Two graduates of the School of Architecture had already worked in Le Corbusier's office during 1930–1932 and participated in major projects before returning to practice in Greece. Furthermore, the organisation of several meetings at CIAM IV, and the exhibition of delegates' projects at the School of Architecture, were greeted with enthusiasm by the professors and the general public and exerted a strong influence on students, among whom were George Candilis and Constantinos Doxiadis.

The first journal that included architectural topics was *Archimedes*, issued by the Greek Polytechnic Association in 1899–1914, but which published comparatively few articles on architecture. The second journal primarily addressed to engineers but which included architectural themes was *Erga* (works, projects), published between 1928 and 1932. The few articles on architecture that it published mostly addressed international town planning and housing issues.

The Technical Chamber of Greece was founded in 1926, and the professional body of architects participated right from the beginning. In 1932 the Chamber initiated its bi-monthly publication of *Technika Chronika* (Technical Chronicles) that continued in print until 2000. *Technika Chronika* was a professional journal published continuously during the postwar years, and its readership consisted of all members of the Technical Chamber, including engineers, and architects (whose membership was mandatory). *Technika Chronika* nevertheless also played an important role in the interwar period because it published a few, but significant, articles on architecture – for instance by Le Corbusier and Alberto Sartoris, as well as an invaluable triple issue in 1933 dedicated to CIAM IV. Gathered in these issues were all the speeches of the delegates in Athens, both in Greek and the language in which they were delivered, and notable details about the conference and the question of the Functional City (*Technika Chronika* 44–46, 1933). This issue reached the libraries of many institutions and architects – CIAM delegates' at least – documenting the reciprocal dialogue in architecture journals between Greek and international exponents of modern architecture.

Continuing the exchanges developed in CIAM IV, several articles on Greek architects were published in European journals in the following years, disseminating Greek modern architecture to an international audience.[2] This was a significant architecture in terms of private houses and apartment buildings as well as public-sector schools, hospitals, social housing and other buildings for social welfare, an architecture that shaped the modern legacy of the postwar era (Condaratos and Wang, 1999).

The Second World War began for Greece in October 1940 with the invasion of the Italian army, and ended in October 1944 with the German retreat. Naturally, reconstruction was a primary concern and Constantinos Doxiadis, who was the director of the reconstruction services from 1945 to 1948, played a major part. War in Greece, however, was not yet over. The 'battle of Athens' started on December 1944 and marked the beginning of a civil war that challenged the accession of Greece to the Western or Eastern bloc, and lasted until 1949. This disastrous confrontation delayed the development of both public- and private-sector architecture until the early 1950s. From then on, and especially from 1952, a period of rapid and optimistic, economic, social and cultural growth began, that brought modern architecture to the fore as an exclusive building tradition. Architects, whose numbers had increased by 140 graduates from the Athens School by 1950 (and 241 more before 1959), were now in great demand and socially respected, having to choose between a rapidly growing private sector and an ambitious and modern public one. Apartment buildings formed the mainstream housing practice in Athens and other cities, while around the same time, but particularly in the 1960s, a trend for second homes beside the sea developed. Alongside these, large-scale state programmes for hotels, tourism, archaeological sites and social housing were led by a younger generation of modern architects whose work combined 'international' characteristics with aspects of the *genius loci* (Aesopos, 1999).

For the first postwar generation of architects, who were primarily French-speaking, the main reference point in the international context was still Le Corbusier and the key journal *L'Architecture d'Aujourd'hui*. A second, but less strong influence were architects such as Richard Neutra and Alvar Aalto, and, a little later, Oscar Niemeyer or Kenzo Tange, associated with architectural journals like *The Architectural Review, Architectural Forum, Detail, Casabella, domus* and *Japan Architect*. In the Greek architectural scene, however, there was only *Technika Chronika*, which had developed during the postwar years a much more technical and conservative profile regarding architecture. The few articles addressed to architects were mainly of a technical or informative nature and the *Technika Chronika* typically did not publish built works by Greek or international architects. The demand for a journal addressed directly to Greek architects, showcasing their work, offering information and a platform for debate, and going beyond the confines of language and place, was now more than pressing. Two journals with very different objectives responded to this challenge by the end of the 1950s: *Architectoniki* and *Ekistics*.

Architectoniki's first bi-monthly issue was released in January 1957.[3] The publisher was the young architect Antonis Kitsikis, who had graduated in 1953, but his father, Kostas Kitsikis (1893–1969), was effectively editor and the real inspiration of the journal. He was at the time a professor of building design and dean at the School of Architecture. He had studied in Berlin and enjoyed a busy career in architecture and urban design before being elected professor in 1940. His career developed further in the postwar era, when he became an important architect to the bourgeoisie, maintaining political relationships in Greece and connections with international architectural organisations (such as the UIA). In the editorial of the first issue, which he signed personally, he argued that the publication met a real need which he attributed not only to the work of contemporary Greek architects but also to the long history of Greek architecture (Kitsikis, 1957a). As he explained subsequently, the journal was not intended to be confined to matters 'closely being understood as architectural activity', but also to expand on 'spiritual and cultural matters [...] such as archaeological research and excavations, the history of architecture, [...] urban planning, housing problems, the protection of the landscape and archaeological monuments, tourism, the trends of international architectural movements' and more. Among the journal's aims, according to Kitsikis, was to promote 'the work of Greek colleagues' and to 'raise the architectural level of the country'. Regarding the selection of architectural projects and articles in general, for which he was responsible, Kitsikis expressed the conservative moderation that characterised all his personal work, confirming the release 'of art from prejudices and imitations of old standards' while trying to avoid 'sophisticated excesses' (Kitsikis, 1957a). In other words, a simplified classicism and a moderate modernity could coexist in the journal.

The contents of the first issue confirmed Kitsiki's intentions. The journal was rich and diverse, with short but well-illustrated articles by prominent Greek architects and planners, balancing work from the private and public sectors and generally echoing modernity. The cover photo from the private apartment of the cosmopolitan painter and professor in the School of Architecture, Nikos Hadjikyriakos Ghikas, designed in collaboration with Antonis Kitsikis, suggested a conservative sense of urban life, despite exhibiting visible frames of reinforced concrete.

In the issue's first section there was a sequence of one-page articles: Kostas Biris on the Gardens of Athens; Anastasios Orlandos on the restoration of the Temple of Aphaia; John Travlos on the restoration of the Holy Apostles church in the ancient Agora; and Panayotis Michelis writing in support of the 'necessity of Style'. The first three articles brought forward the importance of historical heritage in modern Greece, while the fourth was expressing a much more personal perspective. Michelis was taking the modern for granted, primarily because of the technical and social change it epitomised, but he criticised its architectural expression, warning that this was 'leading to "inhumanity"', and he argued for attributing to modernism 'a new realistic humanism, without abandoning its principles, but subjecting them to an aesthetic consideration' (Michelis, 1957). In the following pages, a series of new projects of different types and scales were presented: tourist developments on the Saronic coast, especially that of Vouliagmeni; the plans of Doxiadis Associates for Iraq; a sanatorium by Kyprianos Biris; the house-atelier of Nikos Hadjikyriakos Ghikas; a master plan study for the basin of Athens from the Government's Housing Service; the marine centre in the Coast of Glyfada; the reconstruction of earthquake-damaged villages on Santorini; and several villas, mainly in a

FIGURE 8.1   Journal cover, *Architectoniki* 1 (1957). House-atelier of Nikos Hadjikyriakos Ghikas, by Anthonis Kitsikis.

conservative idiom, from which stand out those of Pikionis at Filothei and by Konstantinidis in Korinthia. News and other information were published in the final pages, along with translations of key texts in French, English or German, depending on the author.

The journal's overall image appeared promising in the Greek context, even if it was characterised by an attempt to publish 'something of everything'. In the following years, the issues published continued in a similar vein, covering more extensive articles and better-illustrated buildings, from Greece and abroad, while also seeking to attract an international audience.

For instance, many articles on excavations and restorations from major archaeological sites were published, a subject equally interesting to both a local and international audience, just as the Byzantine era had affinities with modern architecture. Along with these, there were studies, buildings and analyses regarding tourism's rapid growth in Greece and across the Mediterranean. The state-led, and decidedly modern programme of the Greek Tourist Organisation was extensively published, showcasing significant hotels like the 'Triton' Xenia by Aris Konstantinidis in Andros (Konstantinidis, 1959) and the Xenia hotel by Triandafilidis in Nafplion, featured on the journal's cover (Triandafilidis, 1961).

New large-scale buildings, such as the American Embassy in Athens by Walter Gropius (TAC, 1957), were also extensively documented together with emblematic international works such as the Modern Art Museum of Rio de Janeiro by Alfonso Eduardo Reidy (Reidy, 1959) and the National Museum of Western Art in Tokyo by Le Corbusier (Le Corbusier, 1959). In 1959, an entire issue was dedicated to Doxiadis' practice on the occasion of the

FIGURE 8.2   Journal cover, *Architectoniki* 21 (May–June 1960).

FIGURE 8.3   Journal cover, *Architectoniki* 29 (September–October 1961). 'Hotel "Xenia" at Nauplia', Yani V. Triandafilidis.

completion of his own office building in Athens (*Architectoniki* 13, 1959). In this same issue a long article by Doxiadis on the Science of Housing (Ekistics) was published, while his studies and projects in Greece and especially in Asia and Africa were also included. Given the content of this journal issue, *Architectoniki* expressly addressed an international audience (and consequently all the texts were also published in French, English and German). The following issues were to apply the same translation policy, although selectively, leaving several texts of local interest in Greek alone.

Besides and perhaps in contrast to the above, *Architectoniki* in the early years was publishing primarily apartment buildings and villas characterised by a generally conservative residential architecture, which neither represented the vanguard of modernity nor the interests of most architects, but rather appealed to the wider readership of wealthy Athenian society. There were naturally several exceptions, such as the modern house in Psychiko by Takis Zenetos and Margaritis Apostolidis (Zenetos and Apostolidis, 1959) or architectural competition awards where modern architecture was usually celebrated. We can also find articles supporting modernity, such as the defence of the Modulor by Vassilis Cassandras, professor at the School of Architecture, who advocated international modernism and challenged the criticisms addressed by Kitsikis to Le Corbusier (Cassandras, 1957), suggesting that modernity was not the polemical disposition of *Architectoniki*. The personality of Kitsikis remained dominant as evidenced in his editorials, which included open letters to the government on the subject of the city and discussing planning policies, so sharp and detailed that they are, even today, considered to be of significant interest (Kitsikis, 1957b).

This activity continued with relative success, having the support of a large majority of Greek architects. *Architectoniki*, with a print run of 10,000 copies in 1960, reached, with the help of its sales representatives, dozens of countries and was purchased by many international libraries. At the same time the profile of the journal changed. The role of the father figure of Kitsikis decreased and more responsibilities were taken on by his son Antonis and Doris Makris, now the chief editor. At the beginning of the 1960s a new interest arose in the publication of buildings and studies, which focused exclusively on issues particular to Greece. Even if we have doubts today about its ideology, modernist values, or even the integrity of the publishers (publishing many of their own projects), *Architectoniki* represented Greek architecture to an international audience at a time when the architectural press in many countries was promoting representative national 'modernisms' through documentary drawings and photographs rather than explanatory text. The publishers decided to renew *Architectoniki* when they gave editorial control to Orestis Doumanis (1929–2013), a civil engineer who rather surprisingly had previously edited a series of tributes to a young, dynamic and rising generation of Greek architects in the art magazine *Zygos*.

Architectoniki with Orestis Doumanis as chief editor was released in the summer of 1963 with a very different and modern cover showing a photo of an apartment building by Takis Zenetos and Margaritis Apostolides, contrasting with the vertically arranged title, and contents that left no doubt about the new modernist orientation.

In future issues, *Architectoniki* had become a modern international journal, dropping the subtitle of 'decoration' from its cover, and publishing work of a younger generation of the peers of Antonis Kitsikis, who remained as the publisher-director. Meanwhile his father, Kostas Kitsikis, almost entirely disappeared from the journal. It might look like a conflict of generations, but, above all, it is evidence of the dominance of the modern spirit and proof of a successful business policy. During the same period, *Architectoniki* expanded its activities by

FIGURE 8.4 Journal cover, *Architectoniki* (1963). Apartment building, Takis Zenetos and Margaritis Apostolides.

establishing an exhibition centre for building materials by the companies that advertised their products in the journal. The exhibition centre also operated as a nightclub with dance music, gathering the who's who of Athenian society, from Aristotle Onassis to Melina Merkouri.

Doumanis' new *Architectoniki* shaped up definitively in issue 42, the last of 1963, which combined a comprehensive presentation of modern and especially Greek architecture, including flagship projects from the most significant 'young' architects, accompanied by well-timed but caustic editorials by Doumanis himself, and notable articles on history and theory. The architectural projects highlighted the Greek vanguard of the 1960s, with several modern buildings by Takis Zenetos (Zenetos 1963a, 1963b, 1964), Aris Konstantinidis (Konstantinidis 1963a, 1963b, 1964) and Nikos Valsamakis (Valsamakis, 1963a, 1963b).

They stood out on the international stage, being well documented and represented in outstanding photography. Alongside these modern buildings, important historical and theoretical articles emerged; for example, the short history of modern architecture in five extensive sequels by Thymio Papagiannis and Anna Venezi, later reprinted to enrich the limited Greek architectural literature of the period (Papagianni and Venezi, 1964). Similarly Zenetos' and Doxiadis' essays – the former dedicated to modern urbanism (Zenetos, 1963) and the latter on the relationship of the ancient Greek city to the modern (Doxiadis, 1964) – contributed to international publications reflecting on the postwar avant-garde. Discourse on art was also present in the culture of the 'new' journal in the form of occasional but significant articles, both on contemporary art, and the relation between modern and traditional art infused with the spirit of 'Greekness'. This set of journal issues was complemented by the publication of articles on archaeology, decorative and graphic arts and student work. Several remain

FIGURE 8.5   'Villa at Kavouri near Athens', T. Ch. Zenetos and M. Ch. Apostolides, *Architectoniki* 45 (1964).

FIGURE 8.6   'Small G.T.O. [Xenia] buildings at Epidauros', Aris Konstantinidis, *Architectoniki* 39 (1963).

FIGURE 8.7   'Private house at Anavyssos', N. Valsamakis, *Architectoniki* 42 (1963).

interesting more than 60 years later, and the publication of diploma (thesis) projects by then unknown but later 'recognised' architects reveals a degree of editorial insight. One of the most interesting elements of this period was the writing of the chief editor Orestis Doumanis – caustic and often timely, this extended into interpretation of Greek architecture, such as the extensively illustrated 'Introduction to postwar Greek architecture' (Doumanis, 1964), one of the first critical texts on this period. The essay concludes:

> The overall picture of postwar Greek architecture is discouraging, even more so when compared to the work done in the first forty years of our century. But there are encouraging signs in the work of a few young, and even fewer older, architects who are alive to new directions in world architecture. Their buildings have a severe and sober appearance; a spirit of sobriety and simplicity that characterizes new architecture, devoid of the affectation and exhibitionism of the new baroque school that currently threatens to spread throughout the world.
>
> *Doumanis, 1964*

This period would, however, rapidly come to an end. Doumanis left *Architectoniki* in 1965 and the editorial work was assigned to a graphic designer, Spiros Cosmetatos, who looked to carry on in a similar vein. Nevertheless, *Architectoniki* was in decline, one which was not reversed when the editorship was assigned to Franzis Frantziskakis in 1968 – as a former editor of the defunct *Zygos* – taking the journal into another new direction with an emphasis on the plastic arts. There is no doubt that *Architectoniki* had completed a cycle. During this long decade it well represented Greek postwar architecture in general while simultaneously contributing, in its mapping and pro-active publicity, to a Greek architecture known primarily in select international circles. At the end of 1970, when it had changed completely and finally ceased publication, a dictatorship had been imposed on Greece and tough competition had developed mainly because of Doumanis' editorial initiatives, to which we return later. In the meantime, we are concerned with the parallel but entirely different development of *Ekistics*.

Ekistics was not designed as a journal addressed to the general public, but as an English-language monthly bulletin for the international staff of the Doxiadis Office, which gradually developed into a partially independent edition that was released internationally and served as a worldwide forum of ideas focused on human settlements and urban thinking in general. Constantinos Doxiadis (1914–1975) founded Doxiadis Associates in 1953, a private firm of consulting engineers for 'development' and Ekistics, which expanded by the early 1960s to have offices on five continents and projects in no fewer than 40 countries. In October 1955, when the practice had already undertaken studies in central Africa and Asia, a monthly compilation of abstracts from current publications on planning and housing was launched, primarily for internal use, particularly for those in the field and distant from libraries and periodicals. This collection of abstracts was called a 'Tropical Housing and Planning Monthly Bulletin' with a circulation limited to Doxiadis Associates and select research organisations. Two years later, in October 1957, the bulletin was renamed *Ekistics: Housing & Planning Abstracts*, expanding its release to university departments and research institutes (Tyrwhitt, 1957). By January 1965 it had become *Ekistics: The Problems and Science of Human Settlements*, and in the meantime it had already changed subtitle another three times. These changes were minor, but concurrent changes in content were more fundamental. *Ekistics* shifted from a mimeographed internal bulletin to become a regular hardcover journal, published and printed in Athens by Doxiadis Associates, yet edited by Jaqueline Tyrwhitt, professor at Harvard GSD, and circulated worldwide.[4]

Doxiadis organised the central office in Athens, but its activity was global with annexes in various parts of the world with English as its official language. Doxiadis based this activity on personal research and theoretical work that was grounded in the Greek city and Greek literature (Doxiadis, 1937). Keywords in many of his theoretical writings were neologisms, their roots being in Greek words like *dynapolis, ecumenopolis, anthropopolis* or *entopia*. The leading word in this vocabulary was *Ekistics*, which identified the journal and Doxiadis' most important book, published in 1968 (Doxiadis, 1968). In the editorial of issue 95, in October 1963, which was dedicated to the first 'Delos Symposion', Doxiadis wrote:

> Ekistics is the science of human settlements. The term is derived from the Greek verb ΟΙΚΩ meaning settling down, and demonstrates the existence of an overall science of human settlements conditioned by man and influenced by economics, social, political, administrative and technical sciences and the disciplines related to art. [...] EKISTICS, as a journal, by presenting reviews and original articles in this general field, tries to assist in the formulation of this science.
>
> *Doxiadis, 1963*

Ekistics's most significant period started in January 1962, when it was first released in a standard format, now publishing self-contained articles with broader objectives.[5]

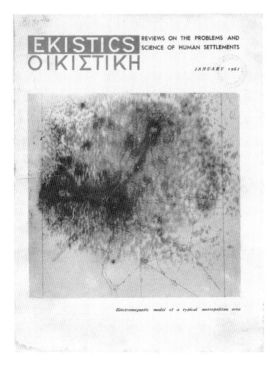

FIGURE 8.8   Journal cover, *Ekistics* 75 (January 1962): 'Electromagnetic model
of a typical metropolitan area'.
Source: *Ekistics*. Courtesy Panayis Psomopoulos.

In the previous year of 1961, *Ekistics* had still been printed as typewritten manuscripts and apart from a few texts written mostly by Doxiadis and his associates (Doxiadis, 1961; Fathy, 1961), it consisted of articles already published in international journals such as *The Architectural Review, Geographical Review, Architectural Forum, Japan Architect* (Tange, 1961), *Bauen + Wohnen* (Chombart de Lauwe, 1961; Jacobs, 1961), and extensive reviews of seminal books, such as *The Image of the City* by Kevin Lynch, reviewed by Jaqueline Tyrwhitt (1961). In the following period, from January 1962 onwards, more articles by Doxiadis and his associates, like the theoretical 'Ecumenopolis, Toward a Universal City' (Doxiadis, 1962), and projects or study reports on Islamabad (Doxiadis Associates, 1962a), Venezuela (Doxiadis and Hadjopoulos, 1962), Ghana (Doxiadis Associates, 1962b) and Greece, were published. In addition, essays discussing social life in settlements and cities around the world were written by freelancers collaborating with the office. From issue 83, in October 1962, onwards the journal became organised thematically. These were either a set of 'minor' themes (three or four per issue), or 'major' themes to which single issues were dedicated. They discussed relevant contemporary issues – for example: 'The Pedestrian Oriented Street' (*Ekistics* 85, 1962); 'Aspects of Urban Form' (*Ekistics* 89, 1963a); 'Activity Spines versus Traffic Arteries' (*Ekistics* 96, 1963b); 'Urban Renewal and Urban Design' (*Ekistics* 105, 1964); or 'Time for Leisure' (*Ekistics* 115, 1965). In many issues the geographic scope was impressive, *de facto* giving *Ekistics* an international status. Issue 81 from July 1962, again typically, included articles on Singapore, Hong Kong, Denmark, Santa Monica (California), Sweden, India, Fiji, Netherlands, Kumasi (Ghana), Thessaloniki and Malaysia. Even the authors of these articles, the majority researchers, had cosmopolitan backgrounds. *Ekistics* had acquired an audience of readers in universities, institutions and large offices, including researchers in other disciplines, but it did not address the general public and, without advertisements, it was not marketed on a commercial basis. Illustrations were limited and tended to be diagrams rather than photographs. It was printed on plain paper, like a scientific journal, and the layout was straightforward, with coloured covers.

Jaqueline Tyrwhitt was the editor from the first issue of 1955 to issue 200 of July 1972 (the focus here is on the period 1962–1972). In these ten years, articles by dozens of now insignificant authors were published. But there were also essays by authors who remain alive in our collective memory, representing the postwar challenge to the modern city, with particular focus on the idea of human scale and the housing of people in less developed countries, also with reference to technological developments such as communication and sustainability.[6]

There is no doubt that *Ekistics* publicised the theoretical and practical activities of Doxiadis Associates, and of Constantinos Doxiadis in particular, but it was simultaneously condensing reflections on the postwar evolution of the global environment, from a perspective that finally addressed the forthcoming millennium and beyond. This future scenario was to overcome the crisis of the postwar modern *dystopia*, which was considered largely a consequence of the Athens Charter, in a future conceived as *entopia* and not as (a futuristic) *utopia*.[7] Amalgamating the concerns of John Turner about uncontrolled urban settlements (Turner, 1965, 1967, 1969) and Edward T. Hall on human needs (Hall, 1969), there was an effort to update the Charter of Athens in a contemporary 'Declaration of Delos'. A symposium was organised exactly 30 years after CIAM IV, to conclude with a declaration at the ancient theatre of Delos.

This became the sole theme of *Ekistics* 95, in October 1963. In this issue the era of the global network is proposed in the words of Marshall McLuhan:

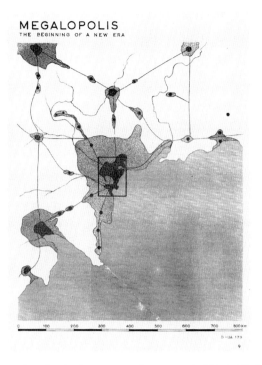

FIGURE 8.9   'Megalopolis, the beginning of a new era', *Ekistics* 75, January (1962).
Source: Ekistics. Courtesy Panayis Psomopoulos.

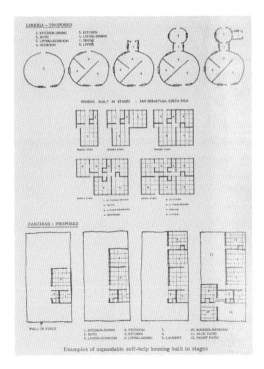

FIGURE 8.10   'Examples of expandable self-help housing built in stages', *Ekistics* 103, June (1964).
Source: Ekistics. Courtesy Panayis Psomopoulos.

FIGURE 8.11   Journal cover, *Ekistics* 103, June (1964): 'Hong Kong Waterfront'.
Source: *Ekistics*. Courtesy Panayis Psomopoulos.

FIGURE 8.12   Journal cover, *Ekistics* 95, October (1963): 'The Delos Symposion'.
Source: *Ekistics*. Courtesy Panayis Psomopoulos.

...sat on the ancient marble benches

FIGURE 8.13   Members of the Delos Symposion, on the ancient theatre's marble benches
at the signing of the 'declaration'. *Ekistics* 95, October (1963).
Source: *Ekistics*. Courtesy Panayis Psomopoulos.

Electronic technology has extended the brain itself to embrace the globe; previous technologies had only extended the bodily servants of the brain. The result now is a speedup of information that reduces the planet to the scale of a village – with this difference, that the volume of information movement on a planetary than a village scale. A global consciousness thus becomes the new human scale.

McLuhan, 1963

Between *Architectoniki* and *Ekistics*, between, that is, a typical architectural journal primarily for Greek architects (simultaneously trying to publicise Greek architecture on the international scene) and a rather scholarly journal that emanated from the same urban neighbourhood of Athens but was addressed, in English, to an international audience, Greek postwar architecture briefly found a powerful field of expression in two other journals with special characteristics. The first was the visual arts journal *Zygos*, published from 1955 to 1966, where Orestis Doumanis acted as architectural editor from 1961 to 1963. During this short period, *Zygos* published several monographic dossiers on the work of young and mostly modernist architects (Zenetos, Valsamakis, Dekavallas, Skiadaressis, Konstantinidis, Papayannis and others), introducing a new pioneering spirit one later identified in architecture with the 1960s Greek spring.

This successful activity led to Doumanis' appointment as chief editor of *Architectoniki*, which he then promptly left in 1965 to take over *Technika Chronika*. As pointed out previously, the journal of the Technical Chamber was addressed to *all* Greek engineers. However, during the two years when Doumanis worked at *Technika Chronika*, while architecture and urban planning gained space, and critical thinking emerged, so also did a technically inclined modernist approach. The role of Doumanis' collaboration with these three journals was important, but ultimately this was only the start. From 1967 he undertook the publication of an annual journal titled *Architectonika Themata* (Architecture in Greece), of which he was also the proprietor, and which was paired in 1970 with another, also annual, journal titled *Themata Chorou + Texnon* (Design + Art in Greece). These two publications were issued regularly until Doumanis' death in 2013, and they represented mainstream 'periodical' publishing in the field of Greek architecture for 45 years. Both moved beyond postwar architecture in time and content, successfully integrating earlier publishing efforts in order for Doumanis to emerge, together with Doxiadis, as a key figure in shaping architectural and urban thinking.

FIGURE 8.14   Motel 'Xenia' at Kalambaka (1959–1960), A. Konstantinidis, *Zygos* 82–83 (1962).

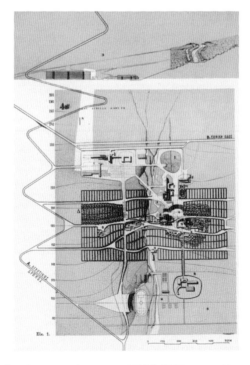

FIGURE 8.15   Agricultural cooperative centre (1954), T. Zenetos, *Zygos* 72–75 (1961–1962).

FIGURE 8.16   Agricultural cooperative centre (1954), T. Zenetos, model of the covered hall, *Zygos* 72–75 (1961–1962).

Periodicals played an important role in the early postwar decades of reconstruction, socio-political restructuring and rapid economic growth, consolidating a dominant modern architecture but also encouraging a critical contestation with this ideology. The internationalisation of problems may go hand in hand with national, or local, formal expression, and the dominant discourse delivered as a universal dictum has to be understood in relation to a structural relationship between centre and periphery in which there are now multiple centres and several dynamic regions. The major international journals have been agents of centrality, though they represent a diffuse centrality of ideas rather than a geographical location, while seeking the globalisation of these ideas and regional interconnection. All major international journals of the postwar period, whether based in Paris or London, had representatives on several continents and in many countries, dedicating special issues to Brazil, Japan or Sweden. Conversely, national journals generally published 'home' projects and, aspiring to be marketed in Paris or London, translated extracts from their texts in French and/or English, thereby challenging their local status. Similarly, all the main international journals reached the major Greek practices, while the Greek publications, primarily *Architectoniki*, only potentially addressed a worldwide audience. However, the relationship was not reciprocal. *L 'Architecture d'Aujourd'hui* may have been read by architects in Athens and Stockholm, but the corresponding Greek or Swedish journals did not equally reach French or other international practices, although part of their texts had been translated. This was, however, hardly a question of language, as architecture is read to a large extent without words, but a challenge in the reciprocity of centre and periphery.

In that kind of confrontation between centre and periphery, the differentiation is not entirely clear because the centre is historiographically defined through publishing activities, while the periphery, on the other hand, is defined by a dependent relationship between the reality of building and enchanting publications. The question is not a simple one. The diffusion, in the global network, of pictures, drawings and also texts on buildings by Richard Neutra, Alvar Aalto, Le Corbusier, Kenzo Tange, Mies van der Rohe and Oscar Niemeyer, or the social programmes in Sweden and the tropical housing in Africa, created, between 1945 and 1965 and for the first time in history, a shared space of information and influence. This represented a form of global database, blurring the idea of a central 'core' and involving a network of centres without geographical, but rather with publishing, coordinates. A condition which made Greek architecture a 'corresponding' architecture for the whole world, without making this relationship reciprocal. Centres have always co-existed with their peripheries. The difference was that Aalto's projects could be at the centre thanks to the central role of the publishing media, while at the same time remaining geographically on the periphery. This meant that there was not, and could not be, a link between peripheries without passing through 'central' publications, Paris and London being a shared destination for Greek and Finnish architects alike. This heterotopic relationship constructed the postwar modern tradition as well as the manner of its contestation.

Transcending the relation between centre and periphery, *Ekistics* and the Doxiadis 'office' attempted to redefine this association for the benefit of the 'global village' and ecumenopolis (Doxiadis and Papaioannou, 1975).[8] The end of colonialism negated the demand for central planning on the periphery, while the dynamic of independence displaced the institutional democracy of colonialism which was returned in principle to its ideological origins. Doxiadis, a man both Greek and universal, identified as he was with the idealism of *Ekistics*, could promote in the post-colonial era – under the peaceful and philanthropic auspices of the United Nations – an emancipated regional centrality, one more emphatic than the commonwealths of Britain or France because it transposed Greek antiquity with the aspirations of a global culture.

This momentum not only provided business for Doxiadis Associates from Aleppo and Baghdad to Islamabad, and from Rio de Janeiro to Caracas, it also gave *Ekistics* a global theoretical scope for promoting a scientific approach to 'planning' internationally. In this case the relationship between centre and periphery remained strong and catalytic. Athens was revived as a centre of influence, and Doxiadis Associates epitomised an international 'community' in which academics, architects, urbanists, anthropologists and historians were welcomed on the condition that they travel on a boat to Delos, just as members of CIAM had in 1933 travelled to Athens. The new complementary centres were above all characterised by political, ideological and economic transformation, in which the discourse of architecture delivered in periodicals, journals and an expanding media, represented a postscripted or predictable modernity, a primary expression of the postwar world in both its most cynical and simultaneously optimistic variants.

Looking back retrospectively to postwar modernity in Greece from 1945 to 1965 we can see the rise of a modern world edging to its geographic and cultural limits, that is insofar as they were represented in international publishing and its penetration into the Greek architectural community. Looking conversely at modern Greece from the outside, it is difficult to explain the dearth of information or critical analysis. In this respect, modern Greek architecture recalled unconsciously, until the 1970s at least, the aura of Doxiadis or Candilis for the creativity they developed outside Greece. The international architects who visited Greece during this period left little evidence of their search for modernity, but rather sought out antiquity. In Greece, however, modern architecture prospered in all its particular expressions, as was the case elsewhere in the world. This self-consciousness sustained a confidence in Greek architects and society in general, projecting a sense of optimism and renewal. This feeling owed much to the perception of the relationship of Greek architecture to its international context, not only to be found published in the journals architects were consulting on their drawing boards, but also in the real place of architecture, when they travelled abroad to experience modernity elsewhere. This flaccid condition of mutual glances and cognitive self-consciousness we understand better today, having moved beyond the ideal coherence of 'historiography', which allows us to see the architecture of the postwar years with new eyes, recognising that the constitution of modernity was a complex cultural condition. It was balanced by inherent tensions and the need to resolve contradictions – a culture difficult to access except through deepening the critical thinking offered in our postmodern era.

Notes

1   Many architects' libraries have been preserved in the Neohellenic Architecture Archives of the Benaki Museum, in the NTUA School of Architecture and in private collections.
2   *L'Architecture d'Aujourd'hui*, *Bâtir*, *Cahiers d'art*, *Bauwelt*, *Baumeister*, *Die Form*, *The Architectural Review* and *L'Architettura*.
3   Sized 24 × 33.5 cm and containing more than 100 pages, half being devoted to independent content, the other half consisting of advertisements.
4   *Ekistics* continued to be published after Doxiadis' death by his colleagues until the beginning of the current century.
5   Sized 20.7 × 28 cm and containing around 70 pages per issue.
6   Contributors during this period included: C. Alexander, W. Cristaller, R. Buckminster Fuller, F. Maki, K. Tange, P. Cook, J. M. Richards, S. Giedion, H. Fathy, L. Mumford, J. Gottman, A. and P. Smithson, J. B. Bakema, H. Hertzberger, A. van Eyck, G. Candilis, S. Chermayeff, A. Tzonis, B. V. Doshi, J. Turner, E. T. Hall, S. Keller, M. Mead, A. Rapoport, A. Toynbee, E. Hobsbawm, N. Negreponte and M. McLuhan.
7   'What human beings need is not utopia ('no place') but entopia ('in place') a real city which they can build, a place which satisfies the dreamer and is acceptable to the scientist, a place where the projections of the artist and the builder merge' (Doxiadis, 1968).
8   Ecumenopolis (from the Greek: οἰκουμένη, meaning 'all of the Earth's inhabitable areas', and πόλις polis meaning 'city'): the coming city that, together with the corresponding open land which is indispensable for man, will cover the entire earth as a continuous system forming a universal settlement.

References

Aesopos, Y. and Simeoforidis, Y. (Eds) (1999). *Landscapes of Modernisation, Greek Architecture 1960s and 1990s*. Athens: Metapolis.

Architectoniki (1959). Doxiadis Associates. *Architectoniki*, 13, pp. 11–72.

Architects Collaborative. (1957). United States Embassy Office Building Athens Greece. *Architectoniki*, 6, pp. 27–34.

Cassandras, V. (1957). Architecture and Modulor. *Architectoniki*, 6, pp. 74–75.

Chombart de Lauwe, P.-H. (1961). A Sociology of Housing. *Ekistics*, 74, pp. 393–397.

Condaratos, S. and Wang, W. (Eds) (1999) *Greece, 20th-Century Architecture*. Munich: Prestel.

Doumanis, O. (1964). Introduction to Postwar Greek Architecture. *Architectoniki*, 48, pp. 1–11.

Doxiadis Associates. (1962a). Islamabad: The Scale of the City and its Central Area. *Ekistics* 83, pp. 147–161.

—— (1962b). The Town of Tema, Ghana: Plans for Two Communities. *Ekistics*, 77, pp. 159–171.

Doxiadis, K. A. (1937). *Raumordnung im griechischen Städtebau*. Heidelberg: Kurt Vowinckel Verlag. Transl. J. Tyrwhitt, C. A. Doxiadis. (1972). *Architectural Space in Ancient Greece*, Cambridge, MA: MIT Press.

Doxiadis, C. A. (1961). Plan for the City of Athens. *Ekistics*, 66, pp. 281–310.

—— (1962). Ecumenopolis, Toward a Universal City. *Ekistics*, 75, pp. 3–18.

—— (1963). To the Reader. *Ekistics*, 14 (95), pp. 281–310.

—— (1964). The Ancient Greek City and the City of the Present. *Architectoniki*, 46, pp. 46–59.

—— (1968). *Ekistics: An Introduction to the Science of Human Settlements*. New York: Oxford University Press.

Doxiadis C. A., and Hadjopoulos, A. (1962). Housing and Urban Planning in the Economic Development of Venezuela. *Ekistics*, 76, pp. 81–84.

Doxiadis, C. A., and Papaioannou, J. G. (1975). *Ecumenopolis: The Inevitable City of the Future.* New York: Norton.

Ekistics (1962). The Pedestrian Oriented Street. *Ekistics*, 85, pp. 289–304.

—— (1963a). Aspects of Urban Form. *Ekistics*, 89, pp. 233–246.

—— (1963b). Activity Spines versus Traffic Arteries. *Ekistics*, 96, pp. 287–308.

—— (1964). Urban Renewal and Urban Design. *Ekistics*, 105, pp. 48–123.

—— (1965). Time for Leisure. *Ekistics*, 115, pp. 324–368.

Fathy, H. (1961). Dynapolis in Africa. *Ekistics*, 71, pp. 206–208.

Hall, E. T. (1969). Human Needs and Inhuman Cities. *Ekistics*, 159, pp. 181–184.

Jacobs, J. (1961). Trial by Cooling. *Ekistics*, 74, pp. 417–420.

Kitsikis, C. (1957a). The Issue of 'Architectoniki': Its Aims. *Architectoniki*, 1, p. 15.

—— (1957b). The 'Fereoikon' State/Need for Public Buildings, *Architectoniki*, 4, p. 21.

Konstantinidis, A. (1959). 'Triton': The New Hotel at Andros built by the Greek Tourist Organisation. *Architectoniki*, 18, pp. 78–85.

—— (1963a). Small G.T.O. buildings at Epidauros. *Architectoniki*, 39, pp. 38–47.

—— (1963b). Motel Xenia at Olympia. *Architectoniki*, 40, pp. 2–12.

—— (1964). Hotel Xenia at Poros. *Architectoniki*, 47, pp. 16–31.

Le Corbusier. (1959). National Museum of Western Art in Tokyo. *Architectoniki*, 18, pp. 10–11.

McLuhan, M. (1963). Contributory Papers. *Ekistics*, 95, p. 257.

Michelis, P. A. (1957). Need for a Style. *Architectoniki*, 1, p. 18.

Papagianni, T., and Venezi, A. (1964). *Modern Architecture: Birth, Establishment and Future.* Athens: Architectoniki.

Reidy, A. E. (1959). Modern Art Museum of Rio de Janeiro. *Architectoniki*, 18, pp. 8–10.

Tange, K. (1961). A Plan for Tokyo, 1960. *Ekistics*, 69, pp. 9–19.

Technika Chronika. (1933). The 4th International Congress of Modern Architecture in Athens 'The Organic City'. *Technika Chronika*, 44–46.

Triandafilidis, Y. V. (1961). Hotel 'Xenia' at Nauplia. *Architectonik*, 29, pp. 23–34.

Turner, J. (1965). Lima's Barriadas and Corralones: Suburbs versus Slums. *Ekistics*, 112, pp. 152–155.

—— (1967). Uncontrolled Urban Settlements: Problems and Policies. *Ekistics*, 135, pp. 120–122.

—— (1969). Architecture that Works. *Ekistics*, 158, pp. 40–44.

Tyrwhitt, J. (1957). Editorial. *Ekistics*, 4 (25), p. iii.

—— (1961). *The Image of the City* by Kevin Lynch. *Ekistics*, 65, pp. 203–207.

Valsamakis, N. (1963a). Amalia Hotel. *Architectoniki*, 41, pp. 20–23.

—— (1963b). Private House at Anavyssos. *Architectoniki*, 42, pp. 16–24.

Zenetos, T. Ch. (1963). Town and Dwelling in the Future. *Architectoniki*, (42) pp. 48–53.

Zenetos, T. Ch. and Apostolidis, M. (1959). House at Psychico. *Architectoniki*, 14, pp. 42–45.

—— (1963a). Block of Flats at Amalias Avenue. *Architectoniki*, 39, pp. 48–53.

—— (1963b). A Brewery in Athens. *Architectoniki*, 41, pp. 10–16.

—— (1964). Villa at Kavouri near Athens. *Architectoniki*, 45, pp. 30–37.

9

ARCHITECTURE D'AUJOURD'HUI, THE ANDRÉ BLOC YEARS

Nicholas Bullock

Launched in November 1930, *l'Architecture d'Aujourd'hui* (*AA*) proclaimed from its very first page a determination to shout the case for modern architecture and to denounce the old, the ugly and the corrupt. With its dark sans serif typeface, the bold contrast of its photographs and its punchy layout, André Bloc, the editor, set out to differentiate his new publication as sharply as possible from the staid imagery of the established journals. Best known were *L'Architecture*, whose soft half-tone reproductions served the interests of the architectural elite associated with the *Bâtiments Civils et Palais Nationaux* (BCPN), or *La Construction Moderne* that served the well-financed needs of architects working in the commercial sector and their friends in the building industry (Badouï, 1990; Jannière, 2002).

During the 1950s and 1960s, *AA* dominated the way that modern architecture was understood in France. It celebrated the work of Le Corbusier and documented the architectural highlights of the country's postwar reconstruction. As the economy boomed and the memories of bitter colonial wars gave way to a new national self-confidence, issue after issue covered the triumphs of Gaullist modernisation, the office blocks, the public buildings and the programme of city centre renewals that were transforming France. The modern architecture promoted by the journal became the style of choice for France's *trente glorieuses*, the 30 years that ran from the Liberation to the petrol crisis that brought the French economy to a halt in 1973.

During the course of the 1960s, however, like so many ageing radicals, *AA* appeared to be losing its former edge. It still published the projects of the great and the good – the mundane along with the inspired – but without editorial comment. It held back from criticism and shied away from debate. By the end of the decade, *AA* seemed out of step with the changing world around it: the 'events of May' 1968, for example, passed largely unremarked.[1] Claude Parent, agent provocateur and long-term collaborator of Bloc, described the journal irreverently if accurately as having become 'the sumptuous, the superb and sacrosanct Queen Mother' of France's architectural publications (Parent, 2005, p. 170).

By the mid-1970s *AA* had revived and changed direction. With new editors, it recovered a sense of intellectual energy and swagger, a willingness to look abroad towards Italy and the US, and to take on ideas like semiology, structuralism and postmodernism.[2] But why had the journal 'aged' as it did during the course of the 1960s? Was it the editorial board, no longer so

FIGURE 9.1 (a) André Bloc at his editorial desk, *L'Architecture d'Aujourd'hui* 133 (1967).
Source: © L'Architecture d'Aujourd'hui.

FIGURE 9.1 (b) One of Bloc's habitable sculptures or *habitacles* in the grounds
of his house in Meudon.
Source: © L'Architecture d'Aujourd'hui.

young and vigorous?[3] Or is it that journals, particularly those that most effectively shape and reflect the values of the moment, have a finite life tied perhaps to a key editorial figure or the passing of a particular cause, and fall victim of their own success?

The pre-war champion of modern architecture

From the first issue in August 1945, the new postwar *AA* radiated a sense of purpose. In contrast to its contemporaries, *Techniques et Architecture* (*T+A*) or *Architecture Française* (*AF*), which initially struggled to recover a sense of identity as they negotiated the transition from Vichy and collaboration to freedom and peace, *AA* appeared ready to resume the role it had played during the 1930s. Indeed, André Bloc's priorities – to champion progressive and radical architecture – seemed as pressing in 1945 as they had done in 1930. Working in the same offices with the same editorial team who had run the journal four and half years before, the new postwar *AA* owed much to its pre-war self.

The early years of the journal, both before and after the war, are a period of precarious survival (Ragot, 1990a; Vago, 2002). The *AA*'s history begins with a virtually unknown engineer Marcel-Eugène Cahen, owner of a little gallery specialising in modern art, who wished to publicise his exhibitions by launching a journal. In this he was aided and abetted by his wife and André Bloc, a close friend, also an engineer but seized with a passion, indulged at weekends, for his activity as a sculptor. Unexpectedly, however, just before the appearance of the first issue, Cahen died. Bravely his wife and Bloc decided to carry on, with the production

 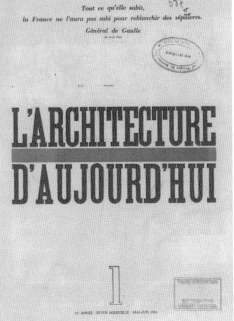

FIGURE 9.2   (a) Journal cover of the initial issue of *L'Architecture d'Aujourd'hui* (November 1930). (b) Journal cover of the first postwar issue (May/June 1945).
Source: © L'Architecture d'Aujourd'hui.

'office' in Cahen's flat in Passy and the editors based in a small room lent to them by Bloc's employers. Without capital or financial backing of any kind, the new journal was to pay its way through advertising, an act of faith that turned out, surprisingly, to be justified. By the end of the 1930s, *AA*'s circulation had long overtaken its rivals (Vago, 2002, p. 115).[4]

Bloc, as editor of the journal of his employers, the *Syndicat du Caoutchou*, was meant to know about the technical side of publishing but had in fact no idea how to run a journal. So, to make up for his lack of experience, Bloc brought in Julius Posener, a young Berlin architect then visiting Paris to see the work of Le Corbusier and other modernists who had marginally more experience of publishing. Posener in turn invited first Pierre Vago and then André Hermant and Jacques Tournant, all former students of Perret at the École Spéciale d'Architecture, to join him. They made a disparate team, whose skills and character fortunately complemented each other and whose constructive disagreements lay at the heart of the journal's long years of success. Vago, a Hungarian, Hermant, a Belgian and, after the war, Alexandre Persitz, a Russian Jew who had grown up in Germany, would be the editorial 'engine-room' of the journal. Vago, central to *AA*'s success before and just after the war, was very much a follower of Auguste Perret. This gave him a suspicion of flamboyant gestures and a view of architecture rooted in an appreciation of structure, materials and programme, values that he shared with Hermant and Persitz.

In striking contrast to the other members of the team was the mercurial Bloc. Intellectually restless, fired by his interest in sculpture, painting and architecture and possible collaborations between them, he was equally excited by the forms and structures to be found in the worlds of science and technology. As Vago and Persitz recalled later, Bloc was as demanding of his team as he was of himself: furious disagreement would give way to intense collaboration, these rapid changes in mood made possible by Bloc's sheer generosity of spirit (Vago, 2002, p. 253). Until his death, as is clear from the tributes of all those who worked with him, he was the animating genius of the journal.[5] It was the combination of the soaring imagination of Bloc and the restraining professional orientation of Vago and then Persitz that enabled *AA* to become the dominant force that it became.

Backed by an impressive, if largely honorary and inactive, editorial board, the journal established itself quickly as the mouthpiece for an uncompromising view of modernism (Jannière, 2002; Vago, 2002). It not only provided generous coverage for leading modernists, notably Perret and Le Corbusier, but through its correspondents it also offered an international perspective unmatched in France at the time. For the first issue Vago was able to persuade Perret to contribute a lapidary article while the following issue carried a review of Villa Savoye and an article by Adolf Loos. Subsequent issues contained articles contributed by figures of equivalent standing and covering canonical buildings like Lurçat's school at Villejuif, Beaudoin and Lods' Maison du Peuple at Clichy, Laprade's Citroen Garage in the XVIe and housing by Pingusson. André Bloc's belief in the importance of the links between the arts and architecture, a recurring theme in the postwar years, was already evident in the journal's early issues, as was its support for the designs for furniture and furnishings of members of the Union des Artistes Modernes, like Charlotte Perriand or Roux Spitz. The journal also harboured campaigning ambitions, arranging a conference in the Salle Pleyel to debate the subject of a contemporary architecture true to its age. With material gathered worldwide by a growing number of foreign correspondents, there were reports on the state of modern architecture in other countries, from Italy and Germany, but also Holland, Austria and Czechoslovakia. Space was also given to buildings from further afield: public buildings in the USSR, Howe and

Lescaze's PSFS building in Philadelphia, and Lubetkin's Penguin Pool at London's Zoo. Finally, *AA* took an active interest in technical issues. From 1934, it started to publish a supplement, called *Chantiers*, edited by André Hermant, that covered construction and materials with issues on Nervi's structures, or Beaudoin and Lods' approach to prefabrication in their housing at Drancy (Ragot, 1990a; Vago, 2002).

As the 1930s drew to a close there was, however, a sense in which the avant-garde was already under threat from the forces of reactionary academicism and *AA* reported with evident disapproval on the monumental architecture of Nazi Germany and, in Paris, Carlu's buildings for International Exposition of 1937, a grandiose marriage of stripped classicism and Beaux Arts composition (*AA*, 8, 1938). It comes as no surprise to see that the journal should reach out on occasion to the political left. In June 1936, for example, it published 'Pour un Plan' to mark the election of the Popular Front (*AA*, 6, 1936).

Wartime closure and rebirth in the summer of 1945

In the summer of 1940, the defeat of France found the editorial team scattered between Paris and the Mediterranean coast (Ragot, 1990b). Bloc wrote to them saying he was unwilling to bow to the demands of the Vichy state to support its programme of cultural renewal and suggested either closing down or, as a fall-back position, selling the journal to a group headed by the architect Albert Laprade, less opposed to the new regime. In response Vago suggested that Bloc should temporarily scuttle the journal with a view to starting again when circumstances permitted, arguing that in Vichy France a journal owned by a Jew, with a Hungarian editor and known for its international contacts, stood little chance of success. After some complicated manoeuvring, Bloc was able to sell the journal in December 1940 with a stipulation that he might repurchase it after the war. Meanwhile in September 1940, Hermant used the material he had assembled for the *AA*'s technical supplement to launch a new journal, *T+A*, with an issue on sport, a subject dear to Vichy and acceptable to the Germans. Thereafter, however, the new journal focused on apolitical questions of technique and construction, themes on which it would concentrate throughout the war and on into the postwar years.

The rebirth of *AA* after the Liberation was difficult and further complicated by the loss of the journal's pre-war records (Vago, 2002). However, with the support of Eugène Claudius-Petit and the backing of members of the pre-war editorial board, by early 1945 Bloc was able to secure an allocation of paper and permission to publish. With Vago heavily involved in reconstruction work, Bloc acted as principle editor assisted by Alexandre Persitz who had, miraculously, survived Auschwitz. Their first issue opened with a manifesto, 'Construire en France', written by Bloc and Vago as a re-statement of the journal's core values and their relevance to the immediate tasks of reconstruction (*AA*, 1, 1930). This was, in turn, backed by a series of statements by the leading modernists of the pre-war years: Perret, Le Corbusier, Lurçat, Lods, Laprade; but also by younger figures, Zehrfuss, Lopez and Herbé.

Perhaps the postwar journal lacked the visual 'attack' of the early years. The design of the covers, brightly coloured, served to attract attention, but *AA*'s pages lack that consistent quality of style and invention to be found in foreign journals like *Casabella* or *The Architectural Review* (*AR*). Run on a shoe-string and lacking the resources that J. M. Richards at *AR* could 'borrow' from its publishing 'parent', the Architectural Press, André Bloc could not afford a production team or develop a close working relationship with photographers or typographers: *AA* could not count on the services of a Dell and Wainwright, there was no equivalent to the editorial eye of Eric de

Maré nor the regular contributions of a draughtsman like Gordon Cullen. The overall impression of the journal's layout and the typography was of energy rather than consistency, a determination to carry the journal's message without being too precious about style (Vermeil, 1990).

While Vago was again establishing his network of international correspondents, Bloc was recreating an editorial committee that would be more directly involved with the production of the journal. With most of the committee's members heavily involved in reconstruction work, it was agreed that for the first few years each member would be responsible for a particular issue on subjects ranging from prefabrication by Gigou (*AA*, 4, 1946) and urbanism (*AA*, 7/8, 1946) by Vago to Bloc's issue on France Outre-Mer, the country's remaining colonies where architectural experimentation was less constrained than in the 'hexagon' of metropolitan France (*AA*, 3, 1945). Alongside these themes the journal was already resuming its old campaigning activities, attacking what it saw as back-sliding and compromise, singling out, for example, the 'New Humanism', actively championed by the *AR* as a softer more 'approachable' form of modernism, as a betrayal of modernist orthodoxy (Vago, 2002, p. 246). Nor did age soften these campaigning instincts; ten years later in an editorial on BBPR's Torre Velasca, entitled 'Causus Belli?', it was belabouring *Casabella* for betraying the values of the modern movement (*AA*, 77, 1958).

By 1948 Persitz had effectively taken over from Bloc the daily details of production to become editor-in-chief. In this role, he prepared around half of all issues until the early 1950s, with those devoted to special subjects still being produced by members of the committee. By around 1953 even Persitz was finding that this was too much for one person and a new pattern of working was established with Bloc and Persitz taking charge of alternate issues.[6] The result was a publication that offered two different perspectives. On the one hand there was Persitz, the former student of Perret, who remained true to the journal's commitment to an architecture founded on the primacy of construction and structure. On the other hand there was Bloc, increasingly engaged with his activities as a sculptor and his collaboration with members of the *Groupe Espace*. Vago recalls him as being permanently on the lookout for the new, the novel and the fantastical, and driven by what he, Vago, saw as essentially painterly and sculptural rather than architectural priorities (Vago, 2002, p. 155).

For the readers of *AA* this collaboration of differences at the heart of the journal seemed to work well, perhaps because by 1949 Bloc had found a new outlet for his belief in the overarching importance of a synthesis of the arts with architecture, technology and science. To pursue his interests but also to jolt *AA* out of what might already have appeared to be a certain predictability, Bloc launched a new journal. Initially called *Art d'aujuourd'hui*, he changed the title in 1955 to *Aujourd'hui, art et architecture* (*A*).[7] Edited by Bloc alone, with the occasional assistance of Pierre Lacombe and later of Claude Parent, it initially gave greater coverage to art and design than architecture, a bias reflected in its advisory committee of artists, poets and critics. However, with the change of title to *Aujourd'hui* it began to cover architecture more actively, challenging and even competing directly with *AA*.

Can we see *A* as the vehicle by which Bloc, more adventurous than the rest of the team at *AA*, broke free to address the issues that he found most interesting? It certainly gave him an immense freedom. This he exercised to the full. In *A*, Bloc ranged freely across the arts, reviewing exhibitions and museum collections from Brazil to Australia. The journal publicised new furnishings and furniture and explored the use of new materials like plastic, plywood and fibreglass and the opportunities they offered to designers. It also ran a regular feature, 'Art Science Technique', edited by Nicolas Schöffer, which provided coverage not just of the

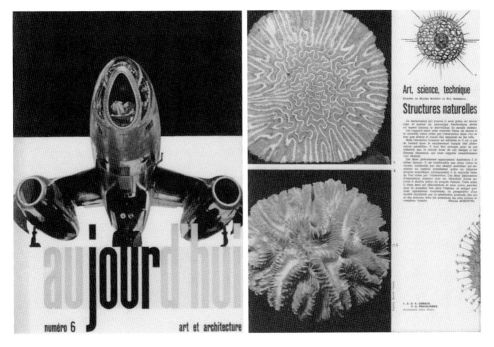

FIGURE 9.3   (a) Journal cover, *Aujourd'hui* 6 (1956). (b) The 'structures naturelles',
Aujourd'hui 14 (1957).
Source: © L'Architecture d'Aujourd'hui.

potential of new technologies and advances in scientific research for new applications, but for the way that they might enable artists and designers to see the world afresh. Another regular feature, 'Formes pour le Movement', reported on the advances in transport and the innovative forms that these might generate, from the delta-winged Vulcan bomber to the muscular elegance of touring cars like the new Lancia Aurelia B20. It should come as no surprise that articles on America's counter-culture appear in *A* long before they appear in *AA* (*A*, 55/56, 1966).

With Bloc thus freed to explore his wider interests, *AA* retained its architectural focus. Even so, it stood apart from the other contemporary journals in its choice of subject and its indifference to many of the issues discussed so actively by its rivals, whose character in turn differed sharply one from another. *Construction Moderne* (*CM*), first published in 1885 and still influential in the interwar years, became, during the late 1940s and 1950s, the refuge for a conservative mainstream that embraced regionalism and stripped or diluted classicism. By the late 1950s, *CM* had drifted into supporting mainstream and commercial modernism, but was struggling to find a way of appealing to a younger generation and losing circulation. Launched in 1940, the aims of *AF* were initially more clearly set, faithfully reflecting the values of the Vichy regime until 1945 when it took as its brief the defence of more traditional approaches to reconstruction.[8] However, from the early 1950s onwards it too appeared to lose a sense of identity. By the 1960s it was publishing the work of established and commercial offices while offering little coverage of progressive architects.

More important, but also more obviously focused on constructional and structural issues in architecture, was *T+A*.[9] At its launch in 1941 it was edited by André Hermant, the member of the team at *AA* responsible for technical matters, and *T+A* was to remain an important vehicle for the discussion not just of technical issues but also for progressive architecture more generally. It was edited for much of the postwar period by Hermant, who remained sympathetic to the ideals of Perret and his followers and as editor emphasised the way that construction, structure and environmental issues might shape architectural form. Individual issues were dedicated to particular materials, or to a building type, and leavened by occasional issues providing a review of recent buildings. During the reconstruction years, the journal not only reported on the development of the industrialised building systems that were being promoted by the Ministry of Reconstruction and Urbanism (MRU), but generally supported the Ministry's line on the reform of the building industry and its approach to the housing crisis of the 1950s.

Degrees of difference

So how did *AA* differ in its coverage of key themes? On reconstruction, a central strand of debate in France from the Liberation to the mid-1950s and a subject assiduously reported by its rivals, *AA* took a selective view. Thus, it was willing to report in some detail on the 'Exhibition of American Housing and Planning Techniques' at the Grand Palais in 1947, made possible by Paul Nelson, somebody close to the journal (*AA*, 12, 1947). It was prepared to run an issue on prefabrication but privileged the lightweight folded metalwork of Jean Prouvé, another friend, rather than the ponderous systems of prefabricated concrete urged by MRU. It provided extensive, if again selective, coverage of reconstruction plans. Playing down the early reconstructions carried out in regional styles, the journal focused instead on those schemes that reflected the influence of the Charter of Athens and CIAM: the plans for Sully-sur-Loire and Orléans were virtually ignored while Le Corbusier's plan for Saint-Dié and Lurçat's plan for Maubeuge were given star billing (*AA*, 7/8, 1946).

As the demands of reconstruction eased, the housing crisis and the urgent need to build affordable housing quickly came to dominate the architectural debate. *AA* did not altogether shy away from discussing these issues but, by contrast with its competitors, it showed scant regard for MRU and its policies. It offered only occasional coverage of the competitions for industrialised building organised by the Ministry in the late 1940s and early 1950s, though it did unbend to provide more generous coverage of Beaudoin's Cité Rotterdam project of 1950 for one of the last and most successful of the industrialised building competitions. It was Persitz, not Bloc, who edited the issues of *AA* that reported on the *grands ensembles*, the large-scale housing developments being built in the Paris region and in other major cities, providing a coverage that seemed more duty than pleasure. *AA* was also the first of the architectural journals to criticise the approach to mass housing encouraged by MRU and to single out Sarcelles, one of the largest developments in the Paris area, for a grim photo-essay on the day-to-day difficulties suffered by its inhabitants (*AA*, 95, 1961). The stark image of the densely-packed deck of a slave ship chosen for the inside cover of a special issue on mass housing is an indication of *AA*'s stance on a subject covered a great deal more enthusiastically, and more regularly, by other journals (*AA*, 57, 1954).

For and against Le Corbusier

A significant difference between *AA* and its contemporaries was the treatment of Le Corbusier. *T+A* offered occasional coverage but lacked sympathy for his work and his use of materials: favouring

Perret's use of reinforced concrete as a point of departure for his architecture, the journal found Le Corbusier's creative use of materials like rough concrete to have little relevance for the issues it regarded as important, such as the industrialisation of the French building industry. *AF* was actively hostile. It pointedly ignored, and on occasions actively attacked, Le Corbusier, providing publicity for those denouncing the supposed dangers to physical and mental health posed by the construction of the Unité d'habitation (*Architecture Française*, Special Supplement, 85/86, 1947).

By contrast, Le Corbusier was lionised by Bloc. Who could better exemplify Bloc's conviction in the primacy of form and the importance of the links between sculpture and architecture? From the first postwar issues of *AA* onwards, Le Corbusier's work from his plans for the reconstruction of cities like Saint-Dié to la Rochelle-la-Pallice, to his recent paintings and sculptures, were generously covered. For Bloc, Le Corbusier exemplified the artist/architect who in buildings like the pilgrimage chapel at Ronchamp could achieve that synthesis of the arts and architecture for which Bloc campaigned. This enthusiasm for Le Corbusier was not, however, shared by the other members of the editorial team. Pierre Vago, a figure with a keen sense of his own worth as a designer, was not only critical of what he saw as the formal emphasis of Le Corbusier's work at the expense of structure and function – a view he shared with his fellow 'Perretist' Hermant – but was clearly stung by the patronising manner in which he was treated by that 'supremely arrogant man' (Vago, 2002, p. 163). In 1948, however, Bloc was still able to override the reservations of the rest of the editorial team to produce a handsome special issue dedicated to every aspect of Le Corbusier's work, from architecture and urbanism work to his latest paintings and sculptures (*AA*, 17, 1948).

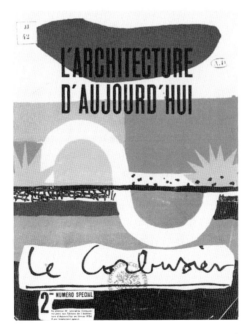

FIGURE 9.4 Journal cover of the special issue devoted to Le Corbusier. *L'Architecture d'Aujourd'hui* (April 1948).
Source: © L'Architecture d'Aujourd'hui.

Can these editorial divisions be seen in *AA*'s limited coverage of the Unité at Marseille – one of the single largest reconstruction projects of its time? Instead of including it in the numbers on housing or urbanism edited by Vago and Persitz, Bloc chose to showcase it as one of a series of articles assessing the French contributions to the development of modern architecture, placing Le Corbusier in the elevated company of Viollet-le-Duc, Eiffel and Perret, and giving the Unité pride of place among his achievements (*AA*, 46, 1953). Ronchamp was barely covered in *AA*. It was, for example, excluded from the issue reviewing postwar church building that chose instead to flatter Vago's recently completed basilica at Lourdes (*AA*, 71, 1957). However, Bloc more than made good this omission by publishing it at length in *A*. Here it was celebrated as the great modern synthesis of the arts, of painting, of sculpture and architecture, with an extended photo-essay, including – exceptionally for the time – a number of images in colour, and an enthusiastic appreciation by Bloc's friend, the poet and painter Gigou (*A*, 4, 1955). By the late 1950s, with Vago increasingly busy with his practice and engaged only at arm's length with *AA*, the journal's coverage of Le Corbusier appears to have been less contentious: his work, from the great government buildings of Chandigarh (*AA*, 101, 1962) to the triumph of the monastery at la Tourette (*AA*, 96, 1961), was published in full. In 1963 *AA* devoted a special issue to Le Corbusier's seventy-fifth birthday, celebrating his status as the grand old man of French architecture (*AA*, 106, 1963). At his death in August 1965, tributes from France and from across the world flowed into *AA*. No longer the troublesome outsider, *AA* could now at last present him as the modern champion of that grand tradition of French architectural creativity running back through the centuries from Viollet-le-Duc to Labrouste, and beyond to Perrault and Mansart.

France and international mainstream modernism

Such differences within the editorial team were part of the creative tension that drove *AA* forward. Bloc might exercise his freedom at *A*, but at *AA* the central priority remained the promotion of the cause of modern architecture. The journal did not define an editorial position as did Ernesto Rogers at *Casabella* or J. M. Richards at *AR*, nor did it encourage the kind of architectural criticism exemplified by the writings of critics like Colin Rowe and Reyner Banham or practitioners like James Stirling or Alan Colquhoun. But the journal's editorial values can be inferred to some extent from what was published, and what was not.

Far more than other French publications, *AA* was outward-facing and the number of issues devoted to developments in other countries was high: between 1955 and 1959, for example, there was extensive coverage of architecture and urbanism in Mexico, North Africa, Poland, Japan, the US, Venezuela, Black Africa, Berlin and Brussels. Many of the buildings selected tended to be those that might be characterised by the term *un fonctionalisme tempéré* (Lucan, 2001), an approach to architecture that, in keeping with Persitz's admiration for Perret and Mies van der Rohe, emphasised rationality of structure and construction and the way in which architectural form might be shaped by function. Typical exemplars – taken at random – might be Saarinen's General Motors Technical Centre in Warren, Michigan; Jacobsen's SAS Hotel in Copenhagen; Gropius' flats at the *Interbau* Exhibition in Berlin; the office buildings of Skidmore Owings and Merrill; and the Case Study Houses. If the architecture of the US, public and private, served as one of the unstated but ever-present paradigms of a new international mainstream modernism, the journal – perhaps the contribution of Bloc – also included the work of architects who stood out as being different. The work of Kenzo Tange and his Japanese contemporaries, covered in a number of issues, suggested another approach to modernity, as did the work of Alvar Aalto the occasional extravagant building from Brazil and the odd late works of Frank Lloyd Wright.

By the late 1950s, with the challenges of reconstruction and the housing crisis receding, French architects and planners could explore new avenues and *AA* could at last match its coverage of modern architecture abroad with the major buildings of a rapidly modernising France. The journal's relationship to the new architectural establishment may be illustrated by its coverage of the work of Bernard Zehrfuss, winner of the Grand Prix de Rome in 1939, from his designs for the new Renault factory at Flins (*AA*, 47, 1953), whose bold colours were a product of collaboration with the painter Félix del Marle, to his collaboration with de Mailly, Camelot, Esquillan and Prouvé on the design of the Centre National des Industries et Techniques (CNIT), fêted as a triumph of French architectural engineering set in the service of de Gaulle's modernising agenda (*AA*, 83, 1959). By the start of the 1960s the pages of *AA* regularly presented the work of this new establishment, showcasing major state projects such as Henry Bernard's Maison de la Radio in the XVIe or Vicariot's new airport at Orly, which were not all as sophisticated formally or as advanced technically as Raymond Lopez's new building for the Centre for Family Allowances. Despite *AA*'s best efforts to open up France to the outside world, it was difficult to escape the sense that French architects lived in what Huet was unflatteringly to call an 'aquarium' where they could swim safely protected from the threat of creative competition from outside (Le Dantec, 1990, p. 181).

FIGURE 9.5   French mainstream modernism: the CNIT, *L'Architecture d'Aujourd'hui* 97 (1961).
Source: © L'Architecture d'Aujourd'hui.

Championing an alternative vision: towards an architecture of fantasy and protest?

AA's success as the dominant chronicle of modernist orthodoxy would soon have its price. For those who had entered practice soon after the war and who had in a sense grown up with *AA*, the journal had come to define the very nature of modern architecture in France. Its clear ambitions and its circulation – larger in the mid-1960s than all its rivals put together – gave the journal a commanding voice (Vago, 2002, p. 250). For the modernist architectural establishment, the journal's contemporaries, this might be reassuring. But for a younger generation, trained postwar and encouraged by *AA* itself to look beyond France for new ideas, the reprising of the conventional wisdom was no longer enough. Perhaps more important, Bloc too recognised this loss of momentum. His response was both to shake up *AA* from within and to use *A* to mount a challenge from without.

From the start of the 1960s, *AA* was already adopting a more critical view of much of what passed for modern architecture. In an editorial looking back over 30 years of championing the cause of modern architecture, Bloc and Persitz quoted the editor of *Progressive Architecture* on the quality of French architecture:

> Today [...] what is there to see? Hesitation, "modernism" (in the form of inferior copies of clumsy American architecture), planning poorly conceived, an absence of organic expression, an absence (to be brutally frank) of talent. In fact, an absence of everything, apart from the crucial consideration that there is still so much to do.
>
> *AA, 91/92, December 1960, p. 197*

An early sign of this disaffection with official architecture and planning came in March 1961 with its denunciation of the new plan for Paris, proudly exhibited under the rubric *Demain … Paris*, as a pusillanimous capitulation to property interests and a betrayal of the city's past, proposing instead a new administrative city, *Paris Parallèle*, to be built 25 kilometres to the east (*AA*, 88, 90, 95; 1960, 1960, 1961).

What Bloc and Perstiz wanted above all was to showcase an architecture and urbanism transformed by creativity and imagination, not held back by the dull constraints of money and timing. From 1960 until 1968, roughly every third or fourth issue of *AA*, with titles like 'Tendences', 'Recherches' or 'Architectures Fantastiques', would highlight some aspect of radical thinking to provide cumulatively a survey of avant-garde thinking in France in all its diversity. The contributors included both 'possibilists' like Candilis, Josic and Woods, those working innovatively in the realm of the currently feasible, as well as 'visionaries' whose work could only be realised in a future, more or less distant. The subjects treated might range from the structural innovations of Robert le Ricolais to designs on the border between architecture and sculpture, such as those by Claude Parent in collaboration with André Bloc. Speculation on urbanism might be even more extreme, with ideas for 'spatial urbanisme', a design approach to the future city, represented by the works of Yona Friedman, which had been appearing in the journal since 1959 (*AA*, 87, 88, 93, 101; 1959, 1960, 1962), or Nicholas Schöffer, an artist and Bloc's fellow member of the Groupe Espaces whose kinetic sculptures, some conceived at the urban scale, were promoted by André Bloc both in *AA* and in *A* (*AA*, 102; *A*, 6 and 8, 1956).

Meanwhile, with *A* Bloc was exploring new ground. Here his collaborator (Persitz having resigned in 1964) was Claude Parent, a provocative and contradictory figure: a polemical

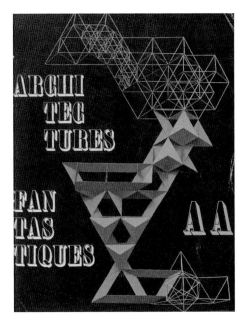

FIGURE 9.6   Journal cover of the issue on Architectures Fantastiques, *L'Architecture d'Aujourd'hui* 102 (1962).
Source: © L'Architecture d'Aujourd'hui.

defender of positions, mostly unwarranted and indefensible; a draughtsman with real skill but irrational subject matter; a utopian with cynical beliefs; an agent provocateur who enjoyed baiting the cultural and architectural establishment but who, in later life, became a member of the very Académie he so affected to despise. Unlike its elder sister, *Aujourd'hui* was free to publish Archigram or Venturi, and to run debates on everything from inflatables to the form of the E-Type Jaguar. It could attack the establishment. On occasion it might go too far, publishing an attack on Le Corbusier's theories of urbanism that had the misfortune to appear the week after the Master's death (*A*, 50, pp. 1–3). The consequences were swift and drastic; the editorial committee of *AA*, outraged at this shocking show of disrespect, required Bloc to disown Parent, who was summarily sacked.

1966, the death of André Bloc and new directions

André Bloc died suddenly and unexpectedly on 8 November 1966. His wife, Margueritte, who had shown no interest in either *AA* or *A* while Bloc was alive, now took control of both. One of her first actions, urged on by *AA*'s editorial committee, was to close *A* (Parent, 2005, p. 173). Though it had struggled to find its bearings since the death of Bloc and the departure of Parent, its closure represented a major loss to Bloc's legacy. Her second major initiative was to launch the search for a new editor for *AA* and, after barely a year, Marc Émery was appointed editor-in-chief.[10] More a planner than an architect and much influenced by an extended stay in Philadelphia where he studied city planning and fell under the sway of Louis Kahn, he was already known to the journal for his work on a special issue on urbanism. However, his choice as editor-in-chief was to prove difficult, marked by continuing disagreements with the old guard of the editorial committee.[11] Perhaps they had hoped that as the son of Pierre-André Émery, Le Corbusier's veteran Algerian assistant, Marc Émery would uphold the values of the journal's founding years. A vain hope. Working in the changed times that followed the 'events of May' 1968, Émery responded to the expectations of a younger generation that wished to see the end of a distinction between architecture and urbanism, and who demanded that architects should engage with sociologists and others in an attempt to understand the society for which they were working. Gone was the journal's closeness to the bow-tied establishment of the 1950s and 1960s. It now published articles by Henri Lefebvre and Françoise Choay and dedicated special issues to subjects such as man and the environment, squatter settlements in Rio or the prospects of underwater living. Nor was *AA* any longer the only champion of radical modernity. With the appearance in 1968 of *Architecture Mouvement Continuité*, a journal that spoke for the younger generation of *soixante-huitards*, *AA* needed to find a new voice, a new way of promoting ideas that belonged between outright activism and a new reading of modernity in architecture (Jannière, 2008).

As disagreement piled on top of disagreement with the editorial board, Émery left at the end of 1973 only to be replaced by Bernard Huet, with whom the editorial board was soon on no better terms. A provocative choice given his well-advertised role in bringing down the Beaux Arts, he too was to leave after only three years, sacked by the editorial board for launching a blistering attack on the *Ordre de Architectes* that in turn led the *Ordre* to launch a successful suit for defamation (Violeau, 2005). Huet's championing of new ideas, notably from Italy, came at a cost. The impossible relationship between an ageing and increasingly reactionary editorial board and the journal's young editors determined that *AA* should reflect – as they believed André Bloc had done before them – the latest developments and ideas of the moment, is a reminder of how far-reaching were the changes that followed the 'events of May'. Perhaps for an older generation it was possible to insist that it was business as usual; for a younger generation the world, and architecture with it, could never be the same. The members of the editorial board, most trained just before or after the war, could not accept this. As they slowly resigned or retired during the mid-1970s, the struggle for the soul of *AA* was eventually won by the young, by Huet and by Émery, who returned as editor in 1977. The journal was once again as free to document and promote new directions in architecture and urbanism as it had been under Bloc in the 1930s. It did not, nor has it since, lost its power to speak for the best in French architecture.

Notes

1 By chance the issue of May 1968, *AA* 137, devoted to university buildings, had a photograph of students at Nanterre, including Cohn-Bendit. However, the journal's immediate coverage of the events was limited to printing the statements of the General Assembly of the students of the former ENSBA and counter statements by those still seeking to defend the Grand Prix de Rome (*AA*, 138, 1968).

2 The journal's editors in the decade after Bloc's death in late 1966 were: Marc Émery from 137, 1968 until 166, 1973; Bernard Huet until 188, 1976; and Marc Émery, again from January 1977.

3 The size and composition of the journal's editorial board changed considerably over the years. In the late 1940s Bloc and Pertsitz had reduced it to those who were prepared to be actively involved with editorial policy; by 1958 it included, *inter alia*, Candilis, Chemineau, Ecochard, Fayeton, Ginsberg, Heaume, Herbé, Lagneau, Le Ricolais, Lods, Mirabaud, Perriand, Prouvé, Rotival, Roux, Sebag, Sive, Trezzini and Zehrfuss. By the late 1960s it had become considerably more conservative than the journal's much younger editors.

4 That this was so is largely due to the abilities of Honoré Bloch, a publicity agent with a flair for selling advertising.

5 Bloc's achievements are celebrated in the tributes collected in the joint special number of *AA* and *A* published in January 1967.

6 The editor and assistant for each issue is recorded on the title page.

7 *Art d'Aujourd'hui* was first published as a monthly in June 1949. From January 1955 it appeared bimonthly with the new title *Aujourd'hui, art et architecture* until 1967; Bloc is listed as editor and Pierre Lacombe as his assistant.

8 *Architecture Française* was first published in November 1940, initially with André Hilt as editor and an editorial board of traditionalists and 'safe' modernists. By 1945 Roux-Spitz had taken over as editor with a new, more progressive editorial board. Even so, it remained the journal for cautious modernists, those of an older generation or those working institutionally and for corporate interests.

9 The launch of *A+T* September–October 1941 out of *AA* is described by Ragot (1990b, pp. 164–167). It was edited by André Hermant into the 1960s and continues to this day. Its architectural orientation, much influenced by the architecture of Auguste Perret, can be gauged from the three editorial committees each uniting leading modernists and the leading engineers of the period, though not Prouvé.

10 In the period after Bloc's death, Marguerite Bloc took over the running of the journal assisted by a group that included Vago, Charlotte Perriand, Candilis and a number of guest editors: Parat for issue 130 and then François Herbert-Stevens from 131 until Émery's arrival, though Émery had already acted as a guest/assistant editor for 132 and 136.

11 The divisions between Marc Émery and the editorial board are evident in the issue on 'Doctrines' (*AA*, 138, 1968), with statements by Vago's allies among the older generation and his attack on developments since May 1968.

References

Badouï, R. (1990). D'hier à Aujourd'hui. *L'Architecture d'Aujourd'hui*, 272, pp. 61–76.

Jannière, H. (2002). *Politiques editoriales et architecture modern: L'émergence de nouvelles revues en France et en Italie 1923–1939*. Paris: Éditions Argument.

—— (2008). La critique architecturale à la recherché de ses instruments: *L'Architecture d'Aujourd'hui* et *Architecture Mouvement Continuité* 1974. In A. Sornin, H. Jannière and F. Vanlaethem (Eds), *Architectural Periodicals in the 1960s and 1970s: Towards a Factual, Intellectual and Material History*. Montréal: IRHA, pp. 271–294.

Le Dantec, J. (1990). La période Huet, une entreprise critique. *L'Architecture d'Aujourd'hui*, 272, pp. 174–178.

Lucan, J. (2001). *Architecture en France (1940–2000): Histoire et théories*. Paris: Editions du Moniteur.

Parent, C. (1990). Souvenirs d'aujourd'hui'. *L'Architecture d'Aujourd'hui*, 272, pp. 170–171.

Ragot, G. (1990a). Pierre Vago et les débuts de L'Architecture d'Aujourd'hui 1930–1940. *Revue d'Art*, 89, pp. 77–81.

—— (1990b). 1940, Eupalinos ne répend plus. *AA*, 272, pp. 164–167.

Vago, P. (2002). *Une Vie Intense*. Paris: Éditions archives d'architecture moderne.

Vermeil, F. (1990). Entre les lignes. *L'Architecture d'Aujourd'hui*, 272, pp. 28–29.

Violeau, J.-L. (2005). *Les Architectes et Mai 68*. Paris: Éditions Recherches.

10

AGAINST THE CONTINGENCIES OF ITALIAN SOCIETY

Issues of historical continuity and discontinuity in Italy's postwar architectural periodicals

Paolo Scrivano

Between 1945 and the end of the 1960s, Italian architectural journals witnessed the transformation of a country that, after defeat in an ill-advised war, passed from being an agricultural nation of limited industrial capacity to one of Europe's economic powers. They also observed the way the professional culture struggled to adapt to the ongoing change by redefining its working methodologies as well as its identity. Moving from cheaply produced and politically engaged publishing endeavours to graphically rich and intellectually sophisticated magazines, architectural periodicals testified to the passage from an economy marked by scarcity to one based on increasing material and cultural consumption. The efforts to adjust to the times led to mixed results, however. Confronting unsettled questions on the relation between past, present, and future, journals such as *Metron* in the 1940s, *Casabella* in the 1950s and 1960s, or *Controspazio* at the threshold of the 1970s devised diverse responses to the events that marked Italy's history.

Postwar hopes for renewal

In 1946, reflecting on its first year of existence, the journal *Metron* described its mission as one aimed at fostering a 'renewal based on culture' and at promoting an approach to architecture grounded on 'precise criteria of planning and serious methodology [derived from] technical studies' (*Metron*, 1947).[1] *Metron* was first published in Rome in the summer of 1945, a few months after the end of the Second World War and when communications between the North and the South of Italy were still problematic.

With the intent to bridge the geographical gap that existed between different parts of the country, the journal's editorial board included architects and planners such as Piero Bottoni, Luigi Figini, Luigi Piccinato and Mario Ridolfi, representing both the Milanese and Roman professional milieus.[2] While not mentioned in the first issue's headings, *Metron*'s real initiator and indefatigable driving force was Bruno Zevi, a young architect and critic who had returned from exile wearing the uniform of the US Army and holding a degree from Harvard University.[3]

Immediately after the end of the conflict, Italy saw the proliferation of countless publishing initiatives dedicated to architecture. Albeit at times short-lived, the dozens of architectural

FIGURE 10.1   Journal cover, *Metron* 1 (1945).

periodicals that were either founded or relaunched in the postwar years placed Italian architectural culture centre stage in the international debate, and in a way that had little historical precedent. As the first major 'voice' to gain recognition in 1945 (*Casabella* and *domus* – both founded in 1928 – resumed their publications only in 1946), *Metron* focused primarily on the question of reconstruction. This subject was not the journal's exclusive prerogative in its early days since it had surfaced in several Italian periodicals even before the cessation of hostilities, in a fashion that did not much differ from other European countries. *Metron*, however, distinguished itself with a militant stance towards the themes of the reconstruction, and for the overt goal to cast its influence well beyond the confines of the professional world.

With its austere layout typified by one-colour covers and rare illustrations in black and white printed on matte paper, *Metron* during the first two years of publication fully embodied the reconstruction spirit. Among those recurrently discussed in the journal's pages were themes that were central to contemporary debate, in particular the question of popular housing and the possible widespread use of prefabrication techniques to expedite rebuilding. While it is probably an overstatement to depict it as an explicit advocacy of prefabrication, it is certainly true that *Metron*'s looking with favour at an industrialised approach to the reconstruction effort was one of the journal's initial distinctive traits. For example, contributors such as Eugenio Gentili authored in the first issues several articles dedicated to this topic, offering readers detailed overviews of comparable initiatives worldwide in the same field. Behind this determination to support prefabrication lay a major debate concerning the direction of Italy's postwar recovery and the dispute between those favouring investments in technology and those defending a low-tech strategy that, by maximising the employment of unskilled labourers, would amplify political consensus.

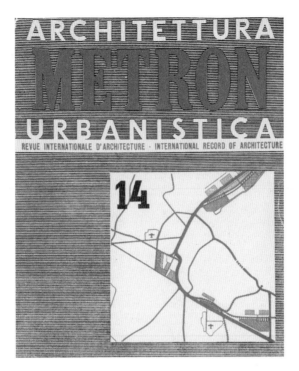

FIGURE 10.2 Journal cover, *Metron* 14 (1947).

Metron's editorial line underscored the main issues at stake in Italy's postwar culture. In many ways, the end of the war marked a rite of passage for Italian architecture, insofar as it implied an internal process of cultural redefinition. In fact, the remodelling of the profession's identity rested on wider questions regarding the part played by architects in the reconstruction effort as well as during the fascist years. The anxiety derived from the ambiguous relation that Mussolini's regime had established with modern architecture was reflected in the difficulty that key opinion leaders experienced in pointing at specific cultural and aesthetic perspectives, a problem that would be common to many publishing initiatives in the following decades. It was also expressed by what appeared as an intensified desire for de-provincialisation.

The latter might explain the recurring reference to foreign examples in the pages of *Metron*. Experiments in prefabrication carried out in France, Finland, USSR, and Sweden were featured as evidence of the possibilities that reconstruction could offer the modernisation of the country. For example, in an article published in the first issue of the journal, Zevi equated the British and Italian situation at the end of the war, pointing to common 'reconstruction problems', only to remark that if England had won the war through 'the most inflexible national planning', it was because it possessed 'the organs and the habit to plan in time of peace'. Italy, on its part, having lived 'in fascist inefficiency, in both peace and war', now needed to retrieve 'the energies and the work culture necessary to plan for the reconstruction' (Zevi, 1945).

The reality was that Italian architects were forced to confront contrasting problems after the end of the war. One was the daunting task of participating in the physical reconstruction of the country; the other was the remodelling of the cultural identity of the profession, since architecture had been heavily involved in the fascist regime's propaganda effort. In many ways, the renewal of the profession coincided – at least in the eyes of the architectural elites – with the renewal of Italian society, and this entailed facing thorny issues of continuity and discontinuity with the past. The delicate question of the relationship with fascism concerned first and foremost the state apparatus, where institutions and government bodies had been either transformed or left untouched by the war, the resistance, and Mussolini's fall;[4] but it had an impact too on the design profession, insomuch as numerous architects and engineers who emerged after 1945 as protagonists of the reconstruction had started their careers under the dictatorship.

The question of continuity (and discontinuity)

During fascism, different tendencies aspired to represent the regime's aesthetic choices in the realm of architecture, and a variety of modern approaches to design had been promoted in official building campaigns. Having been supported by the 'progressive' fringes of the fascist cultural apparatus, modernism could not be conveniently associated with the instances of moral regeneration that Italy's postwar culture and society so often sought. In the early 1950s, coinciding with assuming the directorship of *Casabella*, Ernesto Nathan Rogers gave voice to these anxieties produced by fascism's ambiguous patronage of modern architecture. Published since the 1920s but discontinued in 1943, *Casabella* had briefly resumed its publications in 1946 under the direction of Franco Albini and Giancarlo Palanti.[5] In January 1954, the journal reappeared with the new title of *Casabella Continuità*. Rogers assembled around him an editorial board formed by young and promising architects, including Marco Zanuso (with whom Rogers had been at *domus* between 1946 and 1948), Giancarlo De Carlo and Vittorio Gregotti.

Accounting for the change in the journal's title, Rogers reflected upon the role architects should play in postwar Italy in an editorial titled '*Continuità*' (Continuity) that appeared in the first issue of *Casabella Continuità*. In Rogers' words, continuity meant in the first place to take up the baton of *Casabella* from the years of Giuseppe Pagano Pogatschnig and Edoardo Persico, who, as director and co-director during the 1930s, had steered the publication 'beyond the dark years' of fascism and towards the 'always postponed goal of definitions, discoveries, inventions, fantasies' (Rogers, 1953–1954). This legacy was justified not only owing to Pagano and Persico's active role in *Casabella*, but also because of their complex linkage to fascism: while the two had successfully guided the journal during the second part of the *Ventennio*, the fact that Persico had been imprisoned several times before his untimely death in 1936 and that Pagano had died in 1945 in the Nazi concentration camp of Mauthausen-Gusen fully qualified them as victims of the repression.[6] If they were still alive, concluded Rogers in the editorial, 'they would certainly be different from what they were ten years ago', having completed a trajectory, in his view, both continuous in time (and in terms of architectural interests) and discontinuous in relation to the historical events.

For Rogers, however, the real issue at stake was the continuation of pre-war modernism in postwar architectural practices, attained while marking the change brought about by the political and cultural climate of the postwar years. A relationship to, and a concomitant reworking of the past (even the most recent), could not be questioned: 'There is no true modern work', Rogers wrote in the editorial, 'that has no authentic roots in the tradition, and yet ancient works retain a meaning today insofar as they are capable to resonate through our voice.' There was a 'coherence' to be pursued with the 'historical moment we participate in', he added, just as the historical context of the fascist years had 'conditioned' Pagano and Persico's action. In this light, Rogers championed for *Casabella Continuità* to retain an intellectual position that rejected the uncritical assimilation of 'badly absorbed ideologies' of international origin as well as nostalgia and 'folklorism' (Rogers, 1953–1954).

With Rogers at its helm, *Casabella Continuità* developed an editorial line based on a cultural approach that encompassed the arts, politics, history and also philosophy, reflecting in this last case a penchant for phenomenology, as regular contributions by Enzo Paci, professor of theoretical philosophy at the universities of Pavia and then Milan, make evident.[7] The question of tradition, intended to be seen in relation to both history and popular culture, became central during the first half of Rogers' tenure (Baglione, 2012). It was during this period, for example, that Rogers perfected his idea of design in connection to the historical built environment, what he called the *preesistenze ambientali* (environmental pre-existences) – a concept perhaps epitomised by the realisation of the Torre Velasca in Milan, a building whose visible structural elements and turret-like shape established a dialogue at a distance with the city's cathedral and the tower of the Castello Sforzesco (Rogers, 1954).[8] Within this cultural climate, *Casabella Continuità* placed the spotlight on a new generation of architects who revisited the canons of the modern movement and created the conditions for the growth of future key figures of the Italian architectural landscape, like Gae Aulenti (who was in charge of the journal's graphic layout), Aldo Rossi, Guido Canella, Giorgio Grassi, and Carlo Aymonino, all involved at some point in *Casabella Continuità*'s editorial activities.

Rogers would return to the question of continuity with another editorial published in 1957, pertinently titled 'Continuità o crisi?' (Continuity or crisis?). Posing the question of whether contemporary architecture should follow the postulates of the modern movement or change its course, he questioned the potential co-existence in an architect's work of an uninterrupted connection to the past *and* a detachment from it. In the article, Rogers argued that 'the concept of continuity implies that of the mutation of the order of tradition', while crisis 'is the break [...], the moment of discontinuity due to the influence of new factors'. Resuming a position already delineated in previous writings, in 'Continuità o crisi?' he insisted on rejecting the opposition between 'traditionalists' and 'avant-garde artists' in favour of a more nuanced scrutiny of the recent architectural past's legacy (Rogers, 1957).

Rogers had a precise example in mind for the use of history he advocated in contemporary design, and it was the handful of projects that had advanced a reinterpretation of 'Liberty', the name which in Italy identifies the style echoing at the beginning of the twentieth century the wider European movements of the Art Nouveau. For Rogers, any retrospective view of the past – and, in particular, of that of 'Liberty' – could either lead to a 'correct' evaluation of the historical context (something identified primarily with historical expertise), to the anti-historical repetition of bygone languages, or to the recuperation of specific 'values' – such as the quality of materials and detailing, the elegance, or the visual inventiveness – that could be successfully reintroduced in contemporary design practices. Needless to say, the latter was Rogers' preferred option, the one he indicated as the most programmatically desirable.

What was novel to Italy's architectural scene in the second half of the 1950s – and which prompted Rogers' reflections on history – was the advent of a new generation of architects whose projects challenged uncompromising ideals of modernism. The measure of how culturally disruptive the emergence of these architectures was, and not only at the national level, is given by the polemics about the so-called 'Neoliberty', which reached their peak with a 1959 article published by Reyner Banham in *The Architectural Review* (*AR*) that disparaged the new tendencies promoted under Rogers' directorship (Banham, 1959). The specific object of contention was a project published by *Casabella Continuità* in 1957, the Bottega d'Erasmo by Roberto Gabetti and Aimaro Isola, built in Turin between 1953 and 1956 (Casabella Continuità, 1957). A five-storey (plus attic) apartment building whose first three levels were occupied by an antiquarian bookstore (whose name, 'Erasmus's workshop', recalled the philosopher who graduated in theology at the University of Turin in 1506), the Bottega d'Erasmo established a subtle visual dialogue with the surrounding urban context, in particular with the eclectic language of the imposing Mole Antonelliana, a tall brick-built tower by Alessandro Antonelli (constructed from 1863).

Banham implied that contemporary Italian architects (or, at least, those championed by *Casabella Continuità*) had 'retreated' from a progressive notion of modernism, one capable of expressing both social responsibility and formal purity. While accorded the status of myth in the British critic and historian's view, this image of Italian architecture had been shaped by the exemplary works of Giuseppe Terragni, Luigi Figini, Pietro Lingeri and, of course, by the theoretical contributions of Persico. For Banham, the 'baffling turn' taken by a handful of young practitioners – derisively termed 'Neolibertarians' – signalled a 'more than historical interest' in turn-of-the-century architecture and, ultimately, presented a deviant anti-modernistic design conception. The main target was *Casabella Continuità* itself, which had, not incidentally, published, in the same volume that contained Rogers' article 'Continuità o crisi?' and the presentation of the Bottega d'Erasmo, an essay-review by Rossi of Stephan Tschudi-Madsen's book *Sources of Art Nouveau* (Rossi, 1957; Tschudi-Madsen, 1956).

In his response to Banham's editorial in the *AR*, Rogers returned to the question of historicism, restating the importance for contemporary practices of the continuity with the traditions internal to the profession of architect, provided that they were correctly assimilated in the cultural context of the time and not misunderstood 'by the less [intellectually] prepared' (Rogers, 1959). Ironically referring to Banham as the 'guardian of frigidaires', Rogers concluded by rejecting the claim that a technological 'watershed' had marked the development of modern architecture at the beginning of the century – an interpretation of the evolution of twentieth-century architectural history that Banham would further advance in his 1960 *Theory and Design in the First Machine Age* and that Rogers could not but consider anti-historical.

Other continuities and discontinuities

In reality the international polemics over the Bottega d'Erasmo and Neoliberty only partially reflected the discussions that during the 1950s pervaded a relatively small portion of the Italian architectural community. Around 1955, for example, an informal group of students from the Faculty of Architecture of the Politecnico di Milano, which included Guido Canella, Fredi Drugman, Silvano Tintori, Virgilio Vercelloni, and the same Rossi, engaged their professors in a debate on the use of historical references in their projects. The group was given the name *giovani delle colonne* (youth of the columns) for the propensity of its loosely affiliated members to feature in their academic drawings 'columns, capitals, and flowered pinnacles', as Giancarlo De Carlo put it in a report for *Casabella Continuità* (De Carlo, 1955; Durbiano, 2000). Once again, the question of tradition – and of possible continuities and discontinuities from it – appeared at the centre of the discourse.

But if the issues of continuity and discontinuity, discussed by Rogers and others during the 1950s, mostly concerned traditions limited to the history of Italian and European architecture and to the cultural identity of the modern architect, other forms of continuity and discontinuity with the recent past affected the design profession, often with significantly deeper effects. In fact, the conditions within which most practitioners ended up operating in the postwar years suggested an entirely different social and economic perspective, one in which architects' roles, functions and also relations to the public sphere were under a process of rapid transformation. Among the volatile factors affecting the architectural profession in Italy after the end of the Second World War were, for example, the changed market conditions.[9] Before the conflict, the fascist regime had often acted as an employer, dispensing jobs to many professionals; after 1945, state commissions materialised though various housing programmes of different extent or ambition, such as the largely American-funded UNRRA-CASAS and the more extensive and geographically widespread INA-Casa programmes (Di Biagi, 2001; Pilat, 2014; Talamona, 2001). Favouring a low-tech, labour-intensive approach that was politically motivated in order to maximise employment (with obvious implications in terms of political consensus), these building campaigns provided novel employment opportunities for architects.

A completely different situation emerged in the realm of the private housing market. Owing to a dramatic economic and demographic change between the early postwar years and the 1960s, during the so-called 'economic miracle', Italy took on an increasingly urban character. In the period between 1951 and 1961, for example, the percentage of Italians working in agriculture fell from 43 to 29.6 per cent; from 1951 to 1961 the number of Italian cities with more than 100,000 inhabitants almost doubled, going from 26 to 45 (Scrivano, 2013). Urban growth was accompanied by massive real-estate speculation, well described by Italo Calvino in *La speculazione edilizia* (translated into English as *A Plunge into Real Estate*), a 1958 novel set against the transformation of Liguria's seashore under the pressure of rampant mass tourism.

In this context of high real-estate demand (often to be provided in a short time frame and with a low level of financial investment), architects were forced to confront a substantial metamorphosis of the design and building industry. In particular they had to sustain the competition of other practitioners active in the building sector, such as engineers and *geometri* (surveyors, professionals with college-level degrees and limitations with regard to design competence). Statistics reveal architects' marginality in this context. In the north-western industrial city of Turin, for instance, data on building permits provide significant information about the role played by architects in relation to that of engineers and other specialised practitioners. Between 1945 and 1953, of the approximately 6,200 building permits issued by the city, only 668 were granted to architects: on average, a mere 11 per cent of the total licences were issued to architects, in a range between 9 and 13 per cent (Bonifazio, 1998; Scrivano, 1997). Milan's figures do not differ significantly (Dulio and Rossari, 2009).

One of the most interesting aspects of this degree of marginalisation is the role played by specific typologies of intervention, such as those carried out on existing building stock, in the form of building renovations or extensions. For example, among the 481 building permits for residential use granted to architects in Turin between 1945 and 1953, 155 regarded *sopraelevazioni* (additions of new stories) and variants to already-approved projects, a number considerably higher than the permits accorded for structures up to five floors and for high-rise constructions over six floors, the dominating types in a city destined to rise from 700,000 inhabitants in 1946 to 1,200,000 in 1970 (Scrivano, 1997).

Within the conditions described above, 'high-quality' architectural production was compelled, forcedly but not necessarily consciously, to operate in the interstitial spaces offered by the market. Since engineers or *geometri* largely dominated the industry, architects often concentrated on a limited number of isolated interventions. With the exclusion of those commissioned by large state-run or municipal housing agencies, the majority of buildings conceived by architects in postwar Italy were confined to a particular segment of the real-estate market: a niche demanding high-quality detailing, effective technical performance, and an aesthetic that identified the projects as 'designed', and consequently differentiated them from those geared towards mass production and destined for a market driven by speculation.

As the phenomena that accompanied the rapid growth of Italy's largest cities evidenced, the reality of the postwar era outlined a profile of the architect in large part relegated to the fringes of the design and construction profession. While the degree of their involvement in the housing and building markets would perhaps increase in the following years, for example with the gradual expansion of the sectors of restoration and reuse, Italian architects – in particular those most culturally and intellectually exposed – often remained anchored to a production generally geared to an upper-middle-class clientele. If, over time, additional employment opportunities would materialise, in sectors such as industrial design, advertising, or professional photography, architects stayed by and large on the sidelines of the major territorial changes that the country had required since the 1950s. One can therefore claim that the cultural and intellectual liveliness and sophistication of the debate hosted by the architectural journals of the postwar years functioned as a counterpart to the profession's condition of substantial exclusion from Italy's primary processes of social and economic transformation. In many ways, the glossy pages of publications such as *Casabella Continuità* and *domus*, but also *Urbanistica* and *Zodiac* – launched in 1949 and 1957 and both generously supported by typewriter industrialist and patron of architecture Adriano Olivetti – provided an alternative 'space' for a professional group that was struggling to define its new identity (Zucconi, 1997).

Cultural and intellectual sophistication and social and economic marginality were perhaps two sides of the same coin. In a 2009 article discussing the apparent inability of Italian liberal elites to adapt to contemporary forms of political communication, British historian and political scientist Perry Anderson noted that the refined and yet somewhat old-fashioned cultural traits of left-wing leaderships created a gap 'between educated and popular sensibilities', a gap that in turn contributed to produce a paradoxical effect of detachment between 'high' and 'low' cultures (Anderson, 2009). Anderson retraced these attitudes in the progressive intelligentsia of the postwar years, underscoring Italian intellectuals' poor ability to cope with the ongoing transformations and their patent limits in understanding the contradictions implicit in the rise of the modern consumer society. Whether or not this interpretation is entirely applicable to the architectural elites, it is evident that professional journals often suffered a partial disconnect from the reality within which architecture was socially and economically engaged.

Redefining the identity of the profession

Perhaps revealing their rising awareness of this condition, in the 1960s architectural periodicals redirected their attention to new themes. During the second part of Rogers' tenure as director, for example, *Casabella Continuità* gave regular space to the questions of the city and of large-scale urban interventions: definitions like *città-territorio* (city-territory) and *città-regione* (city-region) were coined and employed to discuss the ongoing transformation of the Italian built environment (Lobsinger, 2009). A number of issues published during this period are worth mentioning: in 1962, those dedicated to the city of Philadelphia and its planning activities (260, with contributions, among others, by Francesco Tentori and Edmund Bacon) and to Italy's directional centres (264); in 1963, those devoted to Boston's Government Center (271), to Japan (273), and to the competition for Turin's directional centre (278) (Lobsinger, 2004). The lively interest in urban problems – in particular concerning the relationship between architecture and the city – was echoed by the publication in 1966 of *L'architettura della città* by Rossi and *Il territorio dell'architettura* by Gregotti, two books written by members of *Casabella Continuità*'s editorial board.

During the latter half of the 1960s, the degree of separation displayed by Italian architectural periodicals from the context of a rapidly changing society unfolded in a contrary fashion. After Gian Antonio Bernasconi in 1965 replaced Rogers at the helm of *Casabella Continuità* (which in the meantime had changed its name to *Casabella*), the journal began to consider industrial design with increased regard, in a move that reflected the presence of Giovanni Klaus Koenig in the editorial board, and of Alessandro Mendini and Tomás Maldonado (the rector of the *Hochschule für Gestaltung* in Ulm from 1964 to 1966) as contributing authors. In the same years, other publishing outlets like *Casa Novità* – launched in 1961 and soon renamed *Abitare* – and *Ottagono* – launched in 1966 – manifested an equal focus on furniture, interior, and industrial design (Mulazzani, 1997).

This shift of interest reflected the rising importance within the Italian economy of the manufacturing sector, a major component of the national trade balance. Specialised publications contributed to the international success of Italian design by shaping an idea of 'Italianness' or 'Made in Italy' that was intended to have a significant commercial impact in the years to come (Scrivano, 2007; Lees-Maffei and Fallan, 2014). This promotion, though, was still confined to the upper-end of the manufacture of goods, barely affecting everyday building and domestic mass production. If the part played by architectural journals in orienting aesthetic preferences, living habits, and cultural and material customs – together with the attitude of architects

FIGURE 10.3 Journal cover, *Casabella Continuità* 260 (1962).
Source: © Casabella Continuità.

and designers towards them – should not be underestimated, the distance that separated the 'official' world of architecture, formed by the most 'representative' figures of Italy's architectural elite, from the 'popularisation' of design witnessed in the everyday lives of the Italians remained in many ways unaltered.[10]

Taking an alternative direction in the second half of the 1960s, several architectural periodicals adopted a radical political stance, often attempting to forge alliances with other discourses and disciplines. While *Lotus* (launched in 1964), under the guidance of editors Giulia Veronesi and Bruno Alfieri, proposed once again the trusted publishing model of an intellectually sophisticated and richly illustrated journal, *Marcatré* explored multidisciplinary collaboration. When it began its publications in 1963, under the direction of Eugenio Battisti, *Marcatré* could sport an editorial board that included art critic and painter Gillo Dorfles, semiotician Umberto Eco, poet Edoardo Sanguineti and architect Paolo Portoghesi. In contrast, *Op. Cit.*, founded in 1964 and directed by Renato De Fusco, concentrated on semiotics and linguistics, two disciplines that gained a degree of popularity in the architectural debate of those years. For each of these publishing endeavours, and for others that appeared in the same period, the common ground was a strong political engagement.

The so-called Battle of Valle Giulia, the violent confrontation between students and police that took place in March 1968 near the Faculty of Architecture of the University of Rome, symbolically marked the peak of this tendency. In fact, two publications open to ideological discussion commenced at this time. *Controspazio*, founded in 1969 and directed by Portoghesi, responded to *Contropiano*, launched one year before by literary critic Alberto Asor Rosa, philosopher Massimo Cacciari, and sociologist and political scientist Toni Negri, as a journal of Marxist criticism.

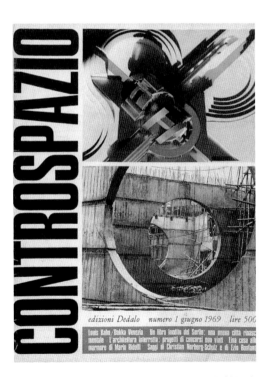

FIGURE 10.4 Journal cover, *Controspazio* 1 (1969).
Source: Courtesy of Dedalo.

While *Contropiano* gave considerable space to architecture (hosting contributions from authors such as Manfredo Tafuri, Francesco Dal Co, Marco De Michelis, and Giorgio Ciucci) without being explicitly dedicated to the subject, *Controspazio* on the contrary focused on the architectural discipline as its almost exclusive interest (Scrivano, 2008). As a result, the journal included articles on ideologically charged questions such as the autonomy of architecture or the latter's relation to politics. Society and its contradictions were indeed central to the journal's publishing project: as Portoghesi wrote in an editorial in the first issue, *Controspazio*'s primary goal was to delve into architectural practice and theory's 'clash with social reality' (Portoghesi, 1969). Dedicated to China, a country whose coeval political underpinnings were the object of fascination for many European left-wing intellectuals, issue 12 of 1971 encapsulated with precision the polarisation of the architectural discourse pursued in professional publications in Italy at the threshold of the 1970s. It also indicated how far this had developed since 1945, when the first issue of *Metron* had seen the light of day.

There is today sufficient historical consensus about the prominent role that Italy, for several decades after the end of the Second World War, played internationally in terms of participation in the cultural and theoretical debate on architecture. No doubt an important contribution to the acquisition of this status came from professional periodicals, thanks to their capacity to provide support for the circulation of intellectually sophisticated documentation, which was often presented in an appealing and captivating fashion. At the same time, however, architectural journals followed in the footsteps of manifold cultural initiatives that strove to gain recognition or to produce a real and effective impact on Italian society. This condition marked

FIGURE 10.5   Journal cover, *Controspazio* 12 (1971).
Source: Courtesy of Edizioni Dedalo.

both a break and a continuity with the past, for it highlighted what had changed since the fascist period, but also the issues that continued to dominate Italian architects' preoccupations. All this resonated distinctly in Rogers' response to Banham in 1959, when he described the context within which *Casabella Continuità*, and many other publications, operated in the postwar years: 'the continuous, dramatic battle of culture [...] against the contingencies of the Italian society (before, during, and after fascism)' (Rogers, 1959).

Notes

All English translations contained in this chapter of passages from Italian journals are by the author.

1 The article did not indicate the name of its author, though the text had likely been written by Bruno Zevi.
2 On *Metron*, see Casciato (2005) and Dulio (2012).
3 On Zevi, see Dulio (2008).
4 Discussion of the continuities and discontinuities within Italy's state apparatus date back to the 1970s and to the pioneering work of historian Claudio Pavone (1974).
5 The periodical changed its name from *La casa bella* to *Casabella Costruzioni* in 1938 and *Costruzioni Casabella* in 1940. In 1946 only three 20-page monographic issues were published (Baglione, 2012).
6 Pagano directed *La casa bella* from 1932 to 1943 (Baglione, 2012).
7 See, as an example, Paci's article 'L'architettura e il mondo della vita' (Architecture and the Lifeworld), referring openly in the title to Edmund Husserl's concept of *Lebenswelt* (Paci, 1957).
8 The Torre Velasca (1956–1958) was the project of the BBPR design group, of which Rogers was part.
9 It has long been accepted that the war led to professional inactivity, while the postwar years, characterized by the reconstruction needs, fostered a design and building boom; a wave of recent studies proposing a more complex interpretation of the time has challenged this trope: see, for example Cohen (2011).
10 The question concerning the forms of living of specific social groups in the Italian society of the postwar years – such as, for example, the middle classes – has received only recently scholarly attention; see De Pieri et al. (2013) and Caramellino et al. (2015).

References

Anderson, P. (2009). An Invertebrate Left. *London Review of Books*, 5, pp. 12–18.
Baglione, C. (2012). Casabella. In M. Biraghi and A. Ferlenga (Eds), *Architettura del Novecento. Vol. 1. Teorie, scuole, eventi*. Turin: Einaudi, pp. 114–121.
Banham, R. (1959). Neo-liberty: The Italian Retreat from Modern Architecture. *The Architectural Review*, 747, pp. 231–235.
Bonifazio, P. (1998). Torino, 1939–1953. Un'ipotesi di lettura dei modelli e delle immagini della città. In P. Bonifazio, S. Pace, M. Rosso and P. Scrivano (Eds), *Tra Guerra e Pace: Società, Cultura e Architettura nel Secondo Dopoguerra*. Milan: FrancoAngeli, pp. 282–289.
Caramellino, G., De Pieri, F. and Renzoni C. (2015). *Esplorazioni nella città dei ceti medi / Explorations in the Middle-Class City: Torino 1945–1980*. Siracusa: Lettera Ventidue.
Casabella Continuità (1957). Bottega d'Erasmo. Un edificio per una libreria antiquaria e per appartamenti a Torino (1953–56). *Casabella Continuità*, 215, pp. 64–69.
Casciato, M. (2005). Gli esordi della rivista Metron: eventi e protagonisti. *Rassegna di architettura e urbanistica*, 117, pp. 45–55.
Cohen, J.-L. (2011). *Architecture in Uniform: Designing and Building for the Second World War*. Montréal: Canadian Centre for Architecture – Éditions Hazan.
De Carlo, G. (1955). Problemi concreti per i giovani delle colonne. *Casabella Continuità*, 204, p. 83.
De Pieri, F., Bonomo, B., Caramellino, G. and Zanfi, F. (Eds) (2013). *Storie di case: Abitare l'Italia del boom*. Rome: Donzelli.

Di Biagi, P. (2001). *La grande ricostruzione: Il piano Ina-Casa e l'Italia degli anni '50*. Rome: Donzelli.

Dulio, R. (2008). *Introduzione a Bruno Zevi*. Rome: Laterza.

—— (2012). Metron. In M. Biraghi and A. Ferlenga (Eds), *Architettura del Novecento. Vol. 1. Teorie, scuole, eventi*. Turin: Einaudi, pp. 597–601.

Dulio, R. and Rossari, A. (2009). Tra cultura architettonica e crescita edilizia: Milano 1945–1961. In E. Cogato Lanza and P. Bonifazio (Eds), *Lex experts de la reconstruction. Figures et stratégies de l'élite technique dans l'Europe de l'après-guerre / Gli esperti della ricostruzione. Figure e strategie dell'elite tecnica nell'Europa del dopoguerra*. Geneva: MétisPresses, pp. 117–129.

Durbiano, G. (2000). *I Nuovi Maestri. Architetti tra politica e cultura nel dopoguerra*. Venice: Marsilio.

Lees-Maffei, G. and Fallan, K. (Eds) (2014). *Made in Italy: Rethinking a Century of Italian Design*. London: Bloomsbury.

Lobsinger, M. L. (2004). Architectural Utopias and La Nuova Dimensione: Turin in the 1960s. In R. Lumley and J. Foot (Eds), *Italian Cityscapes: Culture and Urban Change in Contemporary Italy*. Exeter: University of Exeter Press, pp. 77–89.

—— (2009). The New Urban Scale in Italy: On Aldo Rossi's 'L'architettura della città'. *Journal of Architectural Education*, 3, pp. 28–38.

Metron (1947). La nostra cultura e Metron. *Metron*, 13, pp. 7–11.

Mulazzani, M. (1997). Le riviste di architettura: Costruire con le parole. In F. Dal Co (Ed.), *Storia dell'architettura italiana: Il secondo Novecento*. Milan: Electa, pp. 430–443.

Paci, E. (1957). L'architettura e il mondo della vita. *Casabella Continuità*, 217, pp. 53–55.

Pavone, C. (1974). La continuità dello Stato. Istituzioni e uomini. In E. Piscitelli (Ed.), *Le origini della Repubblica*. Turin: Giappichelli, pp. 139–289.

Pilat, S. (2014). *Reconstructing Italy: The Ina-Casa Neighborhoods of the Postwar Era*. Farnham: Ashgate.

Portoghesi, P. (1969). Editoriale. *Controspazio*, 1, p. 7.

Rogers, E. N. (1953–1954). Continuità. *Casabella Continuità*, 199, pp. 2–3.

—— (1954). Le preesistenze ambientali e i temi pratici contemporanei. *Casabella Continuità*, 204, pp. 3–6.

—— (1957). Continuità o crisi? *Casabella Continuità*, 215, pp. 3–4.

—— (1959). L'evoluzione dell'architettura: Risposta al custode dei frigidaires. *Casabella Continuità*, 228, pp. 2–4.

Rossi, A. (1957). A proposito di un recente studio sull'Art Nouveau. *Casabella Continuità*, 215, pp. 45–46.

Scrivano, P. (1997). Torino. In F. Dal Co (Ed.), *Storia dell'architettura italiana: Il secondo Novecento*. Milan: Electa, pp. 104–121.

—— (2007). Romanticizing the Other? Views of Italian Industrial Design in Postwar America. In L. Molinari and A. Canepari (Eds), *The Italian Legacy in Washington DC: Architecture, Design, Art and Culture*. Milan: Skira, pp. 156–161.

—— (2008). Where Praxis and Theory Clash with Reality: Controspazio and the Italian debate over Design, History, and Ideology, 1969–1973. In A. Sornin, H. Jannière and F. Vanlaethem (Eds), *Revues d'architecture dans les années 1960 et 1970. Fragments d'une histoire événementielle, intellectuelle et matérielle / Architectural Periodicals in the 1960s and 1970s: Towards a Factual, Intellectual and Material History*. Montréal: Institut de recherche en histoire de l'architecture, pp. 245–269.

—— (2013). *Building Transatlantic Italy: Architectural Dialogues with Postwar America*. Farnham: Ashgate.

Talamona, M. (2001). Dieci anni di politica dell'Unrra Casas: dalle case ai senzatetto ai borghi rurali nel Mezzogiorno d'Italia (1945–1955): Il ruolo di Adriano Olivetti. In C. Olmo (Ed.), *Costruire la città dell'uomo: Adriano Olivetti e l'urbanistica*. Turin: Edizioni di Comunità.

Tschudi-Madsen, S. (1956). *Sources of Art Nouveau*. Oslo: Aschehoug.

Zevi, B. (1945). La ricostruzione edilizia in Inghilterra. *Metron*, 1, pp. 33–40.

Zucconi, G. (1997). La professione dell'architetto. Tra specialismo e generalismo. In F. Dal Co (Ed.), *Storia dell'architettura italiana: Il secondo Novecento*. Milan: Electa, pp. 294–315.

11

THE AFTER-LIFE OF THE ARCHITECTURAL JOURNAL

Andrew Peckham

The intention behind this discursive end-piece in two parts (identified with conceptualising and then reading) is to examine how the professional architectural journal changes in its status from an informative and everyday currency to its eventual condition collected and shelved in the library; and to consider what occurs later in its subsequent republication or reproduction.

Part one: conceptualising the journal

To paraphrase Walter Benjamin writing in his essay 'Unpacking My Library': how do journals cross the threshold of the profession and become the property of the archive (Benjamin, 1969a),[1] and equally, how do architecture journals gradually become the property of the historian or the cultural critic? At first the journal is read partially: by architects in practice for professional priorities, reportage and building studies, and by students with contemporary aesthetics, construction details, and 'ideas' in mind. Its identity (appearance, ideology and formatting) is generally taken for granted: in hock to fashion but also to its use as an informative design resource.

Consigned to bookshelves in the office, studio or library, the journal's presence is dulled by handling, rebinding, and the downside of fashion. Set aside, it enters the grey area of occasional retrieval. In limbo, and assigned to a well-worn track record, the contingencies of its relationship with architectural practice and 'policy' in the building industry tend to be blunted or overlooked.

Finally, interrogated for the documentary record, the journal issue, article or page regains the spotlight, reproduced by camera, scanner or in facsimile: sought out as a predictable reflection of the culture of its times, or interpreted contrary to its original formation but still marked by its particular professional affiliation. Scrutinised retrospectively with current issues in mind, its editorials, critiques, advertisements, photographs, case studies, format and covers, acquire a new historical meaning.

The slippage between these different conditions epitomises the double-life of the journal, reflecting professional verities but also exhibiting its own chronology as a specific form of publication (Jannière and Vanlaethem, 2008, pp. 41–42). When does the active participation of

FIGURE 11.1   Journal archive, Marylebone Campus Library, University of Westminster.
Source: © Jonathan Snell.

the journal in professional or cultural dialogue outgrow its immediate usefulness? The notion of an 'after-life' arrives once individual journal issues are systematically archived; their relative rarity consigning them to the status of an exhibit when borrowed from private collections and displayed behind glass, they become tokens of architectural culture. As Theodor Adorno explains in his dialectical essay 'Valèry Proust Museum' (Adorno, 1983): Valèry's conception of the dead art of the museum contrasts with Proust's reading of each exhibit as a fragment of living memory. In the journal archive mortified journals are shelved for posterity (individually or by volume) yet may be perceived by the individual researcher as an active totality; the chronological record of the publication *and* a register of its times.

Envisaging the journal

Should one approach the journal as a historical document, for narrative evidence of its chronological development, or for the insights provided by fluctuations in its identity and status, which constitute a form of architectural 'imaginary'? Whether read initially as 'news' or later examined in the archive, the journal occupies a professional niche and a market condition identified with architecture as an institutional practice in its transit from professional efficacy to the academic context of 'research'. At first the journal enjoys an 'authentic' contemporary presence but one located as part of a 'system' (Barthes, 1990), a media 'complex' or an 'institution' (Jannière and Vanlaethem, 2008, p. 48). Its pages may be viewed as a 'contested site' (Wilson, 2015),[2] and its role is one conditioned by the financial resources and imperatives of the publisher; editorial policy; professional and cultural climate, and the changing role of the architect within the building industry.

   Print journalists have become increasingly displaced from their traditional role as bearers of news, adopting the interpretive slant of the 'columnist' distanced from factual reportage. The gradual change postwar in architecture journals from the descriptive 'documentation' of individual buildings to 'case studies' incorporating statements from the architect – develops into short essays or 'critical' studies by imported critics or theorists. A journal's active currency of information for the designer was increasingly extended into a wider concern with recurrent style, formal idiom and retrospective critique. However, a fusty presence on library shelves tends to dictate that projects (as published) become associated with the formal character of their documentation, as intrinsic to the general culture of the period. This historical identity percolates through all aspects of the journal and its 'image', residing in the often-fractured space given to marginalia: the miscellany; letters to the editor; summary news round-ups; building and product reviews; and advertising; as well as mainstream content.

Contemporary architectural journalists are subject to a particularly volatile contemporary media culture and politics, but immediately postwar practical issues of reconstruction[3] were balanced with a newfound idealism. Journals were particularly concerned to register news of the building industry, but the more culturally aware were also attached to the legacy of their own pre-war past, inhibiting radical change.[4]

After-life

While it may seem contradictory to conclude a book on postwar architecture journals with a focus on their archival condition rather than their 'contemporary' relevance, the depredations of the ageing process highlight that they come from a different place than the present: a past remote, or retrospectively current and informing our interest in them. 'Artefacts', designed, arranged, structured and ordered in a manner commonplace on publication, their style and image at the time negotiated the boundary between the professional and the fashionable. If the universal logic of a physically ageless digital archive is now all-pervasive, ideas, professional routine, design and visual culture, all show their age, much as does the accumulation of dust or the yellowing of paper.

Contrary to the originally pristine state of the single journal issue, the physical condition of the archived journal 'collected' in unwieldy monthly or annual 'volumes' (and indexes), is distorted by the constraints of binding and hard covers.[5] The process of accumulation reforms periodisation, compromising the presence of the original copy which, 'bound', becomes dependent for its individual identity on the legibility of the layout, the repetitive clarity of its structure, and particularly the graphic quality of its covers. The positioning of the contents page, the editorial and disparate secondary items often appear to be compromised by interspersed pages of advertising.

Different stages in the after-life of the journal follow active publication, purchase and display on a current periodicals rack (browsed rather than read cover to cover). Placed 'on hold' subsequently, once loose copies are shelved in the library, stashed in the domestic realm or filed in the office; the journal eventually comes to be 'catalogued' en route to the reference 'stacks'. Finally, years later, the individual issue (Bontempelli and Bardi, 1936), or set of issues (Moller, 1993),[6] may be reproduced in facsimile. More often individual pages serve as illustrations in commemorative anniversary journal issues (Casabella, 440/441, 1978) or extracted texts take the form of an anthology (Spens, 1996). Journal monographs (Baglione and Crespi, 2008; Fiell and Fiell, 2006; Hays, 1998) serve as a more complete 'record' of the journal from the date of initial publication. Occasionally the monograph takes the form of a complete serial republication in book form (Mertins and Jennings, 2010), whereas Rifkind's critical study of *Quadrante* presents an exemplary historical account, albeit of a relatively short-lived journal (Rifkind, 2012).

Consulted or referenced increasingly less often as its contemporary relevance wanes, the apotheosis of the journal arrives in due course when consulted in the archive. While its identity as an individual artefact, more or less pristine on publication, was attached to design and graphic format, this is gradually compromised by wear and tear. Hostage to fluctuating historical fortune – whether seen as iconic, representative or merely typical – the aesthetic value attached to the 'journal as artefact' is as likely to be extrinsic, as it was once intrinsic (consulted beside the postwar drawing board).

Walter Benjamin's essay 'Unpacking My Library' serves as a model for the after-life of the journal, where the initial unpacking of the crates of his personal library is freighted with a dialectical and psychological tension established between disorder and order, utility and enchantment. This correlates with the manner of acquisition and the developing value of ownership. The characteristics of the journal and its 'collection' in the archive, and the accumulation of a personal library, represent contrasting polarities. Benjamin's initially 'militant age', when no book was allowed to enter his library 'without the certification that I had not read it', takes a functional and utilitarian view of books bought with practical intent, read for their immediate and informative value (Benjamin, 1969a). The use-value of the professional architecture journal may similarly be viewed in relation to the professional (or educational) practice of architectural design. Rather than simply endorsing the interests and intentions of the contributing editor, architect-author, journalist or reader, the professional journal, bought individually or by subscription, tends to be complicit with the wider interests of the profession, sometimes owned, identified with or financed by architectural institutes.[7] The 'militant' tag attached by Benjamin to his initial 'collection' of books parallels the journal's contemporary role as 'representative' of the contemporary interests of the architectural establishment while also engaging the current interests and inclinations of architects (and others) engaged in the building industry, its primary audience. But as André Tavares notes, journals are not books:

> Although books and magazines share production techniques and are often intimately connected in content, their formats have different purposes. Magazines are often produced collectively, are released at set intervals of time, and are served by logistical networks that separate them from authored books with their illusion of permanence.
>
> *Tavares, 2016, p. 16*

A journal participates in a collective condition from the moment of publication, and its significance is tied to its serial production. Consequently, while it may be characterised in the form of the ephemeral 'one-off' issue bought on impulse or with a specific intent, the journal's publication is ongoing; continually updated it constitutes a 'cross-section' through the architectural culture and practice of a particular period.

Walter Benjamin discusses the moment of 'inflation' when shelved books acquire a 'real value' registered by their scarcity, and exemplified by the difficulty of purchasing rare books. This 'shift' in value away from the casual or everyday impulse to acquire a book – for edification, as a gift or to relieve the boredom of a journey (as Benjamin puts it) – is paralleled in the temporary value of the individual journal issue, as opposed to the ever-increasing weight of the journal's collection. A successful book is reproduced in multiple editions, whereas the numerical journal issue maintains an archival history.

The visual appearance of the weekly or monthly journal may be a sign of its times, but it is also a component part of its independent narrative content configured by its editor(s), graphic designer or publisher, and experienced in relation to professional mores. Wilson presents the notion of an 'editorial frame' which 'seeks to reconcile the plurality' of journal publication with 'a unifying ethos, a consensual politics constructed across architectural criticism, visual representation and editorial practice' (Wilson, 2015, p. 199). The retrospective researcher seeking out a particular editorial, column, building study, article or sequence of adverts may view them as typical, representative or 'reflective', but it is their critical place in the wider logic of publication and professional ethos, through repetition, evolution and overlapping durations of constituent elements intrinsic to serial publication, that offers a 'reflexive' insight into continuities or change.

Given the difficulty of addressing the totality of the architecture journal in all its complexity as a hybrid compendium (Jannière and Vanlaethem, 2008, pp. 57–59), extracting the chronology of a particular element or aspect of the journal offers a partial view but one caught between two timescales. To treat the journal as a series of self-contained 'publications', albeit of familiar appearance and spatial arrangement, is at odds with the visual armature of its continuing format, placed in a dialectical relationship with the prevailing professional or cultural context (and being continually challenged by, or challenging, this formation). The trajectory of the content of the architecture journal in Western Europe becomes an index of the progress of reconstruction, underpinned as it was by the economic and political imperatives of the Marshall Plan (Grass, 2007, pp. 281–283; Stonor Saunders, 1999).

The journal as chronotype

Interrogating the status of the journal over time and stretching philosophical conceptualisation, the definition of a 'chronotype', defined by John Bender and David Wellbery as 'models or patterns through which time assumes a practical or conceptual significance', might usefully be applied to the life of the journal. Characterised as 'temporal and plural', the 'chronotype' is envisaged as 'constantly being made and remade at multiple individual, social, and cultural levels' (Bender and Wellberry, 1991). The journal occupies a parallel space between linear narrative in its serial publication, and a cyclical periodisation (in forms of graphic convention, recurrent issues or interests, and cycles of editorial renewal).[8]

One might claim in principle that these two primary trajectories are overlaid in the temporality of a journal: a linear chronology tracing news and recurrent professional issues as preoccupations ebb and flow with a 'present future' in mind, and the cyclical return to particular themes, aspects of criticism or architects and forms of architecture, which progressively coalesce to create a certain status, identity, short-term reputation and in the longer term an attendant mythology. Each journal acquires an individual format, one reiterated but whose content may incorporate a familiar annual 'series', recurrent themes, typical or topical 'special issues' or editorials. These vary in literally framing the journal but also metaphorically framing its range of thematic content. Defined by a recurrent return to certain issues, events, modes of criticism or technical developments, the journal retains a febrile perspective following news, fashion and the polemics of debate and professional opinion.

In contrast to presenting a consistent form and 'returning' recurrently to habitual issues, the volatility attached to issues of the moment may also become familiar. The institutional, social and cultural influences that inform the journal are typically interactive and not simply a 'given' (however entrenched the professional ethos). The ambivalent aspect of postwar architecture journals across Europe resides in their similarity as a genre, but also their contingent disjunctures and very real historical differences in negotiating distinct national cultures, political contexts and legacies of the Second World War.

From a temporal perspective, just as the late eighteenth and early nineteenth centuries constitute a historical threshold through the 'temporalization of experience' (Bender and Wellberry, 1991; Kosselleck, 2004), one can speculate whether the tension between a loosening of the ties of modernity, or conversely its 'self-reflexive' 'intensification', created conditions for aspects of post-modernity to register in the nature of postwar journal publication, well before being ascribed to the design of buildings in the late 1960s.

A media trajectory

The influence of the mass media on modern architecture has been traced by Beatriz Colomina, in the case of Le Corbusier, back to nineteenth-century popular journals, advertising and product catalogues, informing his own journals and books which establish a polemical basis for and propagandise his architecture (Colomina, 1994; Smet, 2007). Benjamin's 'The Work of Art in the Age of Mechanical Reproduction', to which her argument is indebted, was not directly concerned with journals, but rather what he maintained was the uniqueness of the work of art 'embedded in the fabric of tradition' and the 'loss of aura' endemic to the process of reproduction, both of which have a purchase on the 'micro-history' of the journal. Likewise, his salutary comments on architecture being ordinarily experienced in a 'state of distraction', through a 'tactile' familiarity and typically an 'incidental' visual perception. Only occasionally is it to be experienced in a state of visual 'contemplation' (Benjamin, 1969b).[9] The journal at first is typically experienced distractively and only much later 'contemplated' in the archive where, unless filed as individual issues, it inhabits a bound volume inhibiting visual access. In his essay 'The Multiplication of the Media', Umberto Eco comments on what he calls its 'genealogy' (with reference to television and film). 'The mass media are genealogical, and they have no memory', he argues, maintaining that the gradual evolution of a 'common language' is without memory because in this 'chain of imitations' any origin becomes opaque and 'authenticity' in the past is displaced by the authenticity of the present (Eco, 1986).

It is the task of the architectural historian to unpick this form of amnesia and refer it back to the particularities of national culture and individual identity, but replication remains intrinsic to the visual style and the typology of the journal as a construct. Periodicals of all kinds accumulate a customary identity in a continuum of similarity (the reader tends to know what to expect between the covers).

FIGURE 11.2 Students reading journals.
Source: © Jonathan Snell.

Part two: reading the journal in retrospect

The question of how a journal is read, when and with what intent raises issues beyond the historicity of the journal itself. Any 'reading' is partial, even if one could read all the text published over the years of the publication of any single journal. Unlike a book, the journal continues in all its changing formats and variants, even on occasion under different titles, and under the auspices of its different editors, until there is a decision to cease publication. Yet it is the individual issue of the journal that typically is the first point of contact: a single document or representative artefact, but one in a series projected into the future. The professional reader reads initially aware of the reputation, status and likely usefulness of the journal.

The move towards reading with the mentality of a researcher pursuing a wider 'historical' agenda may represent a quest for information from particular parts of a journal (within the context of a collection of volumes), or contrastingly focus on the evolution of the journal as a cultural entity. This is typically communicated by exhibiting journal covers as indicative of the fluctuations of aesthetic fashion or periods of editorial responsibility (Baglione and Crespi, 2008, pp. 730–791). The details of changes to graphic formatting (and typography), or the visual culture of the journal expressed over time, are less immediately accessible once the journal is bound and archived. As Wilson notes in concluding his study of architectural media, the individual page is 'a contested site in architectural discourse, containing diverse and contradictory expressions of disciplinary knowledge across image and text' (Wilson, 2015, p. 199), expressions that are muted in the archive.

Paul Valéry's contention in 1926 about two modes of reading the book – that is the text 'read' and the text 'seen' – remain apposite. His distinction between the linear readability of a 'text' – its constructed or rational meaning – and a second way of seeing the page as 'an image' in an 'immediate and simultaneous' fashion, leads on to the notion of a 'common ground', he argues, between typography and architecture (Smet, 2003; Valéry, 1929). This is typically extended in subsequent criticism either to suggest that typography approaches the condition of architecture, or to suggest that the book (or the journal) viewed in visual terms has the artefactual qualities of an object. The design, spatial structure and graphic format of a journal incorporates a particular culture of design which complements or reinforces its written text and architectural documentation.[10]

Rereading

With the rise of 'the new look', and the 'soft power of midcentury design' explored by Greg Castillo – identified with new patterns of domestic consumption (Castillo, 2010) – architecture journals like *domus* and *The Architectural Review* (*AR*) during the 1950s were experimenting with elaborate formats: employing colour to highlight individual texts, editorials and adverts; different papers; inserts of varied widths; fold-outs; sophisticated photography; and contrasting typefaces in a variety of permutations and alignments. This co-existence of a professional concern to document contemporary architecture and project a visual acuity (the sign of a design 'mentality') took on a new character postwar.

The clash of cultures between necessary income from advertising and publicity for the building industry, and concurrent editorial and theoretical idealism, was particularly marked during the period of the emergent postwar economy. In Italy, *Casabella Continuità* only resumed regular publication in 1954 – a stylish Alitalia advertisement preceded the rhetorical stance of Ernesto Rogers' initial editorial '*Continuità*' (Rogers, 1954). Issues of *AR* from the 1950/ 1960s typified the general case elsewhere, bookended with copious adverts for contractors and building products – a culture of manufacture succinctly traced by Stephen Parnell in his 'reading' of glass and glazing adverts representing 'an architectural historiography from the manufacturer's perspective' (Parnell, 2014).[11] The contrast, in issues of *AR*, between the 'aesthetic' scope of the front cover and the pragmatism of the full-page advertisements on the back cover locates the preoccupations of the editors within the emergent context of the postwar building industry. If the restrained 'timeline' fronting the paradigmatic issue of *AR* on 'The Functional Tradition' (*AR* January 1950) was less than typical, the issue's content represented a characteristic mélange of material associated with what was to become an established editorial theme. Arguably, the infiltration of adverts was mediated by the eclectic content of the journal itself, but they presented in this case a more convincing functionality (associated with reconstruction) than the so-called 'tradition' propagated by the editors. This displacement between adverts and editorials highlights how the inter-relationship between design, advertising and the theory and practice of the postwar period produces the 'historical' identity of the *AR*, an identity distinct from the themes habitually revived by contemporary editors in homage to the journal's past.

Nonetheless, the design of journal front covers registered the *AR*'s ambivalent pattern of eclecticism, just as they expressed phases in the life of *Casabella*[12] and projected the illustrative verve that exemplified the character of *domus*. Other journals seemingly followed in the wake of the latter's complementary focus on exhibiting 'design' of all kinds: domestic, product, industrial and graphic; interfaced with an architectural imaginary.

Domus during the 1950s adopted a relatively restrained graphic format formulated as an informative juxtaposition of monochrome architectural plans and photographs documenting residential design and architecture – a range of content which has been 'personally' identified with editor Gio Ponti (Spinelli, 2015).[13] This incorporated the burgeoning commodity culture of American domesticity which acquired a political connotation early in the history of the Cold War, and was gradually displaced by an emergent and exuberant pop sensibility, style and colour range, associated the British culture of the 1960s. The professional journals that aspired to an international status, whether or not they incorporated multilingual captions or provided translated extracts, could also be 'read' visually within the scope of an internationally projected graphic style, even if more conventional in terms of written content. Deyan Sudjic claims, with some justification, the significant influence on *domus* of the 'pioneering typography' of the *AR* (Sudjic, 2016) where this mode of graphic design provided a foil, in a varied[14] set of graphic conventions, for an unstable mix of provincialism, textured brutalism, traditional townscape, attention to the vernacular and expressive polemical outbursts. Perhaps *domus* did assimilate this genre within a culture of Italian design, but it was with an unmatched sophistication and its editors had an uncanny ability to select both the typical and the exceptional international paradigms of the contemporary architectural culture of the period.

Reproduction: the journal and the book

Reproduction is fundamental to the nature of the architectural journal and is considered here with respect to *Casabella* and *domus* – the focus primarily being concerned with what happens when a journal comes to be published as a book.[15] Two aspects of the process of reproduction stand out: re-affirmation through the routine of publication, and the related longer-term

FIGURE 11.3   *domus* bound and reproduced.
Source: © Jonathan Snell.

issue – the republication or replication of the journal, and perception of its periodisation and homogeneity. The first concerns the duration of editorial influence and the format, or content, with which it comes to be identified; the second being the product of a retrospective interest generally by the publisher – to exploit the status, reputation or historical significance of a journal by way of selective republication. Just as the process of 'reproduction' involves the reprint, the facsimile or the copy of the *individual* issue, so a series of issues or a surrogate, partial or sample version of the journal's complete publication constitutes a 'collection', published as a compendium.

   In between these two models lies the 'third order' of the anniversary (or anthology) issue – neither an 'original' facsimile nor the 'reconstruction' of a journal (monograph). This offers the opportunity for editors to reflect on the identity or history of 'their' journal – to reinforce its continuing status, account for its evolution or celebrate its anecdotal 'biography' – generally in decades or as 'centenary' celebrations. These preoccupations highlight how the journal has changed publishers, editors, graphic designers and content over time. *Casabella*'s anniversary issue celebrating 50 years of publication 1928–1978 was a case in point (*Casabella*, 440/441, 1978), intercutting retrospective thematic or interpretative essays with summary descriptions of typical buildings and projects, and including selected *testimonianze* from salient periods of publication. On the cover a configuration of children's wooden building blocks presented an image of construction keyed in with the earlier period of 'costruzione' in the journal's title.[16] Both *Casabella* and *domus* – one focused on architecture as a discipline, and the other engaging a wider territory of design culture (with a bias towards the 'interior') – achieved a genuine international reach during the postwar period, and both journals have now achieved a monographic status.

Two journal 'books': the monograph and a compendium of volumes

The anniversary collection *Casabella 1928–2008* was published by Electa as a weighty book organised according to respective periods of editorial responsibility (Baglione and Crespi, 2008). The ten years from 1954 to 1964 under Ernesto Rogers' influential editorship offer a platform from which to view the earlier and later characteristics of the journal.

Taschen, in contrast, published a substantive box-set of 12 brightly coloured 'volumes': *domus 1928–1999*. Presented chronologically at five-year intervals, the journal title was spelled out in large metallic capitals across their collective colour-coded spines.[17] Volumes III–VI cover the period 1950–1969 and parallel, in a mediated, selective and seductive form, the bound archived 'volumes' of the journal. Their hard, high-intensity covers (front and back) each present representative facsimile 'images' of what were 'soft' covers of the journal. These are set above a silver metallic band which, following similarly coloured title and contents pages, continues at the base of each page, incorporating details of the issues and articles selected for republication. They act as a glossary of the content of the original journal publication.

An alternative cool aura of white space and class (Robertson, 1994) characterises the *Casabella* monograph against which occasional variations are registered: the 'C' of Casabella slips from the front cover onto the spine; red numerals identify the issues from which the selected texts are taken; and their small-scale titles are juxtaposed with an oversized typography applied to dates and authors. Immediately postwar a brief year of publication in 1946 under Franco Albini and Giancarlo Palanti concluded with a valedictory monographic double issue (*Costruzioni Casabella* 195/198, 1946) following the tragic death in 1944 of Giuseppe Pagano (the previous editor 1933–1943). A rupture in publication occurred two years before the end of the war, and another followed after 1946 before publication resumed in 1954.[18]

The narrative text of the *Casabella* monograph opens with four large-print and tightly registered pages with wide margins. An introduction by Chiara Baglione concludes unceremoniously with a black page-break. A spartan title page prefaces an extensive essay covering the first editorial period, which sets the pattern for the sections that follow. In the original issues, Ernesto Rogers' much shorter but decisive 1954 editorials set the tone: 'after this long period of silence … we would like to offer our readers something of the polemics ranging over vital subjects' that were primarily the themes of 'historical awareness', continuity and tradition (*Casabella Continuità* 199 and 202, 1954). The year concluded with extensive coverage of the X Triennale in Milan (*Casabella Continuità* 203, 1954), where the exhibition narrative comes to be visualised in cinematic terms. As Rogers argues, dual narratives of the contemporary *and* the historical – 'the living testimony of architecture, and place' and 'the larger context of history' – mark a return to normalcy (after fascism), transposing the 'history' of the Triennale and the 'tradition' of Italian urbanism. The issue incorporated elaborate fold-outs: a Saul Steinberg cityscape sketching the urban topography of Milan set against the familiar profile of the city skyline; a set of details of the Eiffel Tower and, printed on yellow paper, documentary coverage of CIAM. This disparate content was typical and parallels the contemporary eclecticism of the *AR*. The expansive folded papers were reminiscent of the preceding final issue of *Costruzione Casabella* on Pagano – which incorporated a plethora of fold-outs, construction details, and an expansive plan of 1942 for the development of the Dalmatian coast from Trieste to Corfu.[19] In the Electa monograph, a judicious selection of texts from 1946 includes Rogers' homage to Pagano but disregards the earlier uneven and rhetorical documentation of his work. While the disrupted sequence of the journal stands out on the archive shelves, the journal book promotes an accessible overview whose selective record is conditional and partial, and where in this case the exceptional is rendered homogeneous.

Nonetheless the overall pattern of publication is registered at the back of the book with a comprehensive documentation of the journal covers coded by issue and year. This visual mapping of the trajectory of the journal contrasts with the main content of the book: facsimiles of selected articles set out graphically within the boundaries of each page as if

FIGURE 11.4   Fold-out from *Casabella* 203, 1954.
Source: author.

bound separately into the spine.[20] The respective page numbers, old and new, are juxtaposed at the page corners,[21] tracking the monograph's episodic compendium.

In contrast to the *Casabella* book, the facsimile pages selected for the *domus 1928–1999* volumes coincide directly with the new pages except for the addition of a band at the base of each page which accommodates notation. Throughout the 1950s and 1960s a fluctuating informal visual arrangement of illustrations was combined with narrow caption-like blocks of text.[22] Reproduction, however, altered in places the graphic affect at the page margins where a bright yellow edging (at the head and sides of double spreads) framed selective pages in the original journal copies. In the new volumes, seemingly reprinted from the original pages, the effect is indistinct from natural ageing, so the artifice is lost,[23] as are tangible qualities of visual texture and surface, where photos acquire a coarser grain and stronger contrast. The new slightly matt paper deadens the distinction between the original gloss 'print' and interspersed matt pages, alternately highlighting or muting the colour photographs.[24] These were incorporated among the otherwise monochrome illustrations – a balance gradually altered in favour of colour photography during the 1960s.

Among the selected extracts from the original issues, occasional full-page journal covers and adverts are interspersed arbitrarily as tokens of brand identity out of key with the chronological sequence and displacing the attention paid to the fine arts of painting and sculpture in the original publications. Viewed stylistically in retrospect, the fine arts age more quickly than architecture, while the graphic design of the journal during the two decades under consideration still projects a 'contemporary' equanimity (Spinelli, 2015).[25] It is ironic, then, that *domus* occupied the cutting edge of publicity for *design*, the ideology of brands and spectacle that began to transform material culture during the 1960s.

A retrospective 'image' of the journal comes to convey a timeless quality which is attached to the design and the architecture sampled for republication, despite its original variety and stylistic volatility. The tactical fluencies of the graphic design act, in spite of their collection within individual volumes, as a scenography of the period, while the deletions, insertions and artifice attached to the new volumes, in contrast to their texts, present a 'natural' history of the journal (taken out of its historical context). The process of reproduction in the case of *domus* was taken a stage further by amalgamating pairs of the 2006 volumes at a reduced scale to form two small

FIGURE 11.5   Shelved journals.
Source: © Jonathan Snell.

but substantive books identified with the decades of the 1950s and 1960s,[26] decades that the seductive gloss of the collective volumes dissembled, boxed as they were in a contemporary guise on the cusp of the new millennium.

Conclusion: an elusive entity

In his recent sophisticated and wide-ranging study of the architectural 'book', Tavares is categorical in the prologue about the material 'qualities' through which architectural publications may be conceived to 'embody architectural knowledge', a contention less applicable to the more ephemeral journal. He notes that he intends to depart 'from the chronological cross sections' which characterise his earlier chapters, in order 'to take an anatomical approach to the dissection of the corpus' of architectural books. The 'tools' he presents 'are five concepts – texture, surface, rhythm, structure, and scale – that help to analyse the material qualities of books' and what he warily describes as their 'crossovers' with architecture (Tavares, 2016 p. 20).

While the journal ages more quickly than the book, its legacy as a collection is both looser in content and more substantive in its sequential production. It may be conceived (and analysed) as a visual or a textual artefact, that samples and projects a variety of content in the format of the individual issue, but unlike the integral narration expected of the book, its nature is to be subject to gaps, elisions, contractions and missing links, which are intrinsic to its partiality. This multifarious content offers a range of insight into the complexities of the context in which the journal is produced, but that has to be reconstructed in retrospect.

Arguably, the architectural periodical is primarily concerned with the ongoing dissemination of 'news' about contemporary architecture and its evaluation, yet in celebrating its longevity a journal also reconfigures its own 'history' – just as postwar architectural culture looked to the past for evidence of continuity and stability. Conversely, journals were also engaged with different national attitudes towards the new realities of economic and political transformation, and the social agencies that underpinned reconstruction, whether under the various auspices of the welfare state in the west, or state communism in the east – the contributions to the first volume of Akos Moravánszky's *East West Central* rebalance perception of this duality (Moravánszky and Hopfengärter, 2017). The context of a historian's explanatory 'overview' of a journal's significance, or a critical perception of a journal's autobiography (the internal narrative of editorial policies and personalities – subject to anecdote and potential exaggeration), represent two research strands. Either may be limited by an established chronological inevitability or a preconceived argument.

Viewed in this context the two monographs culled from the longstanding publication of *Casabella* and *domus* represent a constructed after-life, or a conservation of the momentum of publication, that reinforces the mythology attached to both journals, but which may also conversely be unpicked within a wider historical frame, and read as its critical antithesis.

Notes

1 Benjamin asked: 'How do books cross the threshold of a collection and become the property of a collector?'.

2 'whilst the "assemblage" of the architectural report or design review purports to present a position of consensus around the design object through a stable or "generic order" of signification, it also reflexively reveals traces of "repression" within its production' (Wilson, 2015, p. 199).

3 A differentiation between operative issues and the status of completed buildings was clearly expressed throughout the issues of the German journals *Neue Bauwelt* and *Baumeister* immediately postwar, which had resumed publication on cheap paper for building industry content and smooth white paper for, at first minimal, coverage of individual buildings.

4 In an Italian context, Ernesto Rogers' initial editorial setting out the ground for a newly constituted *Casabella Continuita* was symptomatic. He established the theme of 'continuity' as a paradigm for the 'historical awareness' needed to reconstruct a positive relationship between modernism and tradition; between Casabella's past and present, and as something lacking in an aesthetic formalism without ethical content (Rogers, 1953/1954). The assorted content of *The Architectural Review* incorporated similar themes.

5 Depending on dimensions, flexibility, thickness, weight and compression, and also occasionally subject to breaks in publication due to financial or editorial problems, or tampering and theft in the library.

6 The boxed facsimile edition of *ABC* is a special case, being a complete reprint of individual issues, complemented by a supplement providing translations and commentaries.

7 Or affiliated institutions which vary in character nationally.

8 Jonathan Z. Smith argues in his short text 'A Slip in Time Saves Nine: Prestigious Origins Again' that in terms of the structural study of religious myth a duality between 'mythic' and 'historical' time was an invention of the mid-nineteenth century. Questioning the opposing verities of the concept of an 'eternal return' and serial 'succession' he proposes instead an essentially deconstructionist impulse associated with the concept of 'difference' (Smith, 1991).

9 Generally assumed by the architects.

10 Valery goes on to talk about the spatiality of 'the beautiful book' and 'the art of the printer' in terms of spatial integration ('perfect scale'), but he is not talking about the qualities of graphic or book design beyond the boundaries of typography and the 'impression' of text on the page characterized as 'blocks and strata'.

11 Noting the move from advertising initially directed towards the domestic consumer – together with commercials from individual building contractors – to later 'industrial' advertising placed by corporate businesses (and building industry pressure groups).

12 The design and typography is one aspect, but the generic title Casabella also changes from earlier iterations to *Casabella Costruzioni*, *Costruzioni Casabella* and subsequently *Casabella Continuità* under Rogers, 1954–1964.

13 And what has been called ambiguously his 'self-referential and comprehensive universe'.

14 One might loosely say 'picturesque'.

15 It is not the intention, however, to confront the evidently tangled relationship between these journals, their publishers and editors.

16 Acting as a metaphor, perhaps, for the constructive role of critical text or the ongoing constitution of the journal over time.

17 The finish also applied to title headings inside.

18 Ten years later Gian Bernasconi took over as editor under a new publisher.

19 With its imperialistic territorial implications.

20 The margin at the base of each page identifies the issue theme, number in red and extract title.

21 That is the corners of the 'graphic page' and the counterpart on which it is printed.

22 A format sympathetic to later republication at a reduced scale, if then largely unreadable.

23 Where what signified the wilful nature of fashion corresponds with temporal change.

24 Full-colour covers and adverts stand out in this respect.

25 Luigi Spinelli notes perceptively that in 1954 the word 'landscape was added to the titles of all articles'. The concept of a 'typographical landscape' is a plausible description of the graphic design, and Spinelli notes a predilection for day and night views, which certainly heightened that quality in the generally monochrome layout (though whether this was 'mechanic' is questionable).

26 Joining Taschen's longstanding *Bibliotheca Universalis* series of visual 'collections'. What is lost in terms of a slightly reduced content and legibility of detail and text, is gained in accessibility and low price. But the doubling of content produces a directory-like or encyclopedic thickness and a familiar periodization into decades.

References

Adorno, T. (1983). Valéry Proust Museum. In T. Adorno, *Prisms*. Cambridge, MA: MIT Press, pp. 175–185.

The Architectural Review (1950). The Functional Tradition. *The Architectural Review*, January, pp. 1–66.

Baglione, C. and Crespi, G. (Eds) (2008). *Casabella 1928–2008*. Milano: Electa.

Barthes, R. (1990). *The Fashion System*. Berkeley, CA: University of California Press.

Bender, J. and Wellbery, D. (Eds) (1991). *Chronotypes: The Construction of Time*. Stanford: Stanford University Press, pp. 1–4.

Benjamin, W. (1969a). Unpacking My Library. In W. Benjamin, *Illuminations*. New York: Schocken, pp. 59–63.

—— (1969b). The Work of Art in the Age of Mechanical Reproduction. In W. Benjamin, *Illuminations*. New York: Schocken, pp. 221–224, 239–240.

Bontempelli, M. and Bardi, P. M. (1936). *Quadrante*, 35/36 (V edition, 2004).

Castillo, G. (2010). *Cold War on the Home Front: The Soft Power of Midcentury Design*. Minneapolis: University of Minnesota Press.

Colomina, B. (1994). *Privacy and Publicity: Modern Architecture as Mass Media*. Cambridge, MA: MIT Press.

Eco, U. (1986). The Multiplication of the Media. In *Travels in Hyperreality*. London: Picador, pp. 145–146.

Fiell, C. and Fiell, P. (Eds) (2006). *domus 1928–1999*. (v. 1–12, box-set). Koln: Taschen.

Grass, G. (2007). *Peeling the Onion*. London: Harvill Secker.

Hays, K. Michael. (Ed.) (1998). *Oppositions Reader*. New York: Princeton Architectural Press.

Jannière, H. and Vanlaethem, F. (2008). Architectural Magazines as Historical Source or Object. In A. Sornin, H. Jannière and F. Vanlaethem (Eds), *Architectural Periodicals in the 1960s and 1970s: Towards a Factual, Intellectual and Material History*. Montreal: IRHA.

Kosselleck, R. (2004) *Futures Past: On the Semantics of Historical Time*. New York: Columbia University Press.

Mertins, D. and Jennings, M. W. (Eds) (2010/2011). *G: An Avant-Garde Journal of Art, Architecture, Design, and Film 1923–1926*. London: Tate/Getty Publications.

Moller, W. (1993). *ABC: Contributions on Building 1924–1928*. Baden: Lars Müller.

Moravánszky, À. and Hopfengärter, J. (Eds) (2017). *Re-Humanizing Architecture: New Forms of Community, 1950–1970*. Basel: Birkhäuser.

Parnell, S. (2014). In Praise of Advertising. *The Architectural Review*, February, pp. 108–109.

Rifkind, D. (2012). *The Battle for Modernism:* Quadrante *and the Politicization of Architectural Discourse in Fascist Italy*. Venice: Marsilio.

Robertson, K. (1994). On White Space/When Less is More. In M. Bierut, W. Drenttel and S. Heller (Eds), *Looking Closer: Critical Writings on Graphic Design*. New York: AIGA/Allworth Press, pp. 61–65.

Rogers, E. N. (1953/1954). Continuità. *Casabella Continuità*, 199, pp. 2–3.

Smith, Z. J. (1991). A Slip in Time Saves Nine: Prestigious Origins Again. In J. Bender and D. Wellbery, (Eds), *Chronotypes: The Construction of Time*. Stanford: Stanford University Press, pp. 67–76.

Smet, C. de. (2003). The Other side of the Architectural Book. In E. Bresciani (Ed.), *Modern Architecture Books from the Marzona Collection*. Vienna: Johannes Schlebrügge, p. 506.

—— (2007). *Le Corbusier: Architect of Books*. Baden: Lars Müller.

Spens, M. (1996). *AR 100: The Recovery of the Modern – Architectural Review 1980–1995*. Oxford: Butterworth.

Spinelli, L. (2015). Signs of Recovery. In C. Fiell and P. Fiell (Eds), *domus 1959–1962*. Cologne: Taschen, pp. 6–9.

Stonor Saunders, F. (1999). *Who Paid the Piper?* London: Granta.

Sudjic, D. (2016). When Format Speaks Louder Than Words. In C. Fiell and P. Fiell (Eds), *domus 1960–1969*. Cologne: Taschen, pp. 16–18.

Tavares, A. (2016). *The Anatomy of the Architectural Book*. Zurich: Lars Müller/CCA.

Valéry, P. (1929). Two Virtues of the Book. *Wilson Bulletin*, 4, pp. 15–16.

Wilson, R. (2015). *Image, Text, Architecture: The Utopics of the Architectural Media*. Farnham: Ashgate.

FIGURES

INDEX